The Sweat
of Their Brow

Latin American Realities

Robert M. Levine, Series Editor

The Sweat
of Their Brow
A History of Work
in Latin America

David J. McCreery

M.E. Sharpe
Armonk, New York
London, England

Library of Congress Cataloging-in-Publication Data

McCreery, David J., 1944–
    The sweat of their brow : a history of work in Latin America / David J. McCreery.
        p. cm. — (Latin American realities)
    Includes bibliographical references and index.
    ISBN 0-7656-0207-5 (cloth : alk. paper)
    1. Labor—Latin America—History. I. Title. II. Series.

HD8110.5.M33 2000
331′.098—dc21   00-020702

Printed in the United States of America

The paper used in this publication meets the minimum requirements of
American National Standard for Information Sciences
Permanence of Paper for Printed Library Materials,
ANSI Z 39.48-1984.

BM (c)   10   9   8   7   6   5   4   3   2   1

Contents

Series Foreword

David McCreery's study of the history of work in Latin America breaks new ground in several ways. It is the first comprehensive analysis of labor systems spanning the pre-Columbian period to the present. More often than not, historical treatments of social issues deal with either the colonial period or the post-independence period, but not both. We know, of course, that many ways of doing things and forms of behavior in modern times derive from historical experience. This holds true especially in Latin America, where the Spanish and Portuguese imposed their own social and legal institutions on their colonies, sanctioning neither leeway nor flexibility.

The author's choice to write about work, not labor, broadens the book's scope considerably. Labor history, he notes, typically examines the structure of labor unions, the ideological conflicts among their leaders, and the struggle to organize and to influence politics and social policies. The history of work, on the other hand, embraces a much broader perspective. How did the demands of the workplace impact family life? How did changing patterns of labor need affect demographic patterns? How did war (a deadly kind of "work"), insurgency, and revolution affect the rhythm of work? How did the institutions of *encomienda* labor (among American Indian populations); chattel slavery (for Africans), work drafts, debt peonage, forced conscription, sharecropping, and indentured servitude (common among new arrivals as well as the lower classes in general) impact the quality of life?

The issues related to work that this book explores are important as litmus tests of social attitudes and elite behavior. How did local, provincial, and national governments define vagrancy? What attitudes about "laziness" prevailed over time? How did chronic un- and underemployment lead to an "underground" or "informal" economy in many countries, and what impact did this have on working conditions for those formally employed?

The author surveys, as well, the relationships between governments and working people. He investigates the legacy of conservatives, of populists, of military regimes, and of self-described revolutionaries on the world of workers' rights and conditions. He analyzes the impact not only of export agriculture and raw material production, but of rapid urbanization and industrialization during the second half of the twentieth century. His study addresses the issues that make up the debate over free trade and NAFTA, the North American Free Trade Association, which links Canada, the United States, and Mexico. He examines the impact of the lack of social security and welfare nets in Latin America among populations with high (and mostly permanent) populations of unemployment. *The Sweat of Their Brow*, then, is not only a useful guide to the social and economic and labor history of the region, but it will also be useful to future analysts if today's gap between the rich and the poor continues to widen and if unbridled globalization brings further instability to the delicate balance between government, workers, and employers.

Robert M. Levine

Acknowledgments

Above all I wish to thank my family—my wife, Angela, and our children, Anthony ("Shimby") and Elizabeth Carmen—for their love and support. Margie Patterson and the staff of Georgia State University Inter-Library Loan Office are efficient and always helpful. Prof. Diane Willen, Chair, and the History Department of Georgia State University have always generously supported my research and writing, as has the College of Arts and Sciences at Georgia State University. Profs. Seth Fine, Chuck Steffen, and Hugh Hudson read parts of the manuscript and commented on it (when I let them). Beth Burton read the entire manuscript and helped me root out errors. My thanks to all.

The Sweat
of Their Brow

Introduction

This is a history of work, not just of labor. The distinction is important. Although the dictionary defines work as "something that is or was done; what a person does or did; an act, deed, proceeding, business,"[1] our focus here will be on work as it is understood in everyday usage: what someone does to make a living. By contrast, "labor history" too often limits itself to the story of organized labor, of unions and the politics and ideologies surrounding them. This history is attractive both because the records of such groups tend to be among the best available for the working class and because in focusing on unions and militant labor groups, we see workers as active agents of their own history. By contrast, in studies of slavery or indebted labor, for example, the workers too often come across only as victims. Organized, or would-be organized, labor has been an important part of Latin America's history, but it has not been the experience of most Latin Americans. Work has been.

Work involves not only the physical activities of producing and distributing material and intellectual goods, but also the social relations into which individuals and groups enter as a result of these activities, on and off the job. Before the twentieth century a majority of Latin Americans labored in the countryside, but urbanization and industrialization in recent years have opened up new opportunities in the towns and cities. Most worked, and work, to survive, though some have always found the experience rewarding in other ways. Race, class, and gender have conditioned access to work and at least partially determined its rewards, as have the changing economic situations of Latin America's colonies and nations and the external political and economic events impinging upon them.

Five hundred years of history in Latin America have witnessed a wide range of work experiences. These are too diverse to be fully rehearsed, or even catalogued, here, but underlying the kaleidoscope of forms are some basic structures that can be identified. Slavery, for example, existed in Europe and in America before the two continents came violently into contact, but in the New World it became something different, sweeping up indigenous and African populations on an unprecedented scale. Systems of coerced wage labor were widespread from the end of the sixteenth until well into the nineteenth century, including the forced drafts of *repartimientos* and *mitas* and debt peonage or debt servitude, but these showed quite different forms and had different histories from northern Mexico to southern Argentina. Often linked to peonage were "vagrancy" laws that criminalized unemployment among the poor. Least important, though it hardly seems so from a perspective at the beginning of the twenty-first century, has been free labor, the work of men and women who had nothing to sell but their own labor power. In some areas not until the 1930s and 1940s did employers give up direct coercion, and even today the use of state or private violence to combat worker organization and to cheapen labor costs continues. The effort here will be to understand which forms of work developed where and when and why: What were the choices and what were the constraints? What could workers, employers, and the state "think" at a given moment in history, and how and why did these elements change? What, for example, was "women's work," or what could a slave do, and who defined this? Did those disadvantaged by their work situation struggle to change it, or did they accept it as "custom" or "God's will" or the workings of the market?

Our definition draws in activities perhaps not always associated with work. What a bureaucrat does is no less work than the labor of a miner, and a housewife works, though she usually receives no wage for it. For most of Latin America's history, female prostitution was legitimate work, and we will see, for example, how it shifted from a casual part-time activity in the late eighteenth century to a state-regulated industry with international connections by 1910. Crime too is work, at least so far as its purpose is to acquire money or goods, and begging was work sanctioned by the church until at least the middle of the last century. Whatever our best efforts, however, many areas or types of traditional and nontraditional work will escape us. This reflects both the state of what we know about Latin America's history and the constraints of time and space available. The reader is invited to take pen or word processor and fill the lacunae.

The effort is to situate work in the broad historical experience of Latin America, but this book is not a history of Latin America, and it is not even a general economic history of the region. Entirely absent, or receiving only glancing attention, are topics central to such an economic history, including land ownership and use, capital formation, technological change, and trade and commerce. These appear only as they bear on or help to explain specific work experiences. For example, a shift from hand drills and crow bars to pneumatically-operated machinery profoundly altered the work situation of Bolivia's tin miners, if not in ways one might imagine. The transition from slavery to freedom must be one of the most profound experiences humanly imaginable, but even as the social relations of production went through such a dramatic change, the work of cutting and pressing cane remained much the same. Similarly, new crops, transportation links, or markets sometimes generated new work relations. In other instances such innovations instead led to expanding and generalizing already existing forms of work to new areas or taking these forms and putting them to unfamiliar uses. From its colonial inception, Latin America was part of the world capitalist economy, though not necessarily itself capitalist, and it was repeatedly, and sometimes unexpectedly, impacted by capitalism's relentless drive to expand and revolutionize systems and relations of production. Whole regions and populations were mobilized for commercial production, but some of these subsequently found themselves shut out of world markets, as demand or production conditions or politics resituated the colony or country in the world system. These same areas might be subsequently reintegrated on the same or a different basis, or they might be felt to vegetate. Changing politics and new economic conditions altered forms and relations of work. The Bourbon Reformers of late colonial New Spain, for example, sought to enlarge the available labor force by drawing women into wage work, and by 1800 thousands were employed in textile mills and in factories. But the political and economic chaos of independence wrecked the economy. By mid-century unemployed men were taking over jobs that had been "women's work," and women were forced back into traditional, low-paying employments such as domestic service.

Historical overviews sometimes give the impression that systems of labor in Latin America developed in a more or less linear manner: First there was the enslavement of the indigenous population that gave way to *encomiendas*; after the mid-sixteenth century these receded before the spread of forced wage labor and African slavery; then, in the late eighteenth or early nineteenth centuries, or in some areas as much as 100 years later, coercion finally yielded to capitalist free labor. In fact, though, the history of work in the New World was much more complicated. On the one hand, forms of labor mobilization and control rarely disappeared over night, or even over a decade or two, to be replaced by new and different forms. Rather, they tended to coexist, easily or uneasily, in time and place, with one fading gradually into another or perhaps both continuing on parallel or even contradictory tracks for years. Similarly, labor systems overlapped and mixed according to race and gender, with, for example, in some areas free but indebted Indian women working as domestic servants alongside African women who were chattel slaves and mixed bloods who did day service for wages. In the fields, mestizo free workers might tend the cattle while forced wage workers cleaned the fields, and African slaves cut and processed sugar cane. There were also regional variations. Different parts of the New World experienced different labor systems at different times, and in some areas certain labor types, for example, Indian or African slavery, never existed or were found only in vestigial forms. Put another way, whenever or wherever one looked there were different combinations and forms of labor generated by the peculiarities of the time and place.

It is possible to imagine several ways to organize a historical survey of work. One approach might be chronological, but the real difficulties of this should be almost immediately clear. To attempt to cover such a long span of time for such a wide area would create problems for a single time series. The enterprise could easily bury itself in clutter. More promising might seem topical organization: a chapter on slavery, a chapter on forced wage labor, a chapter on industrial labor and unions, and so forth. Quite apart from the mechanical and potentially boring form this imposes, there are two problems. As we noted, labor systems did not exist on their own. And apart from late-twentieth-century capitalist free labor, and perhaps a few slave-based economies in the past, no system so dominated its time and place as to exclude all other forms of work. These competed, coexisted, and influenced each other. By separating labor systems into individual chapters we are in danger of losing the context.

And as we saw, systems of work historically have overlapped each other. On the one hand, different forms of labor routinely have been found together in the same work space. In the 1870s, for example, Brazilian coffee plantations employed chiefly African slaves but were beginning to experiment with European contract workers. Dominant forms change. By 1900 the slaves were gone from these same Brazilian plantations, and few of the free blacks found employment as coffee labor, work which had been taken over by resident Italian *colonos*. Today in the same area free wage labor predominates, hired daily from the side of the road, and it is as likely to be employed producing sugar as in producing coffee. In post-1850 coastal Peru, Chinese contract workers were common on the sugar and cotton plantations, but by 1900 the labor force was primarily made up of Indian and mixed blood migrants from the sierra. Topical chapters might make it difficult to keep in mind that work systems persisted or new ones grew up even as circumstances changed.

The effort here is to combine the two approaches. The book is divided into five chapters, arranged roughly by chronology. This is a chronology of economic not political time. Each chapter focuses on the organization and conditions of the dominant forms of work during the period and considers how these changed, or did not change, and why. Interwoven with these are other, ancillary sorts of work, some peculiar to the time period and others with longer life histories but included at a given point for convenience of exposition. Work, such as plantation slavery or forced wage labor in agriculture, that persisted over long periods and was widely disseminated necessarily turns up more than once, though perhaps in different iterations: African slavery on the coast of Colombia in the eighteenth century, for example, was different from that on Brazilian plantations in the sixteenth century or in Cuban sugar fields in the mid-nineteenth century. Peru's *mitas* and Guatemala's *repartimientos* both were schemes of forced wage labor, but how they worked and what those caught up in the drafts did were quite different. The chapters that follow will address new forms of work as these develop, but they may also return to old forms that changing conditions have revitalized or propagated to new areas.

By way of a preview and an orientation: Chapter 1 looks at Spain, Portugal, and America from shortly before the first contact until the mid-sixteenth century, when conditions in the colonies began to settle down. The emphasis is on slavery of the indigenous population and on the *encomienda*. Chapter 2 shows the routinization of work forms between 1550 and 1750, particularly forced wage labor among the indigenous population and African slavery. Chapter 3 treats the century from 1750 to 1850 by focusing on towns and cities and on work experiences there; it gives special attention to women. Chapter 4 examines the impacts of the nineteenth-century North Atlantic Industrial Revolution on work in Latin America, surveying a period that witnessed more change than any since the conquest. Chapter 5 is about work in Latin America since 1930 and pays particular attention to urban labor, the rise of unions, and worker participation in politics. The concluding chapter makes several broad points about work in the history of Latin America, and those who prefer to begin with the abstract and work toward the concrete may wish to start reading with the conclusions. "Sources and Additional Readings" available in English for each of the five chapters are listed at the end of the book. These include some of the sources for the chapter itself, as well as additional material on these topics and sources about types of work and work experiences relevant to the period but not directly addressed in the text.

Chapter 1

Encounter and Accommodation, 1480–1550

For the people of Castile the best work was war. After Charles Martel stopped the Moorish sweep north at Tours in 732, the small surviving Christian kingdoms of northern Iberia began the *Reconquista* (Reconquest), a 700–year process of pushing Islam back. Individual and social success for these crusaders came from victory in battle, whether in large-scale campaigns or local conflicts. Military prowess elevated lords and peasants alike, if not equally. Centuries later, one of the more unlucky of the New World's Spanish conquerors remembered that his family name Cabeza de Vaca ("Cow Head") and his minor *hidalgo* (lower nobility) status derived from the exploits of an ancestor, a shepherd who had used a strategically placed cow skull to guide Christian armies to a surprise attack on the Moors. What mattered in the Reconquest, and what elevated many an obscure Spaniard in the New World, was personal valor, a capacity for enormous, if typically short-term, physical exertion, and a high confidence in your arm, your God, and your King. Successful men conquered land and honors and put others to work for them.

Background

By the middle of the fourteenth century the Christians had expelled Islam from most of the Iberian peninsula, leaving only the vestigial caliphate of Granada in the southeast. On the flanks of the peninsula the kingdoms of

Portugal, facing the Atlantic, and Aragon and Catalonia, oriented toward the Mediterranean, were shifting their efforts and their economies from war to seaborne commerce. The kings struck bargains with the new, emerging urban bourgeoisies to limit the power of the landed nobility and to pursue policies favorable to trade and manufacturing, in return for financial support for the Crown. These states increasingly resembled commerce-based Italian city-states more than warrior kingdoms, although Portugal, in particular, never entirely abandoned elements of the Reconquest mind set. The kings of Portugal began the modern-day overseas expansion of Europe with the capture of Ceuta on the coast of North Africa in 1415 from Islam. But several hard-fought campaigns soon deflected Portuguese efforts away from direct confrontation with the Moors to explorations down the Atlantic coast of Africa, seeking trade and the possibility of linking up with the almost mythical Christian kingdom of Prester John (present-day Ethiopia). By the 1480s Portuguese ships regularly returned with cargoes of gold, ivory, and slaves obtained at trading posts on the West African coast. In the next decade the king's servants were actively seeking a route around Africa to Asia.

The fifteenth century developed differently for Castile, the most powerful of the *Reconquista* Christian kingdoms and located on the peninsula's high central plateau. Here war had never ceased, although by the mid-1400s this amounted to little more than border raids. Apart from war, Castile's most important economic activity was stock raising, cattle and, particularly, sheep, to supply wool to the textile mills of Castile and Flanders. Large-scale herding of this sort was unusual in late medieval Europe, where economies more generally depended on a peasant farming that mixed agriculture with modest animal production. Ranching on the Iberian peninsula thrived in a warrior tradition that valued mobility and disdained agricultural labor, a tradition reinforced by the association of farm work with a conquered population of Moors, *moriscos* (Moorish converts to Christianity), and slaves.

In the second half of the fifteenth century political events in Iberia accelerated. Isabella, queen of Castile, in 1469 married Ferdinand of Aragon to form the embryonic Spanish state. This touched off an uprising of Castile's nobility, who rightly feared the power of a consolidated monarchy. Victorious after a ten-year war, the Catholic monarchs turned their attention to the remaining Moorish presence on the peninsula. When Columbus brought his brilliant, if flawed, exploration scheme to Isabella, the monarchs were besieging Islam's last citadel at Granada. Thus, in 1492 the proto-nation state of Spain stood unknowingly poised at a historical crossroads. For centuries Castile's population hoped and expected to "make something of themselves" through war, to dominate others and to be respected for valor and martial abilities. But the *Reconquista* was over and, as the Portuguese discovered,

North Africa offered limited possibilities for military success. How would the younger sons of *hidalgos* gain a name or wealth, and how would a warlike and ambitious yeoman peasantry advance? Aragon offered an alternative possible model. At first imitating, and now surpassing, the earlier Mediterranean city-states, Aragon was among Europe's leaders in the development of commercial capitalism, the accumulation of money capital based on long-distance trade. As events unfolded, it was precisely the combination of Castile's military prowess with Aragon's economic power that underpinned Europe's first, though imperfectly realized, nation-state, but it was Castile and Castilian values that framed the empire.

Empire

What might have happened had Columbus not returned to Granada with word of his discoveries, effectively reigniting the Reconquest and securing Castilian predominance in Iberia and in the New World? If not Columbus, someone else would have made the same or a similar voyage soon, and only Spain had the economic and military power at the time to take control of America. Not for more than another century, for example, was England able to launch a successful New World settlement colony. Thinking about alternative possibilities, though, reminds us that there were two models of empire available in the sixteenth century. Portugal's approach was essentially medieval and it followed a pattern that went back at least to eighth or seventh century B.C. Greek trading communities in the Black Sea. Portugal set up "factories" in Africa, in Asia, and on the coast of Brazil, accidentally discovered in 1500 by a fleet bound for Asia. These were manned by agents of Portuguese and Genoese merchants who bartered with local populations for goods of value to Europeans. In the early sixteenth century Portugal made no serious effort to control colonial areas beyond those necessary for their trading stations. This was because the economic relations they developed did not require holding territory and because Portugal's very small national population of perhaps a million in 1500 limited the manpower available for armies and bureaucracies. Even the ships that knitted together this most seaborne of empires increasingly were manned by mixed bloods and local populations recruited in the colonies.

Spain took a different approach to an empire, developed over centuries of the Reconquest and fine tuned in asserting control over the Canary Islands in the 1480s and 1490s. Theirs was an empire of conquest, occupation, domination, and control. Castile, which furnished most of the first-century migrants to the New World, benefited from a relatively large population and one with an appetite for war and conquest. Their experience, which was confirmed repeatedly in the New World, was that militarily they were almost invincible. Emigrants from the peninsula went readily to the New World "to serve God and the King and also to get rich," in Bernal Díaz de Castillo's famous phrase. Valor, heroic energy, luck, and ruthlessness could enrich and ennoble even an "obscure cut throat" such as Francisco Pizarro. This was the Age of Miracles, and it could not last. The first phase was over in the central areas by the 1540s, when Viceroy Antonio de Mendoza mounted the Coronado expedition to rid Mexico City of a turbulent population of would-be conquerors, and a new viceroy in Peru executed Gonzalo Pizarro. But no one knew this yet. For another two hundred years *entradas* (exploratory expeditions) pushed back the fringes of empire, repeating the hardships if rarely the successes of the first generation. War and armed domination unquestionably were work, and the Spanish were their sixteenth-century masters.

Despite the undoubted attractions of conquest, the Spanish did not shun peaceful trade and commerce as paths to riches. What those with social aspirations did avoid was direct involvement in artisan work or retail trade, though they were usually willing to rent property for this purpose and even to be silent partners in small-scale commercial enterprises. Wholesale trade, particularly long-distance overseas commerce, was a world apart from shop tending, and New World elites participated actively in it, often in partnerships with Spanish or foreign merchants. They were also involved in precious metal mining and money lending, as well as large-scale agriculture and stock raising. There was no shame in seeking profit, and a conqueror or a newly arrived viceroy was capable of paying close attention to gains and losses. A figure as prominent as Hernán Cortés spent hours each day preparing detailed instructions for agents and hacienda supervisors who did not seem to be giving enough attention to his income. What those ambitious for social status could not do was to work for others or work with their hands producing goods or services for others. New arrivals who introduced themselves into a community as artisans rarely escaped the social limits this imposed, even if later they prospered, but if they put aside their tools, picked up a sword, and joined an expedition they could move up. The early Spanish colonial world valued hard work and economic success, and like most new societies it was capable of considerable selective "amnesia" about a person's past in the face of present success.

Social mobility was always easier on the edges of the empires than at the center, and in the sixteenth century all of Brazil was a fringe area. Portugal's focus was on the East, and it had few resources to spare for the initially unpromising Atlantic coast of the New World. Several of the Europeans who played key roles in the early settlement of the colony were *degredados*, criminals sent to Brazil for their sins or abandoned on the coast by ships' captains.

In the 1530s men of modest success in India received huge grants of land in Brazil, reinforced by legal and judicial powers of which the Spanish conquerors could only dream. Still, for the first half-century after 1500 the Portuguese presence in Brazil was tenuous, and even after French intrusions and the possibilities of the new crop of sugar stimulated more interest in the 1550s and 1560s, there was no mass migration from Portugal. What arrived instead after 1560 was boatload upon boatload of African slaves, fueling and being paid for by a rapidly expanding export economy. As a result, what emerged in Brazil was a small "white" population immersed in a vast sea of Indians and blacks. Paradoxically, this led the state to reinforce legal race boundaries, while at the same time it prompted and demanded considerable de facto flexibility in the social definition of "white" and of the criteria for membership in local elites.

A term often mistakenly applied to conquest-era Spanish and Portuguese societies, and to much of Latin America since, is "feudal." In fact, a strong Roman heritage and centuries of Moorish influence meant that the Iberian peninsula was the area of Europe in which classic feudalism was least developed. By the mid-fifteenth century much of the continent was moving to restructure economic and social relations to accommodate the development of mercantile capitalism. Spain and Portugal were among the early leaders in these reforms, but after 1500 they fell behind. This was not because they were "feudal" but because a flood of New World wealth made the often wrenching changes seem increasingly unnecessary. Aggravating a growing conservatism was Spain's preoccupation with fighting the Reformation, which drained the state of treasure and the nation of blood. To preserve themselves under the hammer blows of Spain the new nations of England, France, the Netherlands, and the German states dismantled the power of the traditional landed elites, broke up archaic monopolies and production systems, and re-oriented their economies to more capitalist forms. In a short span Spain went from being economically, as well as militarily and politically, the most advanced country in Europe to a laggard that saw its position continue to decline for centuries. The ready availability of New World silver meant that the economic, political, and social contradictions of early modern Spain were not addressed and remained unresolved, hindering modernization.

In Portugal the bourgeoisie by 1500 had made much greater headway in reorienting national policies to support capitalism. Ironically, though, the very size of Brazil, its lack of immediately exploitable resources, and the limited population available for overseas settlement meant that Portugal's New World colony developed a much more "feudal" structure than did Spanish America. In New Spain and Peru within a generation the Crown brought the conquerors under control and imposed on them the rule of urban-based, state bureaucrats, at least in the central areas. For Brazil, by contrast, and even leaving aside the abortive pseudo-feudalism of the donatary captains, the development of sugar meant that the countryside dominated the towns. The weakness of the state fragmented power and put it in the hands of the lords of the *engenhos* (sugar mills) and of the *sertão* (back country). The writ of the king's representative hardly ran beyond the outskirts of the capital Salvador. The most capitalist of the Iberian powers had given birth to the most "feudal" of New World colonies.

Indigenous Populations

Despite evident differences, the culture of the Europeans that arrived in the New World was broadly uniform. This was not so for the indigenous American populations they found there. The outcome of initial encounters and the evolution of the colonies depended on a calculus of clashing social and material cultures, with elements specific to each area. Excepting a few groups that inhabited isolated maritime environments, most Indians in the New World depended on agriculture. Typically, they relied on "slash and burn" cultivation, though the indigenous empires developed more complex patterns of agriculture, and even the Arawaks of the Caribbean built up mounds (*conucos*) for more intensive use. The principal division of labor was by gender. Typically, men did the heavy clearing of the forest, a task that reinforced the skills necessary for hunting and warfare. Women took care of planting, weeding, and harvesting, as well as child rearing and household duties. Occasionally captives were employed as forced labor, but generally subsistence agriculture was family or community based. These units were largely self-sufficient in material terms, producing not only their own food but the tools, housing and bedding, and clothing and ornaments their members required.

With no urgency to produce a surplus above immediate needs, and scant way to store it or transport it if they did, subsistence societies did not usually support a specialized artisan class or an elaborated ruling elite. Where hierarchies did emerge—the Arawaks, for example, had a well-defined strata of *caciques* (local lords)—these seem to have been based more on the control of access to the supernatural, or sometimes to a scarce commodity such as salt, rather than on accumulated material, or class, differences.

The rhythm of subsistence societies alternated short bursts of hard and sometimes dangerous work, for example, hunting or fishing or war, with long periods of leisure. They formed what one anthropologist has labeled the "original affluent societies." Everyone was able to acquire what they needed and were able to use with a minimum of effort, and members of society lacked the means or the rationale to accumulate material capital. As a result, there was little purpose in forcing others to work for them on a large scale. The "improvidence" of these societies and the "laziness" of the population greatly bothered Europeans, particularly when the Indians refused to work under conditions and for the wages set by the new arrivals. Indigenous populations understood and respected work and were capable of enormous bursts of energy when called for. What they could not understand was the accumulation of more and more material possessions, possessions they could not carry, would have to defend, and for which they had little use. Variations on this basic form of subsistence farmer/hunter-gatherer could be found throughout the Americas, from the plains of North America to the cold islands of Tierra del Fuego.

The imperial civilizations of the mainland, most evidently the Aztecs, the Maya, and the Inca, manifested much more highly differentiated production systems that supported complex social and class structures. At the bottom of the socioeconomic pyramid were the peasant farming families, here usually organized into kinship clans called, variously, *calpulli*, *chinamits*, or *allyu*. What set the peasant off from subsistence agriculturalists was the regular production of a surplus, part of which was appropriated by another group for its own purposes. This tax might take the form of agricultural goods or handicraft items such as cloth or worked leather, or natural products or slaves. Where transportation was prohibitively expensive, taxes might be levied instead in the form of "rotary" labor applied to elite or state-owned lands or for public works: men, and sometimes women, were required to work a certain number of days or weeks each year. The surplus they produced supported specialists such as court artisans, a military or priestly class, or a state bureaucracy whose job it was to work full time for the general well-being.

These systems typically involved reciprocal obligations and benefits, and for the mass of the population the very act of generating the surplus reinforced their commitment to society. The early Spanish reported, for example, that pre-conquest Andean peasants had gone "joyfully" to work the Inca's lands. Where, on the other hand, the people doubted the legitimacy of the demands made upon them or saw these as exploitative, the relationship could be tense and might even become dependent on open coercion. For example, in the last days before the arrival of the Spanish, the Aztec imperial state was experiencing growing popular resistance to its demands for victims for human sacrifice.

In the Andes, villages and small city-states had alternated with empires for centuries. The advantages of controlling resources in several ecological zones, including the mountains, the valleys between the mountains, and the coast, prompted repeated efforts to create centralized states, but difficult communications and local discontent again and again split apart and toppled these larger entities. The Inca Empire, consolidated only at the turn of the sixteenth century, was simply the most recent of such supra-village constructions, and it was far from stable, as a destructive civil war in the early 1530s demonstrated. A state policy of *mitmaq* settlements combined the functions of military colonies, to keep outlying areas under control, with guarantees of access to different ecological strata. The Inca's subjects paid tribute chiefly through labor service, *mita*. These demands could be quite extensive. For example, one community of 4,000 "houses" reported shortly after the conquest that its obligations under the Incas had included sending 400 men to the capital for construction work, 400 men to plant food for the military garrisons in the North, shepherds for the Inca's herds, and workers to weave cloth and gather dye stuffs. Others mined salt, harvested peppers and cacao in the hot country, guarded the Inca's fields, transported the products to Cuzco and nearby administrative centers, and carried cargo along the royal highway. The community also furnished to the state various artisan products and sent forty "older" men to guard the women who wove cloth and cooked for the soldiers who passed along the royal road.

Two groups in Aztec and Inca societies remained outside the standard clan and community structures. One was a small number of free laborers, whom the Spanish called *narborías* in the Caribbean and New Spain and *yanaconas* in the Andes. No longer tied to their original villages or kinship groups, *narborías* and *yanaconas* were free of the labor and tax obligations such links entailed but also had lost any claim to community resources or protection. How they came to their anomalous status is not clear, although in some cases villages or families may have expelled them for unacceptable behavior, and others perhaps fled debts or justice or other pressing problems. Some *narborías* and *yanaconas* moved to new villages and settled there as a subordinate population, but most became dependents of elites, whether individual lords or the state. They amounted to no more than about one percent of the population of the Inca Empire when the Spanish arrived, but their dependent condition made them useful, and, not surprisingly, they flocked to the service of the Spanish.

Similarly, many New World societies had slavery, but what exactly this meant varied. The Tupí of Brazil, for example, took slaves in war and made ritual meals of at least some of the men, with great competition to consume parts of the most valiant of these. Captured women and children were assimilated into the kinship group or used as agricultural labor. The Aztecs also took slaves as tribute and in war and notoriously sacrificed them in bloody public religious rituals: Cortés and the surviving Spanish watched their compatriots killed in this manner after the defeat on the Noche Triste. What was generally absent from pre-contact New World societies was chattel slavery in the European sense, the buying and selling of human beings as simple property.

European Impact

Whatever the original organization of the indigenous societies, epidemic disease brought by Europeans provoked massive changes. Apart from simply the demoralization that each new and unanticipated horror caused, an outbreak of epidemic disease could leave the surviving population too weak for agriculture or to hunt and fish, leading to starvation or further weakening from malnutrition: this was the time, one Maya chronicle remembered, when the buzzards came into the houses to eat the dead. Death was indiscriminate, carrying away not just the common people but also the community's spiritual and political leaders. In pre-literate societies the vital knowledge lost with them could not always be reconstituted. There might not be enough survivors left even to fill required positions in the social or political order. When the Spanish attempted to reconstitute an indigenous elite using collaborators, the results were not always successful. In other cases new or traditional enemies seized the chance to move in on weakened communities, killing them or taking their lands or other resources.

Some societies weathered epidemic disease better than others. Widely dispersed family or small kin groups not integrated into a centralized regime had the best chance of surviving. This was one of the reasons the Indians of the Amazon, those in southern Argentina and Chile, and the Chichimecas of northern New Spain proved so resilient to conquest. By contrast, empires dependent on elaborate internal differentiation and living close to the limits of what their environment could sustain, risked, and commonly suffered, collapse. The Aztec state, for example, devolved almost overnight from an empire into a congeries of local communities and regional systems. Intricate mechanisms of tribute collection and community labor collapsed, until the Spanish revived and expanded these for their own purposes.

On a more positive note, contact with Europeans revolutionized many areas of indigenous material culture and patterns of labor use. Iron axes and hoes allowed agriculturalists to complete in hours tasks that would have taken days or months with stone and hardened wood tools. New technologies raised the productivity of labor, but where there was no market for increased output, improved productivity may have resulted only in increased leisure. That is, at least some of the Indians' "laziness" about which landowners and colonial administrators fretted simply reflected higher labor efficiency in a nonmarket economy.

Barter trade with Europeans modified and restructured indigenous economies even without the direct political intervention of colonial rule. Iron was probably the most important item traded in the early years, but the availability of other commodities such as textiles or beads and mirrors and, increasingly, distilled alcohol, prompted indigenous populations to reorient their work to produce goods for which the Europeans were willing to trade. In some instances these changes occurred within the framework of existing socioeconomic structures: in Brazil, for example, the cutting and hauling of logwood to exchange with the Portuguese meshed well with existing Tupí ideas about men's activities. Laboring fifteen hours a day on a sugar plantation did not, and the settlers found it difficult to recruit Indians for such labor. European enthusiasm for products such as gold sometimes prompted indigenous groups to attempt new types of economic activities or to expand existing ones. Where the local inhabitants failed to produce what the Europeans wanted, as for example on Hispaniola, the invaders soon intervened to assert direct control over the economy and to shift the work process to one that more immediately served their interests.

Labor Systems

Almost without exception the first contacts between Europeans and Native American populations, once these moved beyond battle and barter, involved slavery. Indians enslaved European captives, but more importantly and in much larger numbers, Europeans enslaved Indians. Among the first exports of Hispaniola were Indian captives, and the slaving of indigenous populations continued in parts of Latin America into the twentieth century. This enslavement was entirely reflexive. Deeply ingrained racism and cultural prejudice, hardened by centuries of war against the infidel, made it difficult or impossible for most Spanish to view the inhabitants of the New World as equals, or even as human beings. That some New World groups practiced, or were said to practice, cannibalism particularly horrified the Europeans and greatly strengthened their assumption of Indian perversion. The conquerors, by common consent and with little thought, forced the peoples they encountered, and who, it should be remembered, they had often just defeated in bitter and hard-fought struggles, to do whatever they wished. Indians were made to carry heavy loads, to work in the fields and as house servants, to fight in new expeditions, and to provide sexual services. The conquerors took it for granted that they enjoyed the right to dispose of the defeated as they would, and few felt any restraints in the treatment they gave them. For moral and economic reasons the Crown sought to curb the worst excesses of slavery and work abuses, but this took time. Given frequent collusion between Crown agents in the New World and those who exploited Indian labor, the state's ameliorative policies initially had only limited effect.

By 1520 a generation of philosophers, churchmen, and Crown bureau-crats had debated extensively the question of what Europe had encountered in the Indies. With little hesitation Spanish state policy recognized the rights of the indigenous populations to full human status, to citizenship in the empire, and to participation in the church. Columbus was admonished to "treat the said Indians very well and lovingly, without injury . . . and if it should happen that any person or persons treat the said Indians badly in any manner, the said admiral . . . is to punish them severely."[1] As did all the empire's citizens, the Indians had the right to contract their labor freely with whom-ever they wished. Having just in the 1480s released the peasants of Castile from their remaining feudal obligations, the Spanish state now strongly re-sisted recreating a bound population in the New World. But if the Indians were free, they also had the obligation to work, and if they resisted or fell into "vagrancy" they could be made to work: "because our desire and wish [is] that the Indians pay us our tributes and taxes that they have to pay us, as our subjects. You are to compel them to work in the affairs of our service . . . to secure gold and to do other tasks that we are ordering done."[2] For their labor they were to receive fair wages, money with which they would pay their taxes and support the church. But the Conquest kept getting ahead of the state and state policies, pushing into new areas and demanding and requiring immediate rewards. The conquerors tried to impose a labor policy "on the ground" that favored their interests in advance of and, if necessary, in defi-ance of Crown directives, and they held on to this as long as possible. Put another way, few Spanish or creole New World elites could bring themselves to recognize that the indigenous population had any rights worth consider-ing, whether these were "natural" rights or rights elaborated by the Crown's councilors.

When Europeans moved out of the Caribbean and encountered for the first time powerful, centralized empires run by a hierarchical bureaucracy and supported by an extensive tax, or tribute, system, their first instinct was to maintain the structure intact and put themselves in charge. This approach failed for several reasons. Catastrophic population declines undermined the taxing systems, but in most areas this took a generation or two. There were more immediate problems. For one thing, the Spanish generally increased the Indians' tax load. Sometimes this was intentional, but in other cases, and we can tell from surviving records, the new conquerors simply did not un-derstand the forms of indigenous tribute or the quantities these involved. They also changed the nature of the products required. The Spanish had little interest in feather cloaks, for example, but cacao was much in demand. Be-fore the arrival of the Europeans the use of chocolate had been limited to Aztec elites, but now a popular market exploded, and not just in New Spain but in Europe as well. The Spanish quickly made the beans a prime tribute item. Indians residing in areas not propitious for cacao now found themselves forced to trek to the lowlands to obtain it: inhabitants of the highlands of Chiapas and Guatemala, for example, migrated seasonally to the Pacific coast to gather wild cacao or to work in the new cacao plantations. Thousands died when exposed to an unfamiliar climate and new diseases.

Others had no choice but to seek work under sometimes horrific conditions in Spanish-owned mines and mills to earn what they needed for taxes. Before the Conquest elites had reinvested tax income in the local system, as consumption or capital investment or to reinforce the sociopolitical life through ritual and religion. Some of this continued under the Spanish, but now huge amounts of revenue left the New World for the Old, draining the colonies. And the new tax systems exhibited few of the features of reciprocity characteristic of those of the precontact world, weakening their legitimacy.

For the Europeans, slavery was the first and most obvious way to organize indigenous labor in the New World, but its use fell off quickly in the central areas of the empire. Declining Indian populations and growing numbers of Spanish immigrants, together with Crown pressures to end abuses, prompted the development of new forms of labor mobilization and control. Until the end of the colonial period, however, the enslavement of Indians taken in so-called "just war" continued in many parts of both empires. "Just war" was war on indigenous populations that resisted or rebelled against colonial authority or that had fallen into apostasy or heresy, or that could be made to appear to have done so. Such conflicts were particularly characteristic of the lightly populated northern and southern borders, but they persisted too in more central areas.

Before mid-century one of the most notorious regions of continued Indian slaving was that part of the Central American peninsula called Nicaragua. The region had the misfortune to be the meeting point of two streams of conquest, one led by Pedro de Alvarado from Guatemala and the other by Pedrarias Dávila from Panama. Both saw Nicaragua as a frontier zone and marginal to their main interests, and neither had any stake in preserving its population. As early as 1529 Dávila was writing the king describing slaving in the area and making only the slightest pretense that these were legal captives of "just war." By the 1530s the capture and sale of human beings had become Nicaragua's main industry. Slavers each year rounded up thousands of men and women and shipped them down the Pacific coast to Panama and Peru. This was a shortsighted and wasteful process that killed more Indians than it delivered to employers, and by 1550 the trade had largely ended. In one generation slaving and disease reduced the population of the region from perhaps half a million to less than 15,000, and it no longer merited the slavers' attentions.

Brazil

In Brazil Indian slavery had a more protracted history and remained an important form of labor mobilization and control even in the central areas until well into the seventeenth century. Most of the indigenous population of coastal Brazil first encountered by the Portuguese lived in shifting villages based on slash and burn subsistence agriculture, supplemented by hunting and gathering. They spoke Tupí languages, languages the invaders soon shaped into a simplified patois ("*língua geral*") that served along the coast and even into the interior. The Tupí groups had no domestic animals and few possessions, and they considered food and land community property. As in all hunting and gathering societies without techniques for long-term food preservation, a kill or a cache of honey was shared with neighbors, in the certainty that others would do the same another day. Men hunted and fished and cleared the forest for agriculture, while the women grew and prepared agricultural products. The men also fought in the coast's incessant wars. These were not simply ritual occasions: "One could scarcely believe how cruel the combat was. If any of them were hit [with arrows] they tore them from their bodies with marvelous courage, broke them and bit the pieces with their fine teeth like mad dogs. [They were] . . . so furious in their wars that they fight on without stopping so long as they can move arms and legs, never retreating."[3] The purpose of these ferocious encounters was to capture not territory or material goods but prisoners for ritual sacrifice.

For thirty years after 1500 the Portuguese made little effort to control the indigenous population of Brazil but, instead, dealt with them on a more or less equal basis. War racked the coast: Indians against Indians, Indians against the Portuguese, and the Portuguese against the Dutch, the French, and the English. In the indigenous wars and in those pitting Europeans against the Indians, capture and slavery were common. The Europeans put the Indians to work cultivating food crops and cutting and carrying brazilwood, while the Indians integrated into their groups those Europeans they did not kill. Although the Crown and members of various religious orders generally opposed Indian slavery, not until 1570 did Portugal's king declare the freedom of his New World subjects and ban their routine captivity. Even then he left the settlers and Crown agents in Brazil the familiar loophole of "just wars" and the additional one of "Indians of the cord." These latter were Indians unfortunate enough have been captured by other indigenous groups and destined now to be eaten. It was legal to buy or ransom them and then subject them to slavery as the price of their rescue. Through these breaches Brazilian planters and employers propelled centuries of Indian slavery.

Commercial agriculture began to take hold gradually after 1530, and demands for labor increased. The cultivation and processing of sugar in particular required unprecedented numbers of workers, prompting more systematic expeditions into the interior. Slavers invaded the *sertão* on expeditions lasting years and "descended" thousands of Indians to the coast. For the slave catchers it was an arduous but not altogether unattractive life, and one relatively free of state or church restraints: a slaver remembered happily that in the bush he could have as many wives as he wished and eat meat on any day he liked. Areas such as the southern captaincy of São Vicente (present-day São Paulo) specialized in slave raiding and the export of Indians to the northern plantations. But most of the early settlement efforts failed, and the demand for labor before mid-century remained limited.

In both the Portuguese and Spanish colonies the chief impediment to shifting from forced to free labor was the lack of interest the indigenous population showed in working for wages. The Crown's new subjects found ways to meet even their new and higher taxes without seeking wage work, and when they did work for wages their behavior bewildered and infuriated the Europeans. At least for the first century or two most Indians paid their taxes and supported the church in kind. What they did not produce they traded for. When they needed cash, this was almost always for a specific purpose and not part of a larger scheme of accumulation. As a result, they worked only so long as was necessary to get the amount of money they required for the moment and then abandoned wage labor. Whereas in a capitalist economy an increase in wages tends to draw more labor into the market, in a precapitalist environment where workers continued to control the means of their own subsistence and where cash requirements were more or less fixed, higher wages prompted less work. The result is the "backward bending" labor supply curve familiar to specialists in developmental economics. Indians in colonial society responded vigorously to the opportunity to earn better wages but not to the chance to make more money. They were not free workers in the capitalist sense of having only their labor to sell to support themselves, and they showed a distressing lack of interest in either capital accumulation or opportunities to participate in European consumer culture.

Encomienda

The Spanish Crown resisted the general enslavement of its New World subjects, but it also opposed "laziness" and "vagrancy." Laws raised no objections to the coercion of workers when this was seen to be necessary, provided certain conditions were met. This was the origin of the New World *encomienda*, the most important form of labor mobilization apart from slavery up to mid-century. The term *encomienda* derives from *encomendar*, "to give into the charge or power" of another, much the same as the traditional meaning of "commend" in English. The institution had its roots in the peninsular Reconquest. During the long centuries of war the Christian kingdoms with each forward lurch faced the problem of how to incorporate newly captured territories and populations. To do this, kings and princes delegated wide local power to subordinate nobles and churchmen in an arrangement known variously as *encomienda* or *repartimiento* (from *repartir*, to divide up). But these were exactly the magnates Isabella and Ferdinand had struggled to bring under control shortly after their marriage and they had no intention of raising up the same problem in the Indies.

The Crown firmly intended that the institution of the *encomienda* be left behind in Spain, but the conquerors pushed ahead with their own vision of empire, including servile labor. Eventually forced to accept *encomiendas* in the New World, the Crown struggled to limit them and never wavered in denying those who received the grants legal jurisdiction over the Indians.

Encomiendas appeared first in the New World on Hispaniola in the late 1490s. Columbus's inept administration provoked an uprising among the settlers, and to buy them off he distributed *encomiendas*, or, rather, he recognized the distributions the rebels already had made. To quiet complaints among his supporters he made them grants too. The process was entirely predictable, without premeditation, and it followed on historical experiences in Spain. After the fact and very reluctantly, the Crown sanctioned the Hispaniola *encomiendas* as the price of keeping settlers on the island, but at the same time it embarked on a half-century effort to regulate and restrain private appropriation of its citizens' labor. Use of *encomiendas* peaked in the central parts of the empire between 1525 and 1575 and declined rapidly thereafter, but the institution remained strong in some border areas to the end of the colonial period.

To begin with, it is worth pointing out what the *encomienda* was not. It was not a grant of land. This is an error that turns up even today in casual accounts. Except on barren frontiers such as the present southwestern United States, the Spanish Crown rarely granted or gave away land to private citizens. Land was a potentially important source of revenue, and the state sold it wherever possible, typically at auction to assure the best prices. Local officials and town councils sometimes did make land grants, chiefly to themselves and their relatives, and particularly in the second half of the sixteenth century after the huge declines in the indigenous populations. But the new claimants still had to pry recognition of their title from the state, usually through an expensive series of payments called *composición*. Regulations specifically forbade those who held *encomiendas* from owning land in the same area as their grant of Indians, however they obtained this land. Such a prohibition was not easily enforced, and it was widely violated, but the effort was never abandoned, and it clearly indicated the Crown's determination not to allow formation of a "feudal" ruling clique in America.

The New World *encomienda* entitled the recipient to the product of the labor of a specific group of Indians, usually defined as all or part of a town or towns. In some cases the *encomendero* made direct use of these Indians to work in his fields or at mining, but it became more common over time to instead appropriate a portion of the taxes paid by the community. In return, the grant holder was to defend the Indians and to see to their Christianization, usually by employing a priest for them. In theory a map would show a neat division of *encomenderos* linked to certain towns, but the intermingling of subject towns (*sujetos*) in New Spain, for example, and long-standing policies of colonization in the Andes frustrated such precision. Also, to facilitate labor use, tax collection, and evangelization, Crown and church officials resettled and concentrated dispersed Indian populations, creating new towns that sometimes had multiple allegiances. Particularly in the early years, the exact number of Indians in a given grant was often, and purposefully, vague: Cortés's *encomienda* spoke of 23,000 Indians but observers placed the actual number obligated to him at 100,000 or more. For the well-being of both parties, *encomenderos* were not allowed to live in the towns of their grants or, as mentioned above, to acquire land there. In fact, they commonly did both.

Essentially forced upon the Spanish Crown by the New World pioneers, the *encomienda* nevertheless came to be seen by the state as preferable to slavery and the best and most humane way to mobilize the labor needed to sustain the colonies. By "commending" a group of Indians to one Spaniard, the state hoped that the *encomendero* would have a stake in the well-being of these Indians, something absolutely lacking in the first decades when the conquerors treated the indigenous population as spoils of war. In fact, though, and so long as there remained possibilities of new discoveries, consciousness or concern about the well-being of the Indians developed slowly among the conquerors. *Encomenderos* routinely plundered their holding to support new adventures or transferred their grants to others at a pittance to pay for new exploration schemes.

The first Europeans to penetrate Hispaniola found traces of gold in the rivers and saw the inhabitants wearing gold ornaments, without realizing that most of these trinkets came by trade from the mainland. *Encomenderos* imagined that the Indians would pan alluvial gold for them. But the results were disappointing. Local Arawaks never had been much interested in gold and knew even less about mining it than did the Spanish. Still, the techniques involved were simple enough and easily learned. The much more serious problem was population decline. It was in Hispaniola that the Europeans and America's indigenous population first experienced the effects of the introduction of Old World diseases into the New, diseases to which the Europeans had developed some historical immunity. The population of Hispaniola collapsed, falling from several million in pre-contact days to less than 100,000 in 1508 and only a few hundred by the 1540s. Unfortunately for the Indians, the response of the *encomenderos* to this disaster, and to their falling incomes, was to take over direct control of mining and to work the Indians harder. The survivors were subjected to long hours with their feet in cold water and their bodies in the hot sun, almost guaranteeing upper respiratory infections. Those who resisted suffered brutal punishments. Employers underfed them and gave them no time to plant or harvest their own crops. As the local Indians died, slavers fanned out, north to the Lucayas (Bahamas), the so-called "useless islands," to Cuba, and to the mainland of South America, capturing tens of thousands of slaves in what proved to be a futile effort to stem the decline of the island's population.

To most Europeans, such harsh treatment, and even enslavement of the indigenous population, was both logical and necessary, and unremarkable, but a few among the Spanish spoke out against it. The Sunday before Christmas, 1511, the Dominican Friar Antonio de Montesinos startled and enraged the *encomenderos* when in his sermon he asked: "On what authority have you waged a detestable war against these people, who dwelt quietly and peacefully on their own land? Are these not men? Are you not bound to love them as you love yourselves?"[4] Not many in the colony listened, but back across the sea Crown officials in Spain found the devastation of the Indian population worrisome, both for humanitarian reasons and because of its effects on revenues. Worse, events seemed to be repeating themselves in the bloody conquest of Cuba begun in 1511.

In an attempt to rein in the worst excesses and also as part of efforts to harness the New World adventurers to the state's purposes, the king in 1512–13 issued the Laws of Burgos, effectively the first labor code for Spain's American colonies. As they applied to *encomiendas* these laws repeated the requirement that all recipients provide suitable religious instruction for the Indians and a building for services; those with more than fifty Indians were also to employ a teacher to give the children instruction in reading and writing. *Encomienda* Indians could not to be used as carriers and were not to be beaten or whipped or called "dogs." Pregnant women could not be sent to the mines or to do heavy agricultural work, nor could children be made to do adult tasks. All workers were to receive adequate food, housing, and clothing. Finally, no Spaniard could receive more than more than 150 or less than 40 Indians in *encomienda*. However well-intentioned, the laws did little to stem abuses or halt the decline in the indigenous population.

Striving to keep the colonies afloat, the Crown and settlers looked for other sources of labor. One possibility was indentured servants, contracted European workers who would be widely used during the next century in English Caribbean and North American colonies. In the event, neither the Spanish nor the Portuguese employed indentured labor on a large scale in America. They did not have the surplus populations available for this sort of emigration. Portugal, of course, was a small country with a small population and quickly found herself hard pressed to staff a world empire. Not until the late eighteenth century did the mainland and the Azores begin to feel the pressure of excess population, and by then indentured servitude as a form of labor mobilization was outdated. For Spain, the late fifteenth-century laws that freed the peasants tended to undercut any effort to bind Europeans to long-term labor contracts, apart from artisan apprenticeships. Spain also took the lead in the Counter Reformation, and religious wars bled the population of Castile. Not until the nineteenth century, after most of the empire had broken away, did population growth and economic decline on the peninsula make large numbers of emigrants available and willing to work as common laborers in the New World.

The Origins of New World African Slavery

More promising, at least from the perspective of the mine owners and sugar planters, were African slaves. The Jeronymite fathers who briefly ruled Hispaniola recommended the use of such slaves, and in 1517 Bartolomé de Las Casas, later famous as Protector of the Indians, suggested the importation of Africans as one way to build up the labor force and lessen the demands on the indigenous population. Inhabitants of the Mediterranean had a long and uninterrupted familiarity with slavery dating back at least to the Greeks and the Romans. While slavery declined in medieval northern Europe, it flourished in *Reconquista* Iberia: slaves in late fifteenth-century Christian Spain included, in addition to Africans, Jews, Moors and Berbers, *moriscos*, "Turks," and *guanches* (native inhabitants of the Canary Islands). With most of the fighting on the peninsula over, however, and inhibitions about enslaving fellow Europeans or Christians growing, attention focused more on nearby Africa. As early as the 1250s traders had regularly offered African slaves for sale in Portuguese markets. But the real change came two hundred years later as Portuguese explorers and merchants moved down the Atlantic coast of Africa. With regular commerce replacing earlier tentative ventures, Portugal found a ready market for slaves in the new sugar economies of Madeira and the Canaries, and as servants in the urban centers of southern Spain and Portugal: in the 1490s perhaps 6 to 10 percent of Seville was black, and Lisbon may have had twice as many Africans and locally born (*ladino*) blacks. Portugal dominated the slave traffic in the early sixteenth century, and the commercial value of the traffic for the empire at least equaled that of the better-known spice trade.

The Spanish that first arrived in Hispaniola brought African slaves with them, and these proved to be extraordinarily good workers. Across the New World employers routinely rated African workers as being worth three or four Indians. So long as a substantial indigenous population survived, however, the relatively high cost of blacks limited them to the work of servants or technicians and skilled workers in Hispaniola's infant sugar industry. The settlers were hesitant to bring too many blacks to the islands for fear of revolts. For this reason the new governor Nicolás de Obando stopped shipments in 1502, but Ferdinand reopened the traffic in 1505, in the interest of state revenues. By 1514 blacks outnumbered whites on the island, and in the wake of several conspiracies and uprisings Cardinal Francisco Jiménez de Cisneros, Crown administrator of the Indies, again banned imports in 1516. The local indigenous population was effectively extinct, however, and with the mines played out, sugar was almost the only hope for the island's economy and black slaves the only available workers. In what would become a familiar pattern, greed triumphed over fear and slave imports began again in 1518. Two years later Charles V awarded a court favorite an exclusive license to import 4,000 blacks directly from Africa (*bozales*) to Hispaniola. This began the *asiento*, or contract, system that supplied most of the legal slave imports to the Spanish colonies for the next 250 years.

Labor on the Mainland

In the first generation after 1492 African slave imports were but a drop in the bucket compared to the New World's Indians, but the indigenous population continued to fall at an astonishing rate. Moved by this collapse, and convinced of the evident failure of the *encomienda* system to reverse it, Charles V in 1520 declared an end to the grants. Those in place could continue for the holder's life, but *encomiendas* were not to be inherited, and the Crown would sanction no new ones. It was too late. In 1519 Hernán Cortés and a group of adventurers had sailed west from Cuba to land on the shores of what would become New Spain or Mexico. In two years they destroyed the Aztec Empire and took possession of by far the most valuable New World prize won by the Spanish up to that time.

The invasion of the mainland was a process as brutal and violent as had been the devastation of the islands, and on a vastly larger scale, and then and since it provoked outrage. But it was at the same time an incredible feat of endurance and courage that merits our attention, if perhaps not exactly our admiration. The conquerors for the most part were not professional soldiers, though some had experience in the wars on the peninsula and in Italy, and most had participated in earlier expeditions and in the repression of Indian and black slave revolts. What carried the Spanish forward was their self-confidence, their sense of invincibility. In part this was a certainty of cultural and religious superiority that saw Saint James descend to the battlefield to fight at their side, but more practically it was a merited trust in their equipment and tactics. The horse and steel armor and weapons, together with an organization that made Spain's infantry the finest in early sixteenth-century Europe, rendered the conquerors almost impervious to New World arms. Their numbers were small, though, and even under the most favorable of circumstances they sometimes spent weeks fighting every day, constantly wounded and exhausted, short of food and water, and cut off from any possibility of retreat or relief. Of Cortés's march up from the coast, Bernal Díaz de Castillo remembered one day's work:

> A company of Tlaxcalans, more than three thousand strong, who were lying in ambush, began to shower arrows on our horsemen. These Indians put up a good fight with their arrows and fire-hardened darts, and did wonders with their two-handed swords. In the skirmish four of our men were wounded, and I think one of them died of his wounds a few days later. We slept near a stream, and we dressed our wounds with the fat from a stout Indian whom we had killed and cut open, for we had no oil. We were so tired we could hardly stand.[5]

As a reward for such efforts New Spain's conquerors demanded the *encomiendas* that they had become familiar with in the Indies. Initially Cortés resisted, worried that these would do no better for the indigenous population here than they had on the islands. Few among the victors shared his caution, however, and under pressure he soon began to distribute grants. Cortés explained to the king that the *encomiendas* of New Spain would be different from those in the Caribbean, and in 1526 he issued elaborate regulations, banning the use of *encomienda* Indians in mining and limiting the number of days they could be made to do agricultural work. The grants here were of a size unimagined on the islands: in the mid-1530s some thirty *encomiendas* in the Central Valley averaged more than 6,000 Indians each, and the largest was 20,000. And this despite a 1528 Crown rule than limited *encomiendas* to

300 Indians! When the Crown protested such lavish grants, Cortés made the case that they were necessary not only to reward the conquerors but to the tie them to the colony and guarantee Spanish control of New Spain. With little choice the king acquiesced, but he did not give up efforts to bring his unruly New World subjects under control.

The mainland empires of the Aztecs, and later the Incas, proved to be particularly well suited to the *encomienda*, much more so than had been the dispersed populations of the Caribbean. On the islands the Spanish had often found it necessary to group together different communities and impose unaccustomed labor requirements upon them. Inhabitants of the empires, by contrast, were already accustomed to delivering taxes and labor on a regular basis to a hierarchical, centralized state. The Spanish found little difficulty in "decapitating" the state and inserting themselves at its head. But if the shift from an indigenous to an immigrant ruling class did not immediately agitate the masses, these soon found that things had changed. On the one hand, ex-subjects of the Aztecs now were spared the delivery of captives for human sacrifice. On the other, they found that the *encomenderos* and the state forced them to reorient much of their work away from traditional activities to new crops, to mining, and to participation in dangerous expeditions. Overall, labor demands increased, and as the population fell these became that much more onerous. Expeditions were particularly disruptive in the early post-conquest years as ambitious would-be conquerors uprooted thousands of Indians and forced them to serve as carriers and warriors on new adventures where many died and from which few returned: Pedro de Alvarado, for example, took 2,000 from his *encomienda* in New Spain with him to Guatemala and then used thousands more from Central America for his expeditions south in the isthmus, to Peru, and on his final abortive scheme to explore the South Seas.

What did *encomienda* Indians do? The simple answer is anything and everything. Over time the tendency was for the Crown to define taxes in money terms, and this became an important mechanism forcing Indians into wage labor. Before 1550, however, most obligations could be met in kind or labor, and often the two went together. For example, in the 1520s and 1530s the Indians around Mexico City were required to produce food and handicraft items and to transport these to the capital for the *encomendero*'s own use and for resale. Such provisions included corn, beans, spices, cacao, chickens, pigs, and fish, as well as cooking utensils and charcoal and cooking wood, and cloth and clothing. The *encomienda* also provided the servants to prepare and serve the food, and the workers to clean the *encomendero*'s house and the city's streets. Similarly, they delivered construction materials and labor: Tetepango, for example, sent 160 loads of lime every 160 days for the use of the municipality, and Chalco brought stones, sand, and wood. In the wake of the destruction of the Aztec capital, construction work in and around Mexico City was one of the most wearying obligations weighing on the Indians in the years immediately following the conquest.

In the countryside *encomienda* Indians worked in agriculture and stock raising, producing subsistence and cash crops on their own land and on that of the *encomendero*. Those Spaniards favored with *encomienda* grants but who were not themselves engaged in productive activities sometimes, and regardless of repeated laws and Crown injunctions, rented out their Indians to others. Despite Cortés's promises and Crown prohibitions, *encomenderos* did use their Indians in gold and silver mining, at least during the early years. Spurred by widespread abuses, however, the Crown eventually managed to remove most *encomienda* Indians from the actual processes of mining and refining. This was work for slaves and for a growing free labor population. Instead, the *encomienda* Indians produced food, cloth, and construction materials to supply the mines. Others manned the pumps that drained the diggings. As an example of the variety of *encomienda* obligations, Juan Salcedo, *encomendero* of the town of Amatepec, in addition to twenty Indians that worked at his mines, demanded the town provide him every sixty days with sixty loads of corn, twenty *petates* (mats), five loads of beans, five baskets of salt, and ten chickens. Another miner required 200 loads of corn and beans every fifteen days, and Cortés sent 800 loads of food from his *encomienda* to his mines every eight to ten days.

Of all the uses to which *encomenderos* put their Indians, the most notorious, and the one that generated the most Crown attention in the early years, was carrying. At least as early as 1512–13 the Laws of Burgos had sought to regulate this activity, but the problem only became more evident as conquest moved on to the mainland. The Aztec Empire, unlike the Incas who had llamas, lacked either pack animals or wheeled transport and depended instead on a professional group of carriers called *tamemes* by the Spanish. Carrying was a low-status, largely hereditary occupation for which the men trained from childhood or were forced into by poverty. *Tamemes* carried wicker baskets covered with hides and suspended from a tumpline across their forehead; they were said to be recognizable by the loss of hair caused by the abrasion of the tumpline. The standard pre-conquest task was to carry the equivalent of two *arrobas* (*arroba* = 25 lbs.) five leagues, but what a "league" meant in this context was far from clear. Apparently they delivered the load to the next major administrative center, a day or so away, and handed it off there to the next relay.

Human carriers were an expensive form of transport but there was no immediately available alternative. The Crown tried to ban the use of *tamemes* in 1528, but carts required roads that were not yet built, and pack animals remained in short supply for many years. *Encomenderos* increased the carriers' loads, pressed nonprofessionals into service, and held back or refused to pay wages in their drive to get products to markets cheaply. The dilemma for the Crown was a familiar one: how to obtain the labor needed to make the colonies viable without abusing the Indians. The newly arrived *Audiencia* (appeals court) in 1531 gave up efforts to ban *tamemes* and sought instead to regulate the practice. Henceforth, the court decreed, all carrying was to be voluntary, the wage was set at 100 cacao beans (approximately one *real*, or one-eighth of a peso) a day, the load could be no more than two *arrobas*, the journey was to be only a day, and pack animals and carts were to replace human carriers as soon as possible.

It should not surprise us that problems continued. Excessively heavy loads forced upon carriers crippled them, and the work sent them to unaccustomed climates and exposed them to disease. This was particularly difficult for residents of the highlands forced to transport goods to coastal ports, though Indians from the lowlands suffered too in the cold of the high plateaus. Crown laws and regulations for Spaniards did not apply to Indian elites, who also utilized carriers and who proved to be at least as abusive as the *encomenderos*. Not until the seventeenth century did the widespread use of human carriers come to an end in New Spain, and it persisted in Central America throughout the colonial period.

A conqueror fortunate enough to gain an *encomienda* could find it difficult to keep. Francisco Noguerol de Ulloa arrived in Peru in 1535, too late to share in the vast ransom of Atahualpa or to gain an *encomienda* in the central area, but soon enough to become deeply involved in the tumultuous affairs of the new colony. Disappointed *encomienda*-seekers and late arrivals such as Ulloa joined Diego de Almargo on what proved to be a disastrous expedition south into present-day Chile. Returning frustrated and angry, the "men of Chile" constituted a real danger to Francisco Pizarro, and he bought some of them off with *encomiendas*: Ulloa abandoned the Almargo faction in return for a grant of nineteen villages located west of Lake Titicaca and containing some 1,000 Indians. But in 1541 the Almargists assassinated Pizarro and took power, putting Ulloa in serious peril. He escaped to Panama and then returned to Peru in the retinue of the first viceroy, Blasco Núñez Vela. Allied with the vengeful Pizarrists, the viceroy defeated the Almargo faction and regained control of the colony. Ulloa got his *encomienda* back and settled down as one of the founders of the southern Peruvian town of Arequipa, where almost immediately he became embroiled in disputes with other Spaniards who claimed all or parts of his grant.

As an early if not original settler, and one of only some 500 *encomenderos* in all of Peru, Ulloa enjoyed a privileged position, but in 1542–43 the Crown moved once again to attempt to assert control over this group. After years of debate at court, the state issued the New Laws, its latest attempt to regulate work relations in the New World. The regulations forbade Indian slavery, freed all remaining captive Indians, and threatened to punish anyone who abused Indians. The laws gave special attention to *encomenderos*, prohibiting Crown and church officials from holding *encomiendas*, and reducing all grants of "excessive size." No new *encomiendas* were to be given, and all existing grants would revert to the Crown on the death of the present holder. The troublesome *encomenderos* of Peru were singled out for special attention and could lose their grants.

News of the New Laws touched off a fire storm of protest across the colonies. In New Spain Viceroy Antonio de Mendoza frankly admitted that he could not enforce the reforms and responded with the well-known formula of Spanish bureaucracy, "I obey but I do not comply." Instead, he continued to undermine the power of the first settlers by building up the state bureaucracy and to introduce change piecemeal, as opportunities appeared. Peru's new viceroy was less intelligent and less flexible than Mendoza, and the specific provisions of the laws that applied to Peruvian *encomenderos* made the situation there particularly tense. Faced with what they saw as the almost certain loss of their hard-won property, Peru's *encomenderos* revolted under the leadership of Gonzalo Pizarro, defeating and killing Núñez Vela in a battle near Quito in 1546. Evidence suggests the Ulloa supported Pizarro, but when another viceroy arrived, armed with pardons and word of changes in the New Laws, Ulloa again switched sides, allying himself now with the Crown. Gonzalo Pizarro was defeated and executed in 1548. Five months later Viceroy Pedro de la Gasca awarded Ulloa, in "recognition of his devoted service to the Crown," a new and more valuable *encomienda* at Los Collaguas, a holding that once had belonged to Gonzalo Pizarro. Unlike the hundreds who had died in the conquest and subsequent fighting or who fell into disgrace in the civil wars, Francisco Noguerol de Ulloa safely navigated a path through the vicissitudes of early Peru's history.

One of the reasons that many of Peru's *encomenderos* switched back to the Crown and those of New Spain did not revolt was because the state again compromised. In 1545 it bowed to *encomendero* demands and allowed the inheritance of grants for another "life," and subsequently it extended this in some cases to a third life, or even beyond. Rather than taking possession of all *encomiendas* vacated by death or because of rebellious activities as it had threatened, the Crown instead reassigned many of these to loyal subjects, or subjects in which it hoped to stimulate loyalty. These awards gave those who received them a stake in Crown supremacy and made them dependent on

Crown largess; they had the *encomienda* as a gift from the state not as a prize of conquest. Then, in 1549 the Crown banned all personal service to *encomenderos* by the Indians. The Spanish continued to collect taxes in kind or in money from the Indians but they could not demand labor, and if an *encomendero* did employ Indians he had to pay them the going wage. By mid-century the Spanish state had separated political power from *encomenderos'* economic power, converting the institution from a semi-feudal right of conquerors to a government-managed pension system, and had opened access to indigenous labor to a wider range of settlers.

As they had on the islands, the Spanish imported African slaves to the mainland to supplement the indigenous work force. The first black slaves in Mexico were *ladinos*, servants to the conquerors, and there were also free blacks among the soldiers. Over the next several decades Africans and *ladinos* arrived in New Spain at the slow but steady pace of approximately 500 a year, so that by mid-century they numbered about 20,000. Most worked in the urban areas but others were foremen on haciendas, labored in sugar mills and silver mines, or drove mule trains through the mountains from the coast to the capital. Their numbers were small compared to the millions of Indians that still survived. The early pattern of African slavery was much the same in Peru, but here slaves did not arrive directly from Africa or the islands. Instead, they trickled down the coast in ones and twos as part of the trade from Panama, or were marched overland in the contraband traffic with the Rio de la Plata and Brazil. The prosperity of post-conquest Peru resulting from the early discovery of silver made black slavery fairly common. Even the owners of the small truck farms around Lima typically had one or two black slaves to work for them, as did artisans in the capital. The only large concentrations of black slaves in these early days, and this was common to Mexico as well, were on the sugar plantations and in gold panning gangs.

Relations between black slaves, free blacks, and the indigenous population rarely were harmonious. Despite the Crown's fears of servile revolt, *ladino* slaves in particular generally aligned themselves with the masters' culture and looked down on Indians, and the tendency of whites to use blacks to supervise and discipline Indian workers exacerbated poor relations between those groups. Escaped slaves rarely found refuge in Indian communities. The return of a fugitive slave in Peru was so certain that they sold at only a modest discount even before they had been recaptured.

The Frontiers

The *encomienda* in the central areas of the empire died slowly after mid-century, the victim of Crown intervention and Indian population declines.

Those who failed to see this trend developing and continued to rely on *encomienda* income fell into what one writer has called the *"encomienda* trap," finding themselves ultimately impoverished. Those *encomenderos* that prospered recognized early on what was happening and took advantage of their privileged position to expand into agriculture and stock raising, mining, and trade and commerce. Only on the fringes of the empire did the *encomienda* hang on as a viable institution, often developing peculiar local characteristics.

In Nueva Vizcaya in northern New Spain, *encomienda* grants required that the recipient round up and settle the Indians himself from among the Chichimecas on the other side of the frontier. Few among the Spanish had much luck. More promising were mission Indians. The Franciscans and the Jesuits had considerable success in attracting frontier hunter-gatherers to villages attached to the church missions. These settlements offered the Indians not only access to European material goods and the services of the missionaries but also some protection from Spanish slavers and border raiders. But this was limited. When would-be *encomenderos* could not find enough Indians along the frontier to satisfy their pretensions, they turned to the missions, demanding and eventually being granted *"encomiendas"* from among the church-controlled populations. Because the Indians of the North produced little of value to the settlers, and despite the prohibitions of the New Laws, the *encomienda* here remained a labor institution, supplying workers to Spanish- and creole-owned haciendas and cattle ranches. Then, in the 1630s and 1640s governors also began ordering drafts of forced wage labor, called *repartimientos*, from the missions for work on non-*encomendero* properties. *Encomenderos* went to court to stop this, but most cases collapsed into a welter of claims and counterclaims.

To the south in Yucatan *encomiendas* lived on too. The Spanish only managed to gain control of the region in the 1540s and found little there to interest them except a relatively dense Indian population. This blocked nonindigenous access to land but supported a small oligarchy of *encomenderos*. By the 1630s the decline of the indigenous population was undercutting the *encomenderos'* economic base, prompting the more active to move into stock raising or to seek business and marital alliances with merchants in the towns. As the eighteenth century came to an end, the local economy long had passed beyond dependence on *encomiendas*, but the institution persisted as a marker of social prestige and political preeminence.

In Chile, at the other end of the continent, the *encomienda* was an instrument of war. In the 1540s and 1550s Pedro de Valdivia led a drawn out and bloody conquest of the region, founding towns and granting *encomiendas*. Because the local population had little accumulated wealth and produced even less of the value to the invading armies, the wealth of an *encomienda* consisted here too entirely of labor. As in northern New Spain, however, this was labor that the *encomendero* had to capture and coerce. Valdivia died in a 1555 uprising, and the colony settled into two hundred years of frontier violence. Continued Indian resistance to Spanish domination prompted the Crown to accept "just war" against them, and *encomiendas* became essentially slaving licenses for raids across the boundary of European-Indian settlement. The Spanish routinely "killed, maimed and set dogs upon the Indians, cut off feet, hands, noses and teats, stole their lands, raped their women and daughters, chained them up as beasts of burden, burned their houses and settlements and laid waste their fields"[6] in a fruitless effort to terrorize the local population into submission. *Encomenderos* defied orders from the Crown and the Crown's agents to ameliorate treatment of the Indians, and the king ultimately turned a blind eye to the situation, imagining that there was no other way to secure the southern frontier.

But surely the strangest of all the *encomiendas* was that of Paraguay. Only a few Spanish penetrated this isolated outpost before mid-century and those that did found themselves submerged in the local indigenous population. Women did most of the agricultural work among the Guaraní, and families paid taxes to support a modest leadership group by sending female labor to work the leaders' fields. By local reckoning the Spanish settlers fell into the category of leaders, and the immigrants quickly found themselves surrounded by "harems" of women, together with their relatives. This was probably conceived initially as short-term work, but over time permanent agglomerations of indigenous population grew up around the Spaniards, tied together by marriage and kinship. These came to be known as the *encomiendas originarias* (original *encomiendas*). The Spanish quickly "went native," learning Guaraní, eating local foods, and producing herds of mestizo children; it was, in a standard phrase of the time, a "Mohammedan's paradise." The Crown's few isolated representatives had no luck bringing any of this under control or putting family or labor relations into conformity with the law. Instead, in the second half of the century they began to grant *encomiendas* of a more standard form, called *mitayo encomienda* (from *mita*), short-term labor drawn from villages distant from the centers of Spanish settlement. Epidemic disease soon reduced many of these *encomiendas* to only ten or a dozen Indians, hardly enough to support a Spaniard even in impoverished Paraguay. Still, with nothing to replace them, both forms persisted until the end of the colony.

Conclusion

By mid-century the *encomienda* system was collapsing in the core areas of the Spanish American empire. The Indian population upon which it depended was disappearing due to disease, overwork, and the destruction of its social and ideological order. This population collapse accelerated in most areas in the 1560s and the numbers reached all-time lows sometime during the seventeenth century, before beginning a slow recovery. At the same time that the indigenous population suffered 90 percent or greater losses, immigration increased the numbers of Spanish, and the beginnings of a mixed blood population appeared. Few Spanish peasants came to the New World, and even the small farmers and humble artisans in Mexico and Peru who claimed Spanish descent (particularly on the frontiers the definition of who was "Spanish" was quite flexible), expected others to work for them. Within the indigenous communities *caciques* and *principales* (elders) sometimes took advantage of changes provoked by the European invasion to themselves become entrepreneurs and employers of Indians. Thus, a growing European and would-be European population, together with indigenous elites, demanded labor from a declining pool of Indian workers, many of whom remained locked up in a few *encomiendas*. Even as the Crown successfully "tamed" the *encomienda*, new labor systems were emerging to wrestle with these conflicting demands.

Chapter 2

The Colonial System, 1550–1750

The Crown's goal for the New World was a labor force that was able and willing to freely contract its work for wages. The Catholic kings had outlawed vagrancy and ended serfdom in Spain, and for a half century after the Conquest the state struggled to implement a free work regime in the colonies. Black slavery did not contradict this policy because the Crown did not consider the captured Africans citizens, whereas the indigenous inhabitants of the New World emphatically were. But the Indians generally were not eager to work for the Spanish. Most saw little reason to seek out the meager wages and difficult conditions offered. They had to pay taxes, and fees to support the new religion, but until at least the end of the sixteenth century, and in many areas much longer, these could be paid in kind, in the Indians' own products. Alternatively, they could obtain what they needed by trade or by gathering it in the wild. Much of the indigenous population at least initially was able to satisfy its tax liabilities, and even to obtain money to buy new consumer goods, without directly entering the Spanish economy, and, particularly, without working for the Spanish.

If the Indians did not work voluntarily they would be made to work, for their own moral good and to sustain the state and church. As the Crown reined in the *encomiendas* and brought an end to the enslaving of indigenous peoples in the central areas, the Spanish and creole elites, the Indians, and the state worked out forced wage labor systems, called variously *repartimientos* or *mitas*. These had different histories in different parts of the empire, but where forced wage labor did not soon disappear it tended to calcify into a "custom" *(costumbre)* that eventually could prove unnecessary or even counterproductive to further development. In fact, as the indigenous population rebounded and a growing number of mixed bloods crowded the towns and the countryside, direct coercion became less and less important. By 1750 the most common forms of work relations in the countryside were indebted labor and forms of labor rent.

Repartimientos

Indian slavery and *encomiendas* solved the labor problems of the first arrivals, but Crown prohibitions and growth of a non-*encomendero* Spanish population prompted increased demands for a work force not controlled by a lucky few. New arrivals wanted access to labor for commercial food production in the cities, for ranching, for gold and silver mining, and for construction, as well as for servants and artisan craft work. How could these labor demands be met without placing excessive pressures on the population or causing wages to rise to unprofitable levels? The answer proved to be *repartimientos*, also called the *mita* in Peru, or, later, *mandamiento* (from *mandar*, to order). Early administrators of Hispaniola followed the precedent of Castile in giving the name *repartimiento* to some of the island's first *encomiendas*, and later the term applied also to the forced purchase of goods or the production of thread and textiles by Indian women at prices set by Spanish officials. But *repartimiento* most commonly meant a system of forced wage labor imposed upon the indigenous population and regulated by the state. As such, it ingeniously combined elements from both Spanish and the Indian pasts and served as a key link in the transition from *encomienda* to wage labor.

To understand colonial labor *repartimientos*, it is necessary first to understand the tribute (*tributo*) system. In general, all Indian males were required to pay a yearly head tax, or tribute, that varied from a peso or two in some areas to as much as eight pesos in seventeenth-century Quito. In a few areas women paid tribute, and the Crown from time to time tried to impose this tax on free blacks and mixed bloods, but with little success. While in theory tribute was an individual tax, most indigenous communities treated it as a levy on the town, and the Crown based tribute on census counts. Not surprisingly, these censuses were the objects of constant dispute and not just because of taxes but also because the counts determined how many men were liable for *repartimiento* labor. Although the towns sometimes supplied women for specific tasks such as cooking or as wet nurses, and town officials sometimes violated legal age limits under pressure to come up with more workers, officially *repartimientos* fell on men between 18 and 50, less those exempted because of physical impediments or because they held positions in the local government or church. Depending on custom and conditions, a village might be required to supply anywhere from 7 percent to 25 percent of its *repartimiento*-eligible population for forced wage labor, for periods of a week to a year or more. Of course, censuses fell out of date, particularly in the wake of an epidemic or large scale migration. Because Crown agents were loath to recognize this and slow to carry out new counts, what was on paper a quarter of the eligible population might, in fact, amount to a half or more of the surviving workers in a given town. *Repartimiento* labor was paid labor, but it was forced labor, and the wages generally were below those of the free market.

Indigenous community leaders had the responsibility of selecting the men to be sent to satisfy *repartimiento* drafts and for making sure that these turned up on time and at the right place. If they failed, they could be whipped or jailed or fined, but there were also opportunities to take bribes, to exempt individuals, and the chance to favor family members and clients. Once the workers selected for a draft had assembled, usually in the square of the nearest Spanish town, a Crown official called a *juez repartidor* (*repartimiento* judge) divided them among employers. The judge received a small fee for each worker hired, but he might be open to bribes, both from employers who wanted more labor than the law allowed and from Indians who hoped to avoid a notoriously abusive employer or to escape the service altogether. Those who hired *repartimiento* workers were required to pay full wages in advance, "in sounding silver on the table," but again village officials served as intermediaries and sometimes kept part or all of these wages for their own purposes.

Once the labor was parceled out, the men typically walked to wherever the work was to take place, carrying with them their bedding and food, and sometimes their tools. Where the *repartimiento* called for a week's work, for example, they labored until the following Monday, when a new draft might replace them. If replacements did not show up on time, the workers sometimes were forced to stay days longer, even though they might have used up their food by this point. Laws prohibited certain types of work for *repartimiento* Indians, including labor in mines and on sugar and indigo plantations, as well as work that required them to travel long distances or to cross dangerous rivers or that sent them to different and unhealthful environments. Crown officials did not always observe such prohibitions, and employers quibbled endlessly about distances, working conditions, and pay.

The forced labor system of *repartimiento* developed gradually in the years from the middle of the sixteenth until the early seventeenth century. Modified by a thousand local customs and changed over time by law and circumstance, the drafts had their clearest legal expression in the Ordinances of 1609, still the basic law at the end of the colonial period. While the Ordinances made it clear that the Indians were free subjects of the Crown, they also took it as self-evident that the indigenous population could not be left to voluntarily offer its labor for wages because Indians were by nature lazy and given to vice. Therefore, until such time as they were ready to seek wage labor on their own they would have to be forced to work, but only under the supervision of the proper officials and protected by careful regulation. No more than one-seventh of the eligible population could be drafted at one time, and they were to be paid the wage set by the Viceroy and treated well. Wherever possible African slaves or free workers should replace *repartimiento* workers, particularly in dangerous activities, and Indians were never to work even voluntarily at tasks that threatened their health or safety. In particular, the state abolished all *repartimientos* for carrying, except as these served the needs of Crown officials in the performance of their duties. All Indians were to have sufficient time to cultivate their own fields, and employers who received *repartimiento* drafts could not sell or rent these Indians to others.

In the 1630s the Crown issued the first in a long series of decrees abolishing forced wage labor. Although such prohibitions gradually took hold in the central parts of the empire, *repartimientos* persisted in other areas into the nineteenth century. The 1812 Constitution issued by the Cortes abolished the drafts yet again.

An early and important use of *repartimiento* labor, and one that provoked repeated Crown bans, was mining. The first conquerors carried out gold panning in Hispaniola and New Spain with slaves and *encomienda* Indians, but as silver strikes multiplied in mid-century New Spain, would-be miners who did not hold *encomiendas* clamored for access to Indian labor. Already by 1551, for example, Guerrero Indians complained that they were being sent to work in the silver mines at Taxco. *Repartimiento* laborers were not usually worked in the mine itself, because this was prohibited work, because mining at the face involved skills most of them did not have, and because mining's relatively high pay drew many free workers. Instead, the drafted Indians did the sort of work that had occupied *encomienda* labor, including surface construction, wood cutting, and manning the pumps: in 1618 a *repartimiento* draft complained that they had been locked up for eight to ten days at a time, made to work the pumps day and night. A decade later Indians sent to mines of Zacualpán offered a catalog of abuses: the mine owners illegally detained them, stripped and tied them together at the neck, and locked them up at night, and they paid them one real a day instead of the legally prescribed one and a half or the free market wages two to four reales. The mulatto foreman beat and abused them and sold their labor against their will to nearby haciendas. Subsequent investigation showed that mine owners had brought *repartimiento* workers to the mine bound together, had forced the men to work naked in cold water, and had repeatedly beaten them. The injury to

Indians trapped in this situation was threefold: in being made to work against their wishes, in suffering difficult and dangerous conditions for low wages, and in being physically and verbally abused.

The *Mita*

By far the largest and most long-lasting use of forced wage labor for mining was the Potosí *mita*. Potosí, in Upper Peru, was literally a mountain of silver, reaching up some 16,000 cold and arid feet, and the indigenous population had worked it before the Spanish arrived. Early efforts by the Spanish to exploit the deposits made use of *yanaconas* and *encomienda* Indians, who applied essentially pre-contact technology to digging and refining the ore. But the scale and intensity of mining activities expanded enormously in the 1570s with the introduction of the new patio refining process and the regularization of large-scale labor. In Peru this took the name *mita* from the old Inca system of periodic labor in the service of the state. And, unlike New Spain, its chief use here was in mining. Drawing up regulations and carrying out the first of a series of comprehensive population counts, Viceroy Francisco de Toledo organized a labor system for Potosí that endured until the nineteenth century. Eventually the *mita* drew Indians from as far away as Quito in the north and Argentina in the south, furnishing thousands of Indians a year to the mine. Apart from the mercury diggings at Huancavalica where Indians worked under horrific conditions, only Potosí among Peruvian mines benefited from the *mita*. Others operated with black slaves or free labor. Potosí, though, was the first and the biggest of Peru's silver strikes and the focus of the colony's economy for three hundred years.

Because of the distances involved, workers sent to Potosí went not for a week or a fortnight but a year. Legally, only 7 to 9 percent of the population eligible for the *mita* could be drafted at one time, but discrepancies in census counts plagued the villages of the Andes just as they did those of New Spain. Adding to the problem of population displacement was the custom that, because of the time and distances involved, entire families accompanied the drafted workers to the mines. Those who saw the *mita* gangs as they traveled described them as whole communities on the move. Once the Indians reached Potosí, Spanish officials assigned the men to the mines or to refining mills, depending on current labor needs.

After the first years, *mita* Indians did little of the actual ore extraction itself. This became the province of specialized workers, many of whom arrived as *mitayos* and then stayed on. Instead, *mita* workers carried the ore from the mines up a precarious system of ladders, or worked in noisy and dangerous refining sheds, or transported equipment and foodstuffs, or worked in construction and repair of surface facilities. By law only a third of each draft was to be employed at *mita* labor at any one time, with the others resting. Most, however, found that the money they earned from forced labor did not sustain them and their families, and they had to seek wage work during their time off. Free labor had the advantage that it paid wages two or three times those of the *mita*, and some of the men learned skills that prompted them to remain in Potosí instead of returning to their communities. Villages complained bitterly about this drain of tribute payers but found they could do little to force former residents to come back. Others failed to return because they died in Potosí or on the journey.

Conditions in the mines were awful. One vivid, if certainly overwrought, description had the Indians working twenty-three weeks a year day and night, "without light, 1,200 to 1,800 feet down. Those who carry and extract the ore, crawl along like snakes, burdened with ore and if they do not do so quickly, the [supervisors] deal them many kicks and lashes with a whip."[1] Workers could not have survived more than a few weeks of this. Still, recent studies suggest that conditions, if not quite as bad as the above quote suggests, were bad enough. Apart from the dangers involved in the exhausting and perilous work of ascending the ladders with loads of ore, workers in the refining mills risked accidents from the machinery or the effects of inhaling dust, and others absorbed lead and mercury vapors from the patios.

While Crown agents were not always sympathetic to the plight of the Indians or resistant to bribes to overlook unsafe or illegal conditions, some did make an effort to protect the migrants from the worst abuses. They inspected living and working conditions and fined employers guilty of egregious offenses or removed their rights to *mita* labor. Officials were particularly alive to the practice of selling or renting *mita* Indians, a common resort of miners with played-out claims or those who lacked the capital to operate but still had a right to receive Indians from the draft. Although the *mita* persisted until almost the end of the colony, by the mid-seventeenth century free workers already outnumbered coerced labor at Potosí. The *mita* survived, however, as a subsidy to a mining sector important to state revenues even as it fell behind New Spain in output.

The *Desagüe*

Repartimiento Indians labored not just for private employers but for the Crown as well, in public works and government projects. Drafted Indians built roads and ports, constructed and supplied ships for exploration and trade, carried food and equipment on new expeditions, and manned frontier outposts. After an earthquake in 1773 *repartimiento* Indians built a new capital for the

Captaincy General of Guatemala, thirty miles across the mountains from the old city. But most notorious of such state-directed undertakings was the much-feared *Desagüe*, a century-long project to drain water from around Mexico City. Transport in the Aztecs' Tenochtitlán had depended on canoes and canals, but when the Spanish built their new capital they filled in many of the waterways and allowed others to become clogged with rubbish. The result was a series of floods that devastated the city early in the seventeenth century. In 1607–8 the viceroy mobilized tens of thousands of Indians to drive a tunnel through the mountains to divert flood water out of the valley. Faulty engineering undermined these efforts, however, and in 1627–28 the city was inundated, and again the following year, leaving parts of the capital under water for four years. The colonial government revived the drainage project in the 1630s and pursued it intermittently for the next hundred years. Even as the viceroy acted in 1632 to limit and then to ban *repartimientos* for other uses, the state cast an ever widening net for the coerced labor the drainage construction required. The work was dangerous and unpleasant. One observer reported seeing Indians tied to beams and suspended in the water to do dredging and filling operations in the canals, and the tunnels were cold and damp and subject to collapse.

Agricultural Labor

By far the most common use for *repartimientos* was in agriculture. Nowhere was this more evident than in Guatemala, where, under its nineteenth-century name of *mandamientos*, it continued in use until 1920. Forced wage labor took a peculiar form here. By the early eighteenth century the drafts were not allocated by the week or the month but were effectively permanent, at the pleasure of the captain-general. Whereas in New Spain a special court handled Indian affairs, in Guatemala these duties fell to the local *Audiencia*. Those who wished to make use of *repartimiento* workers applied to the court, indicating the number they needed and for how long, what the Indians would do, and the village or villages from which they might be drawn. The *Audiencia's fiscal protector de los indios* (Protector of the Indians) investigated and reported on the request. By custom not more than a quarter of those Indians in any community that were eligible for tribute could be drafted at one time, but this did not always take into account special labor demands such as those for rebuilding the capital or for carrying freight to and from the North coast ports. The *fiscal* was to verify that there were enough workers available within the one quarter of the population before granting a new request, but increasingly he simply approved orders with the stipulation, "if it fits in the one quarter." Who was to make that determination was not clear.

Upon granting an employer's *repartimiento* application the *Audiencia* issued orders to the affected towns to provide the workers. The draft might be given just for seasonal labor, for example, perhaps for several weeks a year to harvest wheat, or it might be for a longer period of time, requiring that the town send men in shifts. Sometimes community leaders protested, usually complaining of a lack of available men, and if this could be substantiated the *Audiencia* directed the order to another village. The right to use *repartimiento* labor belonged to the person to whom the *Audiencia* had granted it and did not attach to a property and could not be sold or transferred. In fact, though, both landowners and Indians commonly acted as though the labor order was part of the assets of an estate, and both expected it to be passed to a new owner when a property changed hands.

In Guatemala the Crown tried to subject mestizos and mulattos as well as Indians to *repartimientos*, and it also sought to draft Indians living dispersed in the countryside apart from the villages. Both efforts failed. The mixed bloods fiercely resisted any attempt to equate them with Indians and took refuge in distant rural *valles*, settlements where, colonial officials imagined, they lived in promiscuous abandon without "God or the King," or on haciendas where the owners shielded them. For their part, many Indians, although they might claim membership in a community, lived much of the year apart from it, cultivating fields in distant valleys or lowlands or involved in long-distance trade. In response, the Crown and the church developed schemes of *reducción* or *congregación*: priests, assisted by the militia where necessary, brought Indians from decayed settlements and others scattered about the countryside together into new towns, where they could be more closely watched and more effectively taxed and their labor tapped. Not all Indians found this attractive, and at the first opportunity many fled back to the countryside.

Though decades and then centuries of use eventually awarded *repartimientos* the grudging legitimacy of custom, Indians hated and resisted the drafts. Officials in the town of Palín (Guatemala), for example, described how difficult it was to get the men together;

> First it is necessary for the justices and the other leaders themselves to go from house to house citing individuals who are to work and to give them two or four reales of their advances, money that they receive with such repugnance that often all you can do is put the money in the house, for no one will take it. On the day indicated for the *repartimiento* the scene is sad. The officials with the policemen round up the men while their neighbors commiserate with them. The women, children and all of the neighbors hurl reproaches and curses on the operation, and finding no escape for their beloved husbands and sons, there are everywhere tears and hopeless cries. It seems more as if they were going to prison or to the gallows.[2]

Repartimiento service meant leaving one's family and community, abandoning agricultural plantings to neglect, and trade and commerce to competitors, and being forced to work under typically unpleasant and hazardous conditions at low wages. Just the travel involved could be dangerous: in 1591 Indians near San Luís Potosí on the northern border of New Spain protested that each week those that were sent to the town of Los Valles had to travel a rough road and cross dangerous rivers, and they constantly ran the risk of attack by hostile Chichimecas. At work, Indians complained, they commonly suffered physical and verbal abuse, problems with housing and hygienic conditions, and shortages of food. The town of San Antonio Palopó (Guatemala), for example, several times petitioned the *Audiencia* detailing the dangers they encountered on a wheat farm near Lake Atitlán: the property was a long distance from their town, and its high altitude, to which they were not accustomed, made them sick; the owners did not pay them adequately for travel and made them work in the rain and sleep in the open on the hard ground. As a result, many became sick and died. The administrator abused them "by word and deed" and demanded bribes before he would let them go home.

Faced with such conditions, it is hardly to be wondered that the Indians did everything they could to evade the drafts. Town officials sometimes had to jail *repartimiento* workers to keep them from disappearing. More and more, Indians fled the communities before they could be tapped for *repartimiento* labor, taking refuge in the towns or, more commonly, as resident workers on Spanish- or creole-owned large rural properties. "For years now," one group of community officials lamented, "they have been abandoning the village, taking their families to the haciendas, ranches, and sugar plantations where they live a life of total license without subjection to our priest or to justice."[3] Others bribed officials to escape the *repartimientos*, or perhaps more imaginatively, accepted wage advances and then ran away or escaped on the road to the work site or from the property itself. Those made to work engaged in all manner of foot dragging, petty resistance, and sabotage, the so-called "weapons of the weak," as well as occasional outbursts of overt violence against their tormentors.

In neighboring El Salvador indigo growers struggled with special labor problems. The law specifically prohibited the use of Indians for indigo production, whether on *repartimientos* or as free workers, because of its reputed damage to their health. Processing the dye involved the workers treading on leaves and stalks covered with spines as these soaked in tanks of water, and the residue of the process attracted swarms of stinging flies. For the Crown the solution was African slaves, but few of the small or medium-sized growers on Central America's Pacific coast could afford these. What developed instead was essentially, and illegally, an Indian "licensing" system. Employers drew Indians from nearby communities into debt with advances of cash or consumer goods and then demanded that they work off what they owned in the indigo fields and mills. This was illegal both because employers routinely manipulated debts to keep workers permanently in the red and because indigo was prohibited work. Inspectors sent out every few years by the *Audiencia* in Guatemala City discovered, to their great surprise, that these practices were going on, and they fined the landowners or, in what amounted to the same thing, took bribes to overlook abuses. Indigo growers treated this as simply a cost of doing business. Inspections, fines, and bribes developed over the course of the late seventeenth and early eighteenth centuries into a regular system that profited everyone except the Indians.

Still, growers were not satisfied and kept pressing for greater access to indigenous labor. As demand for indigo expanded with the Industrial Revolution, El Salvador's producers succeeded first in 1738 in convincing the Crown to lift the prohibitions on Indian free labor in the mills and then in the 1760s in having *repartimientos* approved. These were regularized in the new work rules issued in 1784: villages, and this included settlements of mulattos and mestizos as well as Indians, were required to supply up to one-quarter of their able-bodied men for work in the fields. Wage advances were prohibited, lifting a burden on employers' capital. The hope was, the regulations piously argued, that these new rules would help combat the population's "scandalous laziness," propensity for theft, and the "licentiousness in which they live without shame."[4]

On the Frontiers

Repartimientos also persisted well into the eighteenth century on the northern frontier of New Spain. As we have seen, labor control in this area fell first to the church missions and then to a small group of *encomenderos*. By the late sixteenth century, increasing migration from the South introduced a third group anxious to employ indigenous labor, non-*encomendero* Spanish and creole settlers who sought workers for their agricultural and stock-raising haciendas. New silver strikes opened greater markets for food products and work animals in the mining centers, pushing up potential profits for the supply sector and increasing demand for labor. It was almost impossible for the haciendas to compete for free labor with the silver mines, and black slaves were similarly too expensive. The owners instead demanded *repartimientos*, and, reluctantly, the state complied. As a result, the Indians soon found themselves in the very burdensome situation of being subject to church requirements for taxes and service, to the labor demands of an *encomendero*, and now forced to work for yet a third set of employers as *repartimiento* labor. Not surprisingly, the system depended heavily on indigenous and mixed blood "labor brokers" who earned commissions for rounding up recalcitrant workers. Indians thus found themselves at the center of a three-way tug-of-war for their work but unable to convert this competition into better wages or conditions. For many the best option was to flee the missions for full-time wage work on haciendas or in the mining centers.

Nonmining *repartimientos* seem to have been less important in the Viceroyalty of Peru than in New Spain, or perhaps they simply have been less studied, but they did exist. Around Bogota (Colombia), for example, *encomenderos* dominated labor until the 1590s, when a series of Crown-ordered inspections weakened their power and initiated a *repartimiento* system. The broad pattern is familiar but with local peculiarities. Here the indigenous communities supplied three different types of draft labor: urban workers for Bogota, labor for the mines of Tolima, and workers for nearby haciendas that supplied the urban market. The Indians did day work (*alquiler*) or contracted for up to six months (*concertaje*) at a time, and they seem to have had considerable leeway in determining where they went. Either because conditions were better or because the record is thin, few complaints from the Indians about wages or working conditions survive, and there is little evidence that the communities protested when workers chose to remain on a hacienda at the end of a *repartimiento* stint. By the middle of the eighteenth century, however, the availability of a growing free population of mestizos and of Indians shaken out of their communities allowed an end to *repartimientos*.

While forced wage labor generally applied to men only, the Crown did authorize the drafting of women for special tasks. In 1590, for example, four indigenous neighborhoods in Mexico City complained of being required to supply wet nurses for Spanish children. More commonly, *repartimientos* drafted women to serve as cooks, whether for gangs of free laborers or for men sent on *repartimientos*. The Indian communities resisted these because of the threats they posed to the moral and physical well-being of the women. In the 1790s, for example, the towns of Zacapa and San Pedro (in Guatemala) protested that local women were being sent to cook for the garrisons that guarded the north coast and the Motagua River. Many perished there from diseases before completing their three months' service and now their young children were dying of neglect. The Protector of Indians recommended that instead of Indian women "mulattas in need of correction" should be sent, but the *repartimientos* continued.

Repartimientos made labor available where market mechanisms did not, but they were far from satisfactory. More flexible than *encomiendas* and guaranteeing a broader distribution of workers, *repartimientos* nevertheless left the employer dependent for labor on state intervention. In practice this meant that he was often forced to bribe an array of local and Crown officials to actually obtain workers. Wages had to be paid in advance, and there was little hope of recovering this money if any of the men ran away, died, or worked unsatisfactorily. This could significantly raise the real cost of labor. Because of the turnover in *repartimientos*, there was no chance to train or keep those who proved particularly adept. Even where unlimited *repartimiento* labor was available, which was rarely the case, landowners still had to employ skilled free workers at higher wages for specialized tasks, as the example of Potosí showed. Most important, *repartimiento* labor was forced labor, and its victims generally showed a marked lack of enthusiasm for their tasks. Time and custom may have legitimated the drafts, but *repartimientos* inspired none of the joy and sense of community that pre-conquest communal labor had.

Brazil

Encomienda and *repartimiento* never existed as such in Portuguese America, though coerced labor in other forms did. This was the result both of a rhythm and timing of conquest that differed from that of the core areas of Spanish America, and of indigenous and immigrant populations that resembled those of Spanish America's frontiers more than those of the central areas. In Brazil there was no early experience with the domination of a large, settled indigenous population by a small group of conquerors. By the time the Portuguese began to move beyond their early system of barter trade, King João had made it clear that the purpose of colonization was the conversion of the New World's population to Christianity and its eventual acculturation to full citizenship in the Empire. Only bellicose Indians captured in "just wars" or those rescued from indigenous slavery or Indians guilty of cannibalism could be compelled to work against their will. A half-century of contact with the Portuguese and other Europeans, however, had thinned out the numbers among the coastal Indians and reinforced the warlike tendencies and abilities of those that survived.

To attempt to tame this population, the Portuguese Crown turned to the Jesuits. Created as an order only in the 1540s, the Jesuits were the strike arm of the Counter Reformation, and they now moved enthusiastically into the area around the new capital Salvador to win souls for the church. The Jesuits attracted a high quality of initiate and put these through a rigorous training program; unlike some of the other orders, they took no vow of poverty. Over the next two centuries the Jesuits gained proselytizing successes and material wealth that attracted no small amount of envy in both empires.

After brief and unsuccessful efforts to preach to the Indians in their own villages, the Jesuits in Brazil adopted what became their trademark, the *aldeia* system. The missionaries found that if they left indigenous populations in their communities of origin, communities typically arranged physically to reflect pre-Christian religions, they too readily fell into backsliding and apostasy. Instead, the Jesuits hit on the idea of concentrating potential converts into a few centralized villages under tight control of the order. This prefigured by several decades the Spanish policy of *congregaciones*. Lay settlers around Salvador resisted the *aldeias* because these tended to cut them off from access to indigenous labor, but arrival of the new governor Mem de Sá in 1557 tipped the scales in favor of the Jesuits. By 1561 they had some 34,000 Indians settled in eleven villages, though disease epidemics soon wiped out one-third to one-half of them. Together with an inopportune attack by the unsubdued Caeté, these dramatic declines in the local indigenous population undermined the Jesuits' system and greatly increased settler pressures to get at the pool of workers still harbored in the *aldeias*. The Crown responded by turning over the remaining villages, now reduced to only five, to lay administrators. These instituted what amounted to a *repartimiento* system, parceling out the surviving Indians as temporary workers to the planters.

The evident collapse of the settled Indian populations near Salvador, together with a rapid expansion of the local sugar export economy, provoked a rethinking of the colony's labor situation. The king restated in 1570 the Indians' naturally free condition but insisted too on their obligation to work, and he attempted to clarify the conditions under which they might be forced to do so. To stop was the old subterfuge of "rescuing" and enslaving Indians held captive by other Indian groups. This had become a major source of Indian slaves for the settlers and was widely abused. But settlers reacted with rage and forced the Crown four years later to revoke the ban. The collapse of coastal populations and the resistance of some of those that survived prompted "rescue" columns to penetrate further and further into the interior in search of Indians. The governors continued too to issue licenses for "just wars" that were little more than slaving expeditions. Newly rich sugar planters brought in tough mercenaries from São Paulo who ravaged the backlands in search of labor.

Effectively driven from the main sugar planting areas, the Jesuits turned their attentions north to the Amazon basin, to Maranhão and Pará. Under the leadership of the brilliant and tenacious Father Antonio Vieira, by the mid-seventeenth century they had secured from the Crown a law that restricted, though did not end, Indian slavery in this new area. Because the coastal indigenous populations here had largely disappeared as well, the Jesuits secured permission to "descend" Indians from the many tributaries of the

Amazon and settle them in *aldeias* near the coast. But they soon met opposition and had to compromise. The Jesuits gained overall control of the Indians but were forced to allow these to be recruited for work on settlers' cotton plantations and cattle ranches and to be sent to search the forests for natural products (the *drogas do sertão*) that Europeans wanted. Jesuit-led expeditions ascended the rivers, bringing back tens of thousands of Indians; eventually they controlled some 200,000 in more than fifty mission villages.

In 1663, as the result of yet another Jesuit–settler struggle, the Crown turned these villages over to lay administrators for what proved to be a disastrous two decades. Typically, the directors were men of little education and less concern for the Indians, who exploited their charges in every way they could imagine and allowed others to do worse. Not until 1680 were the Jesuits able to regain control of the survivors and convince the king to issue a ban on all Indian slavery. The settlers of Maranhão counterattacked four years later, throwing the missionaries out of the colony. Back in two years, the Jesuits worked out yet another compromise, one that lasted until the general expulsion of the order from Portuguese America in 1759, though it was marked with almost constant conflict. Effectively, the *aldeia* Indians were made to work part-time for the settlers for what one observer labeled "token" wages, and the Jesuits turned a blind eye to continued Indian slavery in marginal areas of the colony. By the mid-eighteenth century the *aldeia* population had shrunk to some 25,000 (the Franciscans controlled another 25,000) but indigenous labor had made the Jesuits wealthy, with cotton and sugar plantations, as well as huge cattle ranches on Marajó Island, at the mouth of the Amazon River.

Landowners bought and used Indian slaves from all over the colony, not just the *sertão* of the Northeast. Thousands arrived from São Paulo, shipped north by slavers who raided as far west as Paraguay and into Brazil's vast interior. Others were brought overland. But their continued susceptibility to disease, a lack of familiarity with or affinity for plantation field labor, and the relative ease with which they could escape made Indians a far from satisfactory labor force for the sugar industry. Those that survived the initial contacts fled. Some moved inland only so far as necessary to avoid the Portuguese, but seventeenth-century millenarian movements drew tens of thousands of others deep into the interior. Those that remained in the plantation areas became increasingly effective at resistance: the Aimoré, it was reported, were "so barbarous and intractable that we have never been able to tame them or force them into servitude like the other Indians of this land."[5]

By the early seventeenth century the sugar planters of Salvador and Recife deployed a mixed labor system of Indian slaves, poor whites, *mestiços* (mixed bloods), and black free workers, and increasing numbers of African slaves.

The free workers held either skilled or supervisory positions or labored at dangerous tasks such as forest clearing that might risk the lives of valuable slaves. Because slavery generally depresses wages, however, most of the rural poor found the option of small-scale agriculture on lands marginal to sugar more attractive. It was to African slavery that the planters turned for the bulk of their labor force in order to continue the rapid expansion of sugar.

African Slavery

No colony in Latin America was more identified with African slavery than Brazil. The Spanish had brought slaves with them from the earliest days of the conquest, but these remained a minor part of the labor force in most areas. Only after mid-century, with the accelerating decline of the native population and the efforts of the Crown to enforce prohibitions on certain sorts of Indian labor, did blacks begin to gain importance in the colonial Hispanic economy. Even then, as the example of El Salvador shows, where Indians were available it was generally more profitable to illegally exploit them, and pay the occasional fine, than to import Africans. Several other factors slowed the development of African slavery in Spanish America as compared with Brazil and limited its impacts to specific regions. Spain itself did not engage directly in the African slave trade, choosing instead to license suppliers through the *asiento* system. As a result, slaves, whether bought through legal dealers or from contraband traders, continued to be relatively expensive and in short supply throughout the colonial period. Complicating this was the empire's orientation toward the Pacific, which increased both transport costs and mortality rates. Broadly, African slavery for large-scale commercial agricultural production in the New World was viable only under certain circumstances: there had to be either a lack of an indigenous population that could be made to provide needed labor, or a crop or activity effectively banned to Indian workers, and this crop had to be valuable enough to pay the cost of slaves.

Northeastern Brazil in the last quarter of the sixteenth century met these requirements. Not only was the indigenous population small, dispersed, and declining rapidly, but Brazilian planters had a low opinion of the quality and productivity of Indian labor. Portugal was the leading slaving nation operating on the African coast at this time, supplying not only its own colonies but Spanish America and other markets as well. Ships made the passage from West Africa to Brazil in only a few weeks, reducing slave mortality and helping to keep prices down, as did competition among Portuguese suppliers. Estimates are that while there were only some 2,000–3,000 African slaves in Brazil as late as 1570, by 1600 this number had risen to 13,000–15,000, working on 120 sugar mills; between 1600 and 1650 slaves arrived at the rate of 4,000 a year, and this accelerated to 7,000–8,000 after mid-century, so that by 1680 Brazil's slave population totaled at least 150,000 and outnumbered whites.

By the standards of the late sixteenth or early seventeenth centuries, sugar production was a highly capitalized, complex industrial undertaking that demanded sophisticated labor coordination and considerable management skill. How could slaves be trusted with expensive equipment and intricate and easily sabotaged operations? Real or potential physical coercion was always present, and no Brazilian plantation was without its inventory of chains, collars, and whips. But much of the year work went on almost twenty-four hours a day, and no owner or manager could supervise the process closely enough to guarantee that a slave would not drop rocks between the rollers or introduce impurities into the sugar. Clearly many slaves, if some more than others, accepted the situation in which they found themselves enough to take pride in their work. The team that cut more cane, the sugar master on whom the refining process depended, or the artisan who built or repaired machinery and carts won status and respect among peers and earned rewards from the master. Of course, to find that a slave did his or her work well is not to deny the possibility of resistance; throughout the New World the leaders of slave revolts were commonly those of superior skill and intelligence who enjoyed a privileged position in the system.

It is well to remember too that until at least the second half of the eighteenth century few Europeans or Africans saw slavery as morally wrong, however much a slave might regret his or her predicament. The capture and delivery of slaves from the interior of Africa to the coast depended entirely upon Africans themselves, and ex-slaves that returned to Africa from the New World played key roles in the maritime slave trade. In America slavery could not have functioned without the black "drivers" that ran the field gangs or the black "bush captains" that pursued runaways. Even the church lent its moral authority to slavery, and for every Bishop Las Casas that belatedly regretted an enthusiasm for African slavery there were a hundred Jesuits running slave plantations. Only sociopaths consistently reject their environment, and for most Africans, Europeans, and Americans before the late eighteenth century, slavery was simply a given.

Driving the demand for slaves was a huge market for sugar in Europe, undersupplied by plantations in the Mediterranean and on the Atlantic islands. Brazil was uniquely set to supply this market. Whereas sugar cane normally required replanting every year or two, in the extraordinary environment of Brazil's coastal Northeast cane reproduced itself for up to twenty years, and harvests lasted ten or even eleven months a year. Cane cutting was a skilled task carried out preferably in teams, often a man and a woman, one to cut it and the other to clean, bundle, and stack the stalks for pickup. Increasingly after 1600 this was an activity for black slaves. Indian or mixed blood free workers might bring the cane to the mill in ox carts or carry out such ancillary tasks as food production, stock raising, and construction, but the tendency of all slave societies was to replace free labor with slaves, and this was true for Brazilian sugar. Jobs as sugar technicians or artisans that poor white or *mestiço* wage workers might have held in the late sixteenth century, black slaves filled fifty years later. By 1650 African slavery dominated the mill. This lowered costs and gave the master more control, allowing him to reward a slave's good performance by moving him or her to less exhausting and higher-status tasks.

When cane arrived at the mill, it first was crushed between large wooden or copper-covered rollers, powered sometimes by water but in Brazil more commonly by oxen. From there the juice went to the boiling room. One of the most labor-intensive aspects of sugar processing was cutting the wood needed for the fires that heated cane syrup, and gangs of black slaves devastated thousands of acres to feed the roaring furnaces. The sugar master determined the exact moment at which to transfer the boiling cane juice from the huge kettles into molds, where it drained and crystallized. Further processing converted brown sugar into clayed or white sugar, although this was rare in Brazil's early years. When it was ready for harvest, sugar cane could not wait, for if not processed quickly it would begin to ferment and lose sugar content. Thus, the cutting and processing of sugar went on around the clock for many months. A common routine was for a gang of slaves to work eight hours in the fields followed by eight hours in the mill. This was a punishing rhythm that inevitably resulted in accidents with the machinery or boiling cane syrup.

It is easy to imagine an exhausted, frequently injured, and, as sugar expanded and swept aside food production, poorly nourished slave population stumbling from day to day. This was one of slavery's most effective control mechanisms. Overworked slaves had little time or energy to plan or even imagine systematic resistance. Of course, the life soon killed them, but slaves were cheap in Brazil. In the boom years of the late sixteenth century, slaves in the sugar areas could pay for themselves, including upkeep, in eighteen months to two years. Even when sugar prices declined in the seventeenth century, or later when the focus of slavery shifted to mining, four years was a reasonable time to expect to be able to amortize a slave. Under these circumstances there was little reason to provide slaves more than minimum subsistence conditions, and none at all to foster slave families or raise slave children. The ultimate brutality of slavery was not the chains and whips but the reduction of human beings to simple raw material to be consumed at a calculable rate in the production process and then replaced.

Because the Spanish Crown specifically banned Indian labor from sugar, even though growers widely flouted the prohibition, African slavery was associated with commercial sugar production in Spain's colonies too. In Mexico, for example, the use of African slaves in the inland valleys of Morelos probably peaked in the late sixteenth and early seventeenth centuries when mixed blood free labor began to replace them, but on the Caribbean coast the Africans' relative resistance to malaria and yellow fever kept them valuable well into the eighteenth century. A look at the industry in Veracruz gives an idea of the many specialized activities slaves undertook:

In the mill	*Outside the mill*
Sugar master	Ax man (cutting fuel wood)
Mill supervisor	Cowboy
Boiling master	Cane cutter
Mold master	Mule driver
Draining master	Cook
Master carpenter	
Carpenter	
Lighting master	
Water boy	

Here most slaves had more than one task. That is, rather than working in rotating gangs as in Brazil, slaves in Mexico each did several different kinds of work. For example, a slave might be a boiling house worker or mule driver or cane cutter depending on what was needed at the moment. Excepting a tendency for women to concentrate in the areas of cooking and domestic service, there was no particular specialization of work by gender on most sugar mills. Women cut and loaded cane, and even those assigned house duties were drafted at peak times for work in the fields or the mill. The differentiation between field hands and house servants evident in some slave societies had little meaning here. Given the working conditions, and unlike general agricultural haciendas, the slave population on sugar plantations probably did not include many children or old people, but where it did these worked too, herding animals, guiding the oxen that drove the mill, or bringing water and food to workers who ate at their tasks.

Jesuits and Slavery in Spanish America

Of Spanish America's many slave owners, best known and generally most successful was the Jesuit order, which controlled hundreds of agricultural and urban properties from northern New Spain to Chile and Argentina. On the coast of Peru, for example, they operated sugar, wine, and food producing haciendas in the river valleys that led from the Andes down to the Pacific Ocean. Although the Jesuits initially made use of *mita* drafts and also employed wage labor, the largest number of workers, and typically the most valuable assets attached to the properties, were the African slaves: between 1665 and 1767 the average number of slaves per hacienda grew from 99 to more than 250. Unlike Brazil or even Mexico, buyers in Peru rarely obtained slaves directly from Africa, although the Jesuits maintained an agent in Panama for this purpose, and occasionally a cargo reached the port of Callao. More often they acquired slaves a few at a time on local markets or from the La Plata contraband trade. The Jesuits' greater resources allowed them to outbid competitors for recently imported slaves or those sold by their less successful neighbors or from inheritances.

Slaves were given to eat what was cheap and readily available, with little regard to its quality or nutritional value. On the coast of Peru their basic food was *sango*, a mixture of corn, wheat, and grease, seasoned with salt and spices. With this they might receive small amounts of fish or meat and wine or cane alcohol. The extent to which slaves supplemented the rations they received with food they grew themselves varied widely from one slave system to another, and sometimes even between adjacent properties. Where the slaves were employed in producing a valuable export crop such as sugar, owners generally preferred to buy or import the foodstuffs they needed. This worked against the slaves both because most masters provided as little and as cheap food as possible, almost guaranteeing malnourishment, and because in times of war and political crisis communications and transportation breakdowns could impede or cut the flow of food. Where the pace was less hectic or their time less valuable, slaves sometimes received permission to cultivate food on marginal land, to supplement their diet, or even to sell. Such slave self-provisioning could dramatically cut the master's labor costs, but it also left him competing with his own slaves for their labor.

The Jesuits used slaves not just for prohibited crops but also where Indian labor was not available. Chilean *encomenderos* early on had ravaged the present-day Argentine-Chilean border, effectively depopulating the area. When the Jesuits began to develop a group of properties around Cuyo, they relied heavily on black slave labor, supplemented in peak periods by mixed blood contract workers called *conchabados*. These haciendas produced food and wine and *aguardiente* (rum), which the fathers retailed locally and wholesaled to Buenos Aires. Unlike the Peruvian sugar and export plantations where males predominated, on the Cuyo properties there was a near balance of men to women, and the Jesuits went to considerable effort to encourage families and child rearing. Because of the relatively low profits available in this marginal area and the high cost of slaves there, it was good economic logic to maintain and even increase the work force through natural reproduction, rather than to think in terms of working slaves to death and buying replacements. Over the period 1734 to 1767 the slave population on the Jesuits' Cuyo properties went from 28 to 104, almost entirely as the result of self-reproduction.

The living conditions here were relatively good. The slaves grew their own food and seem to have enjoyed an adequate diet and housing. Except for the free labor hired to help with the sugar harvest, slaves did all the work on the properties. There were multiple opportunities for those with the interest or talent to learn skills apart from routine work: slaves trained as cobblers, masons, barbers, in wine growing and alcohol production, and as cooks, and the Jesuits even sent some to learn music in the missions of Paraguay. Rewards for good behavior included extra food, clothing, and money. It was a complete world with rewards as well as punishments, and its isolation contributed to the willingness of the slaves to work within the system. Few tried to escape, and those that did were quickly recaptured and not subjected to harsh punishments.

Farther to the east, around Cordoba and toward Paraguay, Jesuit haciendas took on characteristics more like those of coastal Peru. For one thing, the number of slaves per property was much larger than in Cuyo and totaled some 3,000 by 1767. The main activity here was ranching, cattle for local markets and Buenos Aires and mules for use in Upper Peru. The properties' labor force mixed together the remnants of local *mita* Indians, *conchabados*, and black slaves, who worked as cowboys and grew most of their own food. In the interest of social peace and reproduction of the labor force, the managers here too attempted to maintain a balance of the sexes, but there were few children. Instead, the main form of replacing and increasing the slave population was the purchase of *bozales* from Buenos Aires and, illegally, from Brazil.

Modern calculations indicate that the use of slaves on the Pampas was no cheaper, and may have been more expensive, than free labor. Leaving aside the question of whether the Jesuits made these same calculations, or reached the same conclusions if they did, slaves offered a stable and reliable work force on these open plains that free workers did not. Already Argentina's rural frontier had spawned the *gaucho*, the rootless cowboy and border ruffian that the nineteenth-century Argentine state labored mightily, and with little success, to bring under control and to mold into a docile laborer.

Gold Mining

During the colonial period gold mining consisted almost exclusively of alluvial panning, often in hot, unhealthful areas. The indigenous populations of these regions had been particularly hard hit by the diseases the Europeans brought, and after a few initial disasters those who controlled Indian labor in the highlands resisted sending their workers to almost certain death in the hot country. Free labor similarly avoided these areas. By default, then, black slaves came to dominate gold mining. They survived the climatic and working conditions better than the Indians or mixed bloods, and even if they did not there was no one arguing against using them. And successful mining was profitable enough to pay the costs of slaves.

Typical were Spanish activities in the Chocó region of present-day Colombia. The Chocó was, and is, a hot and disease-infested region along the Pacific coast, and mining activities there supported only a scattering of small settlements and dispersed camps. Europeans first began to move into the region in the second half of the seventeenth century, and after a brief attempt even the Jesuits abandoned the effort to plant missions there. The few Indians that survived their initial encounters with the Spanish avoided further contact, so that when mining began in earnest in the early eighteenth century it necessarily depended on black slaves. This population peaked at more than 7,000 in the 1780s but declined thereafter as the gold played out. Mining techniques were primitive, and there was little attention to the sort of hydraulic engineering used to improve efficiency in other areas. In the Chocó a foreman ran each operation, supervising the slaves, while the owner remained behind in the much more healthful highland town of Popayán. Most of the slaves were *bozales*, and contemporaries estimated that up to half were illegally imported, bought from British contraband traders in the Caribbean and shipped secretly down the Atrato River.

What was most striking about the Chocó was the facility with which slaves gained their freedom. Certainly this opportunity, more than diet or clothing or housing, must have been the central concern of most slaves, and the experience of the Chocó puts the process in clear relief. The manumission rate among slaves in the region was extraordinarily high, so much so that by the 1780s, and despite high mortality, at least a third of the black population in the Chocó already was made up of freedmen. The manumission of a slave in colonial Latin America was rarely the result of the master's good heart or a reward for the slave's devotion. Overwhelmingly slaves became free because they purchased their freedom or someone else bought it for them. Parents freed children and children freed parents, future employers freed workers, and many a slave bought his or her own way out. The key was being able to earn and save money. To do this the slave had to acquire and hold property that was beyond the claim of the master, a radical supposition in a slave society and one that not all owners were willing to honor. Both Portuguese and Spanish law were vague and contradictory about if or how a slave might manumit him- or herself, and, in any event, law and the legal system had limited impact in areas such as the lowlands of eighteenth-century Colombia. Custom, on the other hand, was strong in all parts of the colonies, and generally it sustained the slaves' right to purchase their freedom. Where the masters refused to cooperate, slaves hid money or kept it with a free person, and almost always the courts honored their right to have a fair price fixed and to free themselves by paying this.

But how was a slave to earn this money? Though there might be ways to do this in the city, rural slaves had fewer such opportunities, and most slaves worked in the countryside. From this perspective, and despite the mosquitoes, disease, and isolation, captives in the Chocó were particularly fortunate. Most went about their mining activities with only the loosest supervision, and sometimes they spent days or weeks apart in separate camps. In this environment supervisors could exercise only limited disciplinary power, and the slaves had wide freedoms. They could have escaped, but it was so easy to appropriate some of the gold they found for themselves that it made as much or more sense to seek freedom through legal manumission. Their experiences left most of the ex-slaves so unassimilated to Spanish culture that they promptly withdrew from day-to-day contact with the colonial regime, moving into the interior and supporting themselves by farming and gold panning.

By far the richest of the colonial gold mining areas was Brazil's Minas Gerais, together with its lesser siblings Goiás and Mato Grosso. When it was that Paulista slave hunters discovered gold and diamonds in the region is not clear, but word leaked out in the 1690s, provoking a rush to the region. Whole districts of Portugal were depopulated, it was said, and the decadent sugar economy in Brazil's Northeast sent thousands of whites and tens of thousands of slaves to the gold fields. By 1735 there were more than 100,000 slaves in the mining area. Generally poor whites or free mulattos, called *faiscadores*, prospected the rivers for gold deposits, and if they found gold they did their best to keep the discovery to themselves. Inevitably the news spread, however, and a Crown official quickly appeared, allocated a small part of the site to the original discoverer, and distributed the rest to others. In Minas Gerais mining was only slightly more technically advanced than in the Chocó, with some use of simple machines and the diversion of small streams to expose a promising gravel bed or to provide water to wash gold-bearing soil. African slaves did the actual panning in the river, typically under the close watch of white or mulatto supervisors: "There they work," one observer remarked, "there they eat and often there they have to sleep; and since when they work they are bathed in sweat, with their feet always in the cold earth, on stones, or in water, when they rest or eat, their pores close and they become so chilled that they are susceptible to many dangerous illnesses."[6]

Here too, as in the Chocó, slaves sometimes worked on their own, returning a daily quota to their masters, but owners and public authorities policed their activities much more closely than on the coast of Colombia.

Particularly in the first years, these gold mining areas suffered massive male to female imbalances among both the slaves and the free population. Over time, though, a population of slave women and free blacks and mulattas grew up, doing cooking and domestic work, and women were responsible for most of petty commerce and street trade around the mines. It was in this latter capacity that they particularly worried colonial authorities, who sought repeatedly to ban mulattas and free blacks from the mines or at least to sharply limit their activities. Slaves passed gold and stolen property to women they got to know in the streets, either to fence, to hold for them, or as payment for food or sexual services. Crown officials persecuted female street vendors mercilessly but with little success. They were simply too valuable to be dispensed with.

Because of the sometimes lurid emphasis given to the physical abuse and sexual exploitation of slaves, it is worth remembering the employers bought slaves primarily to make money. Slaves were an important investment and commonly the most valuable part of an agricultural or mining operation. Of course, all societies breed psychopaths and sadists that simply enjoy hurting others, and for obvious reasons slave societies encouraged this. Planters in late-eighteenth-century Saint Domingue (Haiti), for example, were said to have "poured burning wax on [the slaves'] arms and hands and shoulders, emptied boiling cane sugar over their heads, burned them alive, roasted them over slow fires, filled them with gun powder and [blown] them up with a match."[7] In most environments, though, slaves were too expensive and too necessary to the labor process to be abused gratuitously or punished in ways that might seriously affect their ability to work. Observers of slave society not uncommonly confused exemplary punishment with day-to-day conditions. In colonial Latin America, and unlike the antebellum southern United States, slaves and free blacks routinely outnumbered "whites," and owners and the state worried that the hold they had over this naturally resentful population was dangerously precarious. It would have been much more so had Indians and blacks cooperated against their oppressors, but this rarely happened. Racism and economic competition kept the groups apart, and the mixed bloods that might have served as intermediaries and leaders typically sought individual success by dissociating themselves from their tainted past.

To keep the blacks, Indians, and *castas* (mixed bloods) under control the colonial state and employers relied in no small part on terror, on implied and real violence. This was not a totalitarian state, however. Public authorities had limited contact with the lower orders on a day-to-day basis and even less chance of imposing hegemonic ideas upon them. The persistence of religious syncretism was the best evidence of this. Rather, the state and the elites depended on exemplary violence. Slave or peasant uprisings, for example, had leaders, or so the authorities reasoned, and when the outbreak was repressed, the leaders were executed in a public and dramatic manner, the better to frighten and intimidate the survivors or those who might be contemplating resisting the state. Whether those unfortunates whipped or shot or hung actually had been the leaders, if indeed leaders existed at all, was less important than the evidence that any resistance entailed horrifying consequences. By contrast, an owner confronted with an obstreperous slave was much more likely to sell rather than damage him or her, and he was usually very reluctant to lose his investment to state repression.

Free Workers and Peasants

If slaves were rebellious and Indian forced workers sullen and inefficient, what of free wage labor? Put simply, free labor in the true sense hardly existed during the early colonial period, though some forms of employment approached it, but a growing labor pool in the eighteenth century meant that free labor was beginning to emerge as a viable form. In the century or two after the conquest, few workers were free in any sense, and even the apparent liberty of *narborías* and *yanaconas* was constrained by their dependence on a patron. Slaves were the limit case of unfreedom, of course, but the majority of Indians in the villages were unfree too, in a double sense. On the one hand, membership in the community entailed claims on labor and time from kin and village authorities, claims not easily evaded. Local leaders named workers for the *repartimientos* and decided who would pay how much to meet the village's tax obligations. Community membership also required participation in *cofradías* (religious brotherhoods) and village governance, time consuming and expensive activities. A host of claims, then, weighed upon the individual and the family and made it impossible for them to dispose of their labor as they might wish. Similarly, and to the great frustration of would-be employers, much of the indigenous population at least initially did not have to work for wages because they still had access to land and other resources, usually through the communities. Most, that is, were free not to work for the Spanish, and for this reason employers in the sixteenth and early seventeenth centuries relied heavily on forms of coerced labor.

By the end of the sixteenth century, however, a growing population of mixed bloods was competing for land and resources with the Indian villages and the haciendas and might have formed the basis of a free labor force. In theory, of course, these people did not exist. Spanish law forbade "interracial" unions, and the church condemned sexual relations outside of marriage, but neither the church nor the state had much success at imposing their strictures on human sexuality. Significant numbers of *castas* were becoming visible in Mexico City and Lima as early as 1550 or 1560. They dominated the "white" populations in marginal and frontier regions: a visitor to New Spain's remote Tehuantepec peninsula remarked of local elites: "There is no one who dares to classify the *castas*. Such information, if applied rigorously, would be odious and expose dark stains, erased by time, in prominent families."[8]

Indians, as "natural lords of this place," by law and custom had rights to land, even if these were honored in the breach more than in fact, but mixed bloods by the very nature of their being racially inferior and presumptively illegitimate did not. Early on, when they were few, mestizos and mulattos were relatively easily absorbed into one of the parent groups. As their numbers grew, however, they became more obvious and more threatening to the authorities. As people situated literally between accepted groups, some mixed bloods found their best chance in performing middleman functions, working as foremen, mule drivers, and traders, or becoming priests by virtue of their familiarity with indigenous languages. Others insinuated or forced their way into Indian villages and dominated and exploited the indigenous population. Mulatta *regatones* (intermediaries) went out from the towns each morning to meet Indians on the way to market and coerce them into giving up their products cheaply for resale in town. *Castas* survived precariously in the towns as casual day laborers, prostitutes, beggars, and petty criminals. By the eighteenth century urban elites increasingly feared the rootless, disaffected, violent, and growing population of "lepers" that crowded cities' streets.

Most mixed bloods lived in the countryside, though, scrambling to survive in agriculture and stock raising or as wage workers. Many were small farmers, slash and burn agriculturalists in a pattern that pre-dated the conquest. Some produced food only for their own use, while others were peasants or marginally better-off *rancheros* (middling farmers and ranchers) who regularly sold surplus crops and handicraft items on the market. These activities depended on family labor. As in pre-contact society, men generally took the lead in clearing the fields for planting, but now they played a bigger role in the actual cultivation. In part this was because the state had banned the sort of military activities that had occupied men in many of the pre-contact societies, and also it was the result of ecological changes and new property boundaries that limited what and where they could hunt or fish. If women sometimes helped with the planting and the harvest, field agriculture was preeminently a man's job, and boys as young as five or six joined their fathers there to begin learning the techniques of machete and hoe cultivation.

The home and its environs, on the other hand, were the woman's sphere, and a subsistence farmer would have found it almost impossible to function without having a wife or female relative to do this work. Indeed, in most indigenous societies only a stable union with several children conferred full adult status. The woman managed the household economy, including not just domestic tasks but the vegetable garden and the yard animals, as well. Any money made from truck crops or the sale of these animals was hers. The couple might also engage in handicraft production, and normally the wife took this to market if they chose to sell or trade it. In pre-industrial society women were key not just to reproducing but also to socializing the work force. Subsistence and peasant farmers only functioned effectively as part of a family unit, and everyone lost if the family failed.

Transition from subsistence to peasant agriculture was dependent on access to markets. Typically peasants sold small quantities of what they produced to nearby haciendas or plantations, to merchants, or to professional middlemen who traveled the countryside buying up produce and bulking it for resale in the urban areas. With the money they earned peasants paid taxes and fees to the church and bought consumer goods—for example, salt or cloth or alcohol, or food as their own stocks dwindled toward the end of the dry season. Some observers have labeled these small producers "penny capitalists." More properly, though, they were "petty commodity producers." That is, they transferred the mechanisms of their subsistence from simple production for home consumption to production for sale on the market. But they did not profit enough from this to accumulate, reinvest, and expand their output, the fundamental mechanism of capitalism reproduction. More and more they were drawn into the world capitalist system without themselves becoming capitalists, and thus suffered its problems with few of its benefits.

More than through the sale of products, peasants and the rural poor entered the larger market economy through the sale of their own labor. Most who did this were forced into it by land problems. Slash and burn agriculture could be very productive, but in order for the soil to recuperate its fertility farmers had to move every few years and leave the old plot fallow. Population growth in the countryside, together with more formalized hacienda and property boundaries, narrowed the peasants' horizons more and more. To an extent this was not accidental but the result of state and elite policies that sought to force small farmers into wage labor by denying them independent access to land. By the mid to late seventeenth century the indigenous population's declines had bottomed out, at least in the central areas, and the numbers were beginning to inch up again. Taken together with the rapidly expanding strata of *castas*, this meant that more rural inhabitants were searching for land and finding less of it available. An increasingly common resort was to rent land or seek wage work on haciendas and *estancias*.

Employment of nonslave workers on large holdings in colonial Spanish America took a variety of forms and went by many names, whether *inquilinos* (resident workers) in Chile and *conchabados* in Argentina or *peones permanentes* and *arrendatarios* (renters) in northern Mexico or *jornaleros* (day laborers) across the continent. The work varied with crop, region, and time of year but involved the familiar tasks of cultivation, stock care, preparing and processing hacienda products, artisan work, and transportation. What also varied was the manner in which the employer paid for this labor and the workers' degree of independence or insecurity. Least common was genuine free labor, men and women who worked by the day or week in return for payment in cash or goods. On the one hand, a general shortage of money in rural areas slowed the development of wage labor; *hacendados* might be land or cattle rich but all were short of cash. More importantly, reliance on casual labor violated an underlying concern for security characteristic of both the landowners and the workers. An additional factor that made free labor unattractive to the poor was the tendency for wages to remain stable over decades and even centuries, while prices responded more actively to market ups and downs and generally rose in the eighteenth century. In these circumstances *castas* and Indians saw security not as wages but as guaranteed access to land on which to grow food.

The most common nonslave employment relationship for rural workers during the colonial period, and well into the nineteenth century, was the exchange of work for the right to use land—labor rent. A tenant or renter was required to give a certain number of days' work a week or a month in return for the use of a subsistence plot and a place for his house, and perhaps the right to graze a few cattle on the landowner's pasture. They commonly also had the opportunity, or heir contract might make it an obligation, to work additional days for wages, for example during the harvest. On Sundays everyone did *faena*, unpaid cleanup work around the property. Labor rent gave the tenants some security, and this form of labor mobilization also suited the *hacendados*, who typically had large amounts of land of which they made no direct use.

In areas where labor was in short supply, these resident workers were fundamental to the viability of the large properties, and to keep them owners offered various incentives. Favored workers lived near the *casco* (the hacienda center), instead of scattered on the fringes of the property, and received not only access to land but a food ration, as well as cheap credit at the hacienda store. A bit further down the scale, and this might include the children of the resident families, were workers employed as needed for a daily wage, usually at a rate slightly higher than that paid permanent laborers. But this employment was seasonal, and although these workers might be allowed to live at little or no cost on the property, the status carried with it none of the other guarantees provided renters or permanent workers.

Surrounding the hacienda property were likely to be indigenous communities and many small peasant holdings, nominally independent but probably on untitled land or with defective documents. Even where they did not depend directly on the large holdings for land or credit, these less powerful neighbors deferred leadership in social and political questions to local landed elites, sought them out for relations of fictive kinship (*compadrazgo*), and came to them for economic assistance and employment when their own land did not provide an adequate living. It was a symbiotic relationship, if not one of equals. The hacienda needed large amounts of labor only occasionally, for the harvest or the roundup or to make up a clientele for armed disputes, and owners found it convenient to draw this from among the small farmers and peasant communities in the vicinity.

Rural workers of whatever sort rarely received cash for their efforts. More often payment was in kind, in cloth or animals or food, or it might take the form of credit at the hacienda store or with a merchant in a nearby town. The infamous *tienda de raya* (hacienda store) appeared in various manifestations throughout Spanish America and sits at the heart of one of the most debated aspects of colonial agricultural labor—"debt servitude" or "debt peonage." Despite indebted labor's fierce reputation, recent research has demonstrated the real fragility of the institution in many areas. Far from being a burden, debts could be a reward for good performance. The standard notion has it that poor Indians and mixed bloods fell into debt when they accepted advance payments from employers for their labor, payments that their low salaries and the hacienda bookkeeper's manipulations made impossible to repay. Far from being deceived or even desperate, however, it now seems clear that most workers entered debt voluntarily and even enthusiastically, fully aware of what they were doing and counting themselves lucky to have the chance. These circumstances became more evident and the workers' situation more desperate a hundred years later, but already by the mid-eighteenth century many of the rural poor considered themselves fortunate to have a stable rent or work relationship on a hacienda and to be spared having to scratch a living on marginal land or scramble for uncertain day labor. Credit at the store was especially important. Records make it clear that while some purchases at the stores were consumer goods such as cloth or tools, or even ribbons and lace, the biggest item was food. Credit could mean the difference between survival and death by starvation or from disease aggravated by malnutrition.

But what of the coercive aspects of debt peonage, the way it restrained freedom and locked the worker into a presumably exploitative relationship?

Evidence varies widely and probably needs to be examined not just for each region and time but for each property, but we can begin by asking a question: Freedom to do what? Given colonial patterns of power and control, a laborer that escaped one relationship of indebtedness had little alternative but to seek another, or fall into the even less attractive categories of day laborer in the countryside or "leper" in the city. Workers did move from one property to another for personal reasons, or to escape an abusive employer, or to pursue better wages, credit, or working conditions, to the great distress of employers. Genuine "debt peonage" or "debt slavery" would imply and require that these employers or the state had the power and the will to force workers to continue employment under conditions imposed upon them unilaterally, because their debt "bound" them. Apart from moral consciousness, however, nothing about a debt bound anyone in the eighteenth century any more than it does today. Debt is a contract, and the state operating through the judicial system enforces contracts. But it was precisely the absence of a strong state that marked the colonial regime. If sometimes hacienda owners attempted to enforce debts and debt peonage on their own, this was always extralegal. By the second half of the eighteenth century the Bourbon state actively opposed both the use of debts to hold workers and physical punishment to coerce labor.

Apart from agriculture, the biggest employer of free labor was the mining industry. As we have seen, gold mining depended on black slaves, and Potosí and Huancavelica benefited from the *mita*, but even at Potosí free laborers outnumbered drafted workers as early as 1600, particularly in the more lucrative tasks and at the ore face. Similarly, while early silver strikes near Mexico City made use of *repartimientos*, as the center of mining shifted north drafted labor all but disappeared. There were few settled Indians in the mining areas to be pressed into service, and *encomenderos* and *corregidores* (governors) in the colony's more populated regions resisted sending the Indians they controlled to the uncertain conditions of the North. Black slaves were expensive, and although they had the advantage of providing a stable labor force, experience showed that they performed poorly underground, suffering from the cold and damp and easily succumbing to disease. Instead, they worked in the ore processing plants and ancillary activities.

Silver mining in northern Mexico was the province of an elite free labor force made up of *narborías* that had migrated from the South together with a growing number of *castas* drawn by the relatively high wages available there. Best paid were the *barreteros*, the crowbar men who worked at the mine face. They earned five to eight pesos a month, but by custom also were allowed to keep some of the ore they found, the *partido*. Each mine set a daily quota based on local conditions, and the miners kept whatever they dug out above this. The *partido* could easily amount to three to five times the daily wage, and in the eighteenth century miners sometimes made as much as three to four pesos in a single shift. There were other skilled and comparatively well paid activities associated with the mines as well, including: prospectors; stamping mill workers; mine carpenters; mercury/chemical workers; mine drainage workers; amalgamation supervisor; *partido* checkers; labor recruiters; ore classifiers/washers; and refinery workers.

Even given its undoubted risks, mine labor was an attractive opportunity, and men and women poured into the mining areas in the second half of the sixteenth and the early seventeenth centuries. Some lived in the refining compound (the *hacienda de minas*), while others sought out those from the same parts of Mexico or of similar ethnic extraction and formed distinct neighborhoods (*barrios*). The number of workers involved in mining by the early seventeenth century was not large, perhaps as few as 5,000, so the labor supply did not suffer adverse effects from the general population declines that hit the colony after 1560. Mexican mine labor was perhaps the nearest approximation of free labor in sixteenth- or seventeenth-century Spanish America. By their migration the miners had largely freed themselves from the demands of family, kin, and community. At the same time, their lack of property or access to land freed them of anything to sell but their time and skill, their labor power.

Of course, even the Crown's commitment to free labor had limits, particularly for an activity as vital as silver mining. State policy fenced the industry about with regulations and attempted to structure labor relations to the benefit of employers and to increase output. Silver mining was a boom and bust enterprise, as pockets of ore played out and new strikes occurred. Each fresh discovery tended to draw workers away from existing mines, as they sought better wages or a bigger *partido*. Employers had to compete for labor, prompting constant complaints and fruitless ordinances against "poaching." Debt servitude was of little use, both because the state's presence in the North was far too limited to enforce restrictions on the highly mobile miners and because mine owners readily employed and protected good workers, even if these owed debts to others. Instead, some owners hoped to cut down on labor turnover by reducing or doing away altogether with the *partido*, eliminating the incentive to move to newer, richer strikes.

Efforts to cut their share or eliminate the *partido* infuriated the miners and in August of 1766 provoked one of Mexico's first industrial strikes, at the Real del Monte mine in the Pachuca district. When popular resistance blocked the owners' efforts to eliminate the *partido*, they instead instituted a *revoltura* system: at the end of each shift the foreman mixed together the bags of quota and *partido* ore and then redivided this, preventing the miners from keeping the best material for themselves. Workers also were made to pay for such auxiliary services as the mine doctor out of their *partido* bags. Rebelling against this attack on custom, as well as what they felt was mistreatment at the hands of several foremen, the workers addressed a series of protest petitions to royal officials and the viceroy. These had little effect, however, and the conflict soon fell into violence. One of the foremen, as well as the *alcalde mayor* of Pachuca, who ill-advisedly tried to intervene in a riot, died at the hands of a mob. Given the importance of mining and seeing the volatility of the situation, the investigating judge sent to straighten things out moved cautiously. He did not punish the miners for the riots or the deaths and agreed to restore the old *partido* system. When the viceroy issued comprehensive mining regulations in 1778, the first of these warned that "no one will dare to alter the existing system of payments established by custom."[9] The workers of Real del Monte had mounted a successful reactionary protest, but it availed them little. By 1770 most of the shafts in the area had played out and were shut down and flooded.

Apart from Potosí and Huancavalica, hard rock mining in Peru depended on free labor, but this took a different form from that of northern Mexico. At Oruro, north of Potosí, owners of silver mines obtained wage labor from nearby indigenous communities but remained unhappy at what this cost them. Repeatedly they petitioned the viceroy for access to *mita* workers, but the Crown refused, fearing this might disrupt operations at Potosí. In a real sense, though, Potosí and the *mita* did subsidize Oruro labor. The Indians accepted lower wages than they might otherwise have demanded because work in the Oruro mines exempted them from the *mita* drafts. Drawing labor from nearby villages also cheapened wages because the Indians produced much of their own food, cutting the costs of maintaining and reproducing the work force. They could be sent home and not paid when they were not needed, but were unlikely to move elsewhere in search of employment. At the same time, of course, the very availability of an alternative subsistence economy limited the downward pressure that employers could exert on wages: in the late seventeenth century, with Oruro's mines in decline, daily rates fell only to four reales, the same as that paid *mitayos* and above what rural agricultural labor earned. Mine owners never were able to eliminate the customary practices of *corpa*, the casual taking of ore by the miners, and "doubling," the right of the Indians to work the mines for themselves in their spare time. Oruro's miners closely approximated what writers have called a "semi-proletariat." Although they labored part of the time in the wage sector and responded to many of the elements of a free wage market, they still owned or had access to land and were not entirely dependent upon wage labor for their survival. And at least indirect coercion persisted in the form of the *mita*.

Compared to mining, textile mills (*obrajes*), another major consumer of semi-industrial wage labor, had enormous trouble recruiting workers. Most mills produced cheap, coarse cloth for the bottom end of the market and they employed a very diverse labor force. By the middle of the seventeenth century the *obrajes* of New Spain, for example, largely had been forced to abandon *repartimientos*, but they still used black slaves when they could afford them, and some employed convict labor. Colonial jails were notoriously insecure, and in 1555 the Crown granted the *Audiencia* of New Spain permission to sentence criminals and runaway slaves to work for private businesses. Bakeries and *obrajes* were the biggest consumers of convict workers, with bidding for them taking place at judicial auctions or contracts arranged privately with the courts. Sentences rarely exceeded ten years, but employers attempted to pull the prisoners, just as they did their free workers, into debt and hold them after their term of imprisonment had expired. Convicts worked in chains and suffered harsher punishments for infractions than free workers, but most seem to have survived their sentences. How many eventually escaped the mills is unclear. Even free workers sometimes found their mobility limited, and in extreme cases they were locked in the mill buildings or chained to their machines. This sort of restriction tended to be short-lived, however, both because Crown policy opposed it and because the cyclical nature of demand for textiles and the uneven availability of raw materials forced the mills to periodically shut down and dispense with most of their workers.

More than New Spain, the *Audiencia* of Quito (Ecuador) was the great colonial center for *obrajes*. For example, when in the early seventeenth century Mexico City had 49 *obrajes* with 2,200 employees and Puebla had 32 mills with 1,440 Indians, Quito had 51 legal *obrajes* with some 7,300 workers and at least another 150 illegal mills employing more than 20,000. The Quito industry benefited from plentiful supplies of locally produced wool and cheap labor. Laws to the contrary not withstanding, *repartimiento* labor persisted in the Quito until the eighteenth century, and here legal mills mixed free workers, *repartimiento* Indians, and black slaves. Unlicensed mills did not have access to drafted Indians, but efforts by the state to have these demolished or to regulate working conditions came to naught. Local elites, including the Franciscans and Jesuits, owned numerous illegal mills and strongly resisted efforts to rein in their activities, pointing out that cloth production was the only source of wealth in the area and the chief financial prop of the state. Even Indian communities operated illegal *obrajes*, to raise money to pay tribute.

Textile manufacturing involved a series of complicated steps: women washed the raw wool, carded, and spun it, whether on wheels or by hand;

from there the thread went to be dyed and then woven on large looms operated by male workers; final processes included fulling, burling, teaseling, and shearing. The technology was more complicated than a simple summary suggests, but it had been imported whole cloth, so to speak, from late medieval Europe and experienced little innovation before the end of the eighteenth century. The workers labored in gangs organized around specific tasks and were paid piecework rates as a group. Conditions in most mills suffered from poor lighting, inadequate ventilation, and high levels of heat and humidity. Workers wore the minimum clothing possible, to avoid chafing from sweat-soaked garments and to deny a home to the many fleas that arrived in the raw wool.

As bad as the *obrajes* sound, the work paid better than agricultural labor. In most cases, though, wages were still too low to support a family, particularly for Indian workers who had to pay Quito's extraordinarily high tribute. Another problem was the practice of paying wages not in cash but in cloth of the mill itself, and often an inferior quality at inflated values. That workers fell into debt was hardly to be wondered, and these debts functioned more coercively than was typical of agriculture. Employers regularly held workers against their will, and relatives of workers who died or fled could be saddled with their debts. Still, and apart from the *repartimiento* Indians, black slaves, and criminals, those who entered the mills did so largely voluntarily because it was the best opportunity available to them.

Conclusions

The goal of the Spanish and, somewhat less enthusiastically, Portuguese Crowns was the creation of a free labor system for the empires' citizens. But the kings' subjects also were required to work, for their own moral edification and for the benefit of the royal treasury. Of course, the indigenous population had always worked, but they had done so on their own land or in their own industries, and they showed little inclination to seek wage labor on Spanish-owned haciendas or in the mines. For mulattos and mestizos, laboring for others was something Indians did and to be avoided for this reason; for ex-slaves, work was what slaves did. The Spanish Crown's interim solution was *repartimientos/mitas*, forced wage labor the Indians both came to accept as "customary" and legitimate and did their best to avoid. Even the Crown and the employers were at cross purposes about *repartimientos*. The state wanted to make sure that Indians received their wages so they could pay taxes and support the church, while employers sought to cheapen labor by paying the workers as little as possible.

By the second quarter of the seventeenth century conditions in the core areas were turning against the logic of forced wage labor. The decline of the indigenous population had stopped and the number of Indians and mixed bloods in the countryside was growing again, if slowly. In the meantime, Spanish and creole landowners had acquired much of what had once been Indian community land, leaving a growing population of rural poor with little resort but to seek wage work or a rental relationship on one of the large properties, or to migrate to the cities. These changes, the inflexibility of *repartimientos*, and Indian resistance prompted a shift in many areas toward freer labor systems over the course of the seventeenth century.

The century after 1550 saw a diversification of work relations, relations that after 1650 tended become set in "custom" that persisted into the eighteenth and even the nineteenth century. Coerced labor lasted longer on the peripheries, because of the poverty of the economies and because of the mobility of the indigenous populations. African slavery dominated those areas where prohibitions on Indian labor or a scarce local population together with a profitable crop made it viable. For free workers debts seem to have been common, but there is less evidence that these always and everywhere bound them effectively in "debt peonage." Even where growing populations allowed employers to limit or end advances and debts and to shift to freer labor, they continued to threaten or exercise coercive violence where they could, the more effectively to mobilize and to cheapen labor.

Chapter 3

Cities and Towns, 1750–1850

Most of colonial Latin America's inhabitants lived in the country side, but Spanish and Portuguese cultures were urban centered. This was a heritage of Rome and of Islam and reflected too the limited impacts of feudal decentralization on the Iberian peninsula. The first act of the conquerors in the New World was to found a town, or several. Though the wealth of the colonies came from mines, plantations, and haciendas, and from the labor of millions of rural Indians, black slaves, poor whites, and mixed bloods, elites came to the cities either to spend it or to send it back to Spain. With mounting population pressures and expanding commercial agriculture in the rural areas, a growing number of the rural poor also sought refuge in the cities, fleeing village tax and labor demands and declining access to land. By 1790 Latin America had a number of substantial cities, and these and other new ones, grew rapidly over the next century.

Population of Latin American Cities, 1750–1850[1]

	1790	1800	1850	1880
Buenos Aires	22,000	40,000	99,000	187,000
Lima	53,000	54,000	70,000	101,000
Santiago	45,000	90,000	130,000	
Bogota	18,000	24,000	30,000	96,000
Rio de Janeiro		43,000	166,000	360,000
Mexico City	131,000	137,000	170,000	250,000

In Spanish America the towns and cities dominated the countryside. They housed the chief representatives of secular and religious power, as well as the main seats of learning, and here the most important merchants accumulated the wealth of the colonies. This was not an accident but a conscious artifact of state policy. Crown and church authorities sought to better control the population by concentrating it in towns under their watchful eye. The Crown demanded the *encomenderos* live in Spanish towns, not among the Indians, for the well-being of both parties, and the *corregidor* who took over control of the countryside from the *encomenderos* spent as much of the time as possible in urban areas among their fellow Spaniards. By law the only non-Indians allowed to live in the indigenous communities were their priests, but it was notoriously difficult to stir even priests from the capital to take up parishes in remote areas. Landowners, apart from an occasional short visit to their properties, preferred the cities too, and retreated to their haciendas only in times of economic distress. Only the poor and the benighted, and of course, the Indians, lived "in the interior," and by the early seventeenth century there was beginning to appear even a growing and distinctly urban Indian population.

Political independence in the teens and twenties did not greatly or immediately alter work relations in the urban areas or the countryside, though subsequent economic upheavals did. The new republics abolished African slavery, for example, only where it was no longer important or profitable. In Brazil and Cuba, on the other hand, slavery expanded dramatically in the 1830s and 1840s. Many Spanish merchants and bureaucrats stayed on in the new republics and some prospered, while others fell victim to the civil wars and to an influx of British goods and British merchants. Free trade devastated the artisan class and urban handicraft workers. The upheavals of the first half of the nineteenth century were particularly damaging for poor women, many of whom had benefited from new employment opportunities opened by the Bourbon Reforms but now found themselves squeezed out as domestic manufacturing collapsed and unemployed men took what jobs survived.

Bureaucrats

The main square or plaza of any Spanish American city mapped the distribution of power. With a whipping post or a gallows at its center, the square was fronted on one side by the offices of the chief Crown authorities, on another by the main church and its attendant buildings, and on the other two by the houses and stores of the community's most important merchants and landowners. The plaza was the locus of elite life. This elite was a remarkably small group, perhaps 3 to 5 percent of the population, defined by political and social power, wealth and culture, and legal privileges (*fueros*). At its peak were the Crown's direct representatives, and first among these was the viceroy, though the archbishop more than once disputed this ranking. Until the late colonial period there were only two viceroys in the New World, one in Mexico City and the other in Lima, and the post turned over fairly rapidly, with five to eight years in office being typical. In secondary jurisdictions, or *Audiencias*, a president or a military captain-general ruled, depending on the area's defense needs. Although promotion of a viceroy from Mexico City to Lima or to the Council of the Indies was possible, for most successful bureaucrats or military men an appointment to either viceroyalty was likely the culmination of their careers and the reward for long years of service to the Crown. The office carried high prestige and high pay, and viceroys were not allowed to engage in commerce or other activities, though some did. They commonly arrived, too, accompanied by a swarm of relatives and hangers-on (*paniaguados*) who rightly saw this as their best chance to make a fortune or a good marriage.

The often slow and inconsistent nature of imperial communications allowed viceroys considerable room for short-term local initiative, but they worked constrained by law, custom, the policies of their predecessors, and sometimes by detailed instructions from the Council of the Indies. The Council's charge to Antonio de Mendoza, first viceroy of New Spain, for example, ran eighty-two pages. He was ordered to undertake, among other things, the improbable task of visiting each town, city, and village of New Spain and gathering information on the inhabitants, particularly as this would increase Crown revenues. Viceroys suffered *visitas* (inspections) and *residencias* (end-of-term reviews) and the constant carping of their subordinates. Some were incompetent or time servers who had little impact, while others, such as Antonio de Mendoza and Antonio María Bucareli in New Spain or Francisco de Toledo in Peru, left lasting imprints on their colonies. All found the work demanding: "The responsibilities are insufferable, decisions necessary in many cases, and confusion of antecedents more than you can imagine. I spend ten hours a day at my desk, and still cannot complete what I would like, because on Court days they interrupt me at each step with appeals."[2] The relative effectiveness of the viceroys tended to reflect the condition of the Crown and the Spanish state, vigorous and attentive in the sixteenth and eighteenth centuries, and lethargic and place-filling in the seventeenth.

Likely to remain in office longer, the quintessential New World Crown bureaucrat was the judge (*oidor*) on the *Audiencia*. While for most of the colonial period there were only two viceroys, there were at different times some ten to fourteen *Audiencias*, each with up to a dozen judges. The

Audiencia had multiple functions and a broadly defined jurisdiction that not accidentally overlapped those of other officials and governing bodies, guaranteeing conflicts only the Council and the Crown could resolve. *Audiencias* issued laws and regulations and on occasion took over the executive functions of the viceroy or president, but their main work was as a court of appeals.

Positions on the *Audiencias* were greatly coveted. To be considered for a judgeship the candidate had to have a law degree, generally from one of the top schools on the peninsula, and he had to be able to sustain the expense of lobbying at Court for a position. If successful, he was likely to be appointed initially to one of the peripheral courts, for example, Santo Domingo or Guatemala, or, most feared of all, Manila. Over time, with successful work, contacts, luck, and by avoiding entanglements that might compromise his judgment, the young judge could expect to ascend the career ladder to the more prestigious courts of Lima or Mexico City. At some point along the way, however, many of these men traded the prestige of their position and peninsular origins for a favorable marriage, giving up the chance of promotion and "taking root" in the community.

Laws issued in Spain for the New World only took effect in a given jurisdiction when published there by the *Audiencia*. In a notorious case, the *Audiencia* of New Spain did not release the 1609 *repartimiento* regulations until 1624, and then only under escalating pressure from the peninsula. Similarly, many in the New World learned that the 1812 Spanish Constitution abolished both the *mita* and personal service to the clergy before the document became official in the colonies. Such discrepancies led to protests and riots and in the early nineteenth century fed what would become the independence movements.

Beyond their work on the bench, *Audiencia* judges carried out a variety of other bureaucratic functions. For example, *oidores* on the late-eighteenth-century Lima *Audiencia* audited military accounts and state tax records, administered ex-Jesuit properties, and ran hospitals, water districts, pension funds, and royal monopolies, as well as supervised various public works. Judges inspected troops and investigated abuses in the Indian communities, enumerated censuses, conducted *residencias*, and carried out studies for the Crown on subjects as diverse as the mails, taxation, and the slave trade.

But the day-to-day work of the *Audiencia* always dealt with criminal and civil cases, and it was here that their activities most often proved problematic. The *Audiencia* heard appeals from inferior courts such as those of the *corregidores*; the town councils (*cabildos*); the special courts of corporate groups, for example, the merchants' *consulado* and the military courts; and the church, when that institution chose to defer jurisdiction to the civil arm of the state. Most of these cases were the routine stuff of interpersonal mayhem, land conflicts, and commercial disputes. For all but the very wealthy and powerful the *Audiencia* was their last hope, as few could afford to carry an appeal to a superior *Audiencia*, and even less likely was resort to the Council of the Indies. Not surprisingly, the courts' members were subject to constant pressures, importuning, and threats from the civil and political society around them. It was for precisely this reason that they were not supposed to have local connections such as marriage, business investments, or family, and to anticipate upward mobility in a bureaucratic career by adhering to legal norms and pursuing the Crown's interests.

Never perfect, this decoupling of judges from local interests broke down dramatically in the seventeenth century as an impecunious Crown put more and more offices, including seats on the *Audiencias*, up for sale. By law, anyone purchasing an office had to be qualified, but when it came to the price they were willing to pay, local applicants typically bid more, because of the prestige and advantages a judgeship promised them in their home community. Indeed, demand was such, and the Crown's financial situation so ruinous, that applicants bought *anticipados*, positions to be filled in the future as vacancies became available. By the mid-eighteenth century locals dominated the *Audiencias*: in 1774, of the twelve judges on the Peru *Audiencia*, eight were from Lima, two were from Chile, and one from Panama; only one was from Spain. Similarly, in 1767, of twelve judges on the Mexico City *Audiencia* at least eight were locally born.

The Bourbon monarchs that came to power in Spain after 1700 sought to break this pattern and recentralize imperial administration but found themselves hamstrung first by problems in Spain itself and then by a series of wars in the New World. The sale of offices continued up to mid-century. Stung to action by defeats in the Seven Years' War, however, the Crown overhauled its administrative policies and sent out legions of new civil and military bureaucrats to shape up the empire. One of the first targets was the *Audiencias*: the Council of the Indies stopped selling offices, visiting inspectors removed judges wholesale for corruption and influence peddling, new peninsular appointees arrived, and the promotion system again began to operate. The effect was dramatic. By 1804 there remained only two creoles on the Lima bench, whereas in Mexico local representation had been cut to three or four. Interestingly, in peripheral areas such as Chile, after an initial purge, creole domination reemerged. The newly revived *ascenso* system moved effective peninsular-born judges up and out, whereas the Chilean-born preferred to stay, and those Spaniards unable to gain promotion married and made business ties locally.

Until 1751 Brazil had only one high court, the *Relação* founded at Salvador, Bahia. Here the judges were all graduates of the University of Coimbra and had

had several years' experience in Portugal before being assigned to the colony. A few came from service in Africa or Asia, but generally these were career circuits separate from Portugal–Brazil. Positions were not salable. A look at the collective biographies of the judges shows they came solidly from the middle ranks of Portuguese society, the sons of military men, merchants, and even from among the more successful artisans, something that would have been highly unlikely in the Spanish world. Most common of all were the sons of bureaucrats, who, like the military, increasingly formed a professional caste. As in the Spanish American colonies, the Portuguese Crown also tried to insulate its judges from local influences with good salaries, promotions, and honors, but encountered here the same problems. In a society as bereft of suitable elite marriage and business partners as eighteenth-century Brazil, the judges were simply too attractive. *Desembargadores* (judges) routinely traded their status and influence for favorable marriages, local business connections, ritual kinship relations, and association with the landowners and merchants.

Middle Groups

Below the viceroys and the high courts was a small cadre of professional bureaucrats about which we know little for the Spanish American world and next to nothing for Brazil. Apart from circuit-riding judges such as Brazil's *ouvidores* and *juizes de fora*, most of these officials were concentrated in the capital and chief cities. For example, one estimate of Mexico City in the early nineteenth century puts the number of colonial office holders above the clerk level at no more than 500–600, including military officers but not church functionaries. As well as staffing the offices of the viceroy and the *Audiencia*, they worked in tax collection, auditing, and the various treasuries; ran the royal mint and the mail service, and administered the Crown *estancos* (monopolies) of tobacco, alcohol, and gunpowder. Most such posts were purchasable, apart from those involving tax collection. Multiple office holding was common, and probably few could have made a decent living without engaging in outside activities, whether legal or illegal. Most bureaucratic work was boring and repetitive but carried with it the very real advantages of "white collar" status and the opportunities for gain available to those with even limited power in the colonial system. Office holders in Mexico City divided approximately 60 percent–40 percent between creoles and Spanish-born, and of the creoles 40 percent came from the Mexico City area. In the absence of any sort of civil service, or, indeed, in most cases, even a defined career path, employment depended on patronage. Even the *peninsulares* had no secure hope of promotion and many quickly came to identify their interests with those of their creole peers. This became clear after independence in 1821 when the overwhelming majority stayed on to work for the new national government rather than return to Spain.

Around the office holders swarmed a mass of favor seekers, ranging from university-trained lawyers and their empirical competitors (*tintorillos*) to *hacendados* seeking tax relief and humble Indian delegations waiting in the anterooms of the powerful. For those in obviously dead-end positions, the temptation to take money or other bribes in return for favorable attention must have been almost irresistible. For those who had purchased the office with borrowed money this was probably an absolute necessity. Observers reported widespread corruption and abuses.

The colonial officers most notorious for abuse, however, though in some areas the priest gave them strong competition, were the *corregidores* or *alcaldes mayores*, governors of the rural, usually indigenous areas outside the cities. These men typically were not career bureaucrats, and by the second half of the eighteenth century many of those who held the office felt themselves very lucky to gain a single three to five year appointment. The number of literate, and sometimes even university educated, creoles and *peninsulares* seeking white collar employment by now far outstripped jobs available. One result was to bid up the price of *corregidor* positions. Since few of the applicants actually had the required money, they too borrowed it. The new governor then had only a few years to pay back what he owed and set himself and his family up for life. The salary was low, but the *corregidor* found opportunities to enrich himself illegally. He might, for example, appropriate part of the taxes he collected, but his superiors were very watchful for this. He could solicit bribes in his work as judge, but there was not much money there, or he could use his power to exploit Indian labor and perhaps to encroach on their land, but Indians were quick to protest such abuses and sometimes even violent in their resistance. More than one *corregidor* died under the knives and hoes of an enraged Indian town.

The most common way that governors extorted money from their indigenous charges was the notorious *repartimientos de comercio* or *mercancías*. By using his power to control local markets and exclude competitors, the *corregidor* could force Indians to buy the goods he supplied at monopoly prices, goods commonly furnished by the merchant that had financed his purchase of the office. Alternatively, the *corregidor* might deliver raw materials such as cotton or wool to the Indians and require them to spin it into thread or weave thread into cloth, work for which he paid them at best below market wages. Everyone knew that these activities were illegal, and Crown officials periodically blasted them: "They are violent and tyrannical, and useful only to enrich the governors and drive the Indians deeper and deeper into poverty."[3] But the Crown realized that until it was willing and able to pay adequate salaries to the *corregidores*, these would necessarily find ways to supplement their income. Without this no one would take the job.

The Indians knew these *repartimientos* were not permitted, and protested them. Women in particular bore the brunt of much of the forced spinning and weaving and frequently were at the front of mobs that met the official with a hail of rocks and foul language when he came to pick up what he imagined to be his thread or cloth. By the late eighteenth century, however, the practice had persisted for two hundred years and become custom. As with most people, the Indians accepted as inevitable a certain level of abuse and only seriously protested or rebelled when this suddenly surged to intolerable levels. The Crown attempted to alleviate the problem by appointing better-paid intendants starting in 1764, but these efforts failed when the intendants named the old *corregidores* as their deputies. Custom reasserted itself.

The counterpart of the *corregidor* in the cities was the town council, or *cabildo*, a government in theory elected from among the *vecinos* (legal residents) of the city. In most cases this was a smaller group than one might imagine, both because the mass of Indians and mixed bloods in the urban population had no say in politics and because even many of the Spanish and creoles living in the town actually had their legal residence established somewhere else. In most cases a tight oligarchy controlled the government, a circle narrowed even more in the seventeenth century when the Crown began to sell council seats in perpetuity. *Cabildo* service was not a full-time job and there was no mayor or chief executive. Rather, council members took turns administering day-to-day government from the town hall and met as a group periodically to set policy, administer town affairs, and act as a court of the first instance for minor crimes. At a typical meeting, the Lima *cabildo* disputed control of community land with cattle ranchers and the *Audiencia*, dealt with the apparent theft of water from the city system, appointed a market inspector, and confirmed the elections of guild officials. Even town governments as important as Lima's, however, often found themselves short of funds and unable to provide the services the growing urban areas needed. The steady appropriation of power by the Crown in the seventeenth and eighteenth centuries left the *cabildos* with less and less to do. What had been a vital institution in the sixteenth century fell generally into decay. Still, the councils were almost the only opportunity creoles had to practice deliberative politics, and the bodies reemerge in the early nineteenth century as the foci of the independence movements.

At God's Work

Across the plaza from the government buildings, but figuratively next door, stood the church, the ideological arm of the state. Under the patronage system granted them by the pope, Spanish and Portuguese rulers had the right to appoint church officials down to the parish level, as well as to regulate all travel and communications to the New World and to supervise, and veto if they wished, all church building. Typical of the latter was the refusal of the Portuguese Crown to allow more than one convent in Brazil before the eighteenth century. The monarchs delegated day-to-day appointment powers to the bishops and archbishops and did not normally intervene in routine church affairs, but they always stood ready to enforce their prerogatives if they felt challenged, as the Jesuits discovered when the Portuguese king expelled them from his possessions in 1759 and the Spanish king followed suit in 1767. In return for an agreement with the papacy that gave it the right to collect such taxes as the tithe, the Crown guaranteed the church the economic resources and secular support necessary to carry forward its missions of proselytizing and enforcing Christian conformity.

Under a special dispensation from the pope, the Spanish, and less systematically the Portuguese, governments used members of religious regular orders such as the Franciscans and Dominicans, and later the Jesuits, to spearhead conversion and control of indigenous populations. As colonial life settled down, however, secular clergy took over the parishes in the central areas, and the orders typically found themselves shunted to the frontiers, the Jesuits to Brazil's Amazon and the Paraguayan frontier, for example, and the Franciscans and Jesuits to New Spain's north. The Indians generally preferred the regulars and opposed secularization of their parishes, most notably in the highlands of Mesoamerica and in the Paraguay missions. The policy suited the Crown, however, because existing patronage arrangements gave it more direct control over the activities of the parish clergy than the orders. For a growing creole population, secularization promised much-needed employment opportunities.

Although the upper levels of the church hierarchy remained firmly in the hands of *peninsulares*, by the mid-seventeenth century creoles, together with a few mixed bloods who passed as creoles, had come to dominate the ranks of the parish clergy. This continued through independence. There were four types of parish appointments: the most desirable of these was as a *cura beneficiado*, a regular assignment to a parish won through a competition and held permanently, at the pleasure of the bishop. A *cura ad interim* was the same but on an interim basis, and *vicarios* and *coadjutores* were forms of assistant clergy, usually hired and paid directly by the priest and about whose activities the church hierarchy had little direct knowledge. Roughly two-thirds of the priests working in rural New Spain, for example, fell into one of these last two categories, forming a mobile and poorly paid religious proletariat. Whereas, for example, a priest possessing a first-class parish could make as much as 6,000 pesos a year, and 2,000–3,000 pesos was considered a comfortable income, vicarios commonly made do with 200–400 pesos, only slightly more than a poor urban artisan. For a lucky few these positions were simply stepping stones on the way to their own parish, but for most the status of *vicario* or *coadjutor* remained a permanent condition, on the fringes of the church and Spanish society. Of course, all enjoyed the advantages of the religious *fuero*, including exemption from civil jurisdiction and the right to trial in their own courts.

Qualifying for the priesthood normally required a *bachiller* degree, essentially a high school diploma, followed by a year or two of seminary. Only the academically talented went on to university, and most of these did not serve in the rural parishes but remained in the capital, at the cathedral chapter or teaching in the seminaries or at the university. Those with any education, it was said, lost it quickly in the remote parishes. A few priests, and a declining number in the late eighteenth century, bypassed the regular hiring process to gain a parish appointment *a título de idioma*, that is, on the basis of being able to preach in a needed Indian language. Almost all of the small number of Indians who entered the priesthood took this route, but by definition it condemned them to the poorest and most desolate parishes with little hope of promotion.

Once a priest gained a permanent appointment, he remained in one spot an average of six years, at least in eighteenth-century New Spain, though those with desirable parishes were likely to stay longer. There was no system of rotation or regular promotions, and priests did not move unless they initiated it or were removed for misconduct or incompetence. Most sought a new parish to improve their income, but some were also looking for a better climate or to be near the capital or family or business investments. Gaining permanent employment or promotion depended on success in a competition for a vacant post. These involved submission of a resume followed by personal interviews in the capital; some priests applied simply as an excuse to spend a few days in Mexico City. Candidates were judged primarily on their academic accomplishments and secondarily on their work in the parish, particularly on "charity," defined chiefly as rebuilding and refurbishing church properties. At least as important to one's career prospects as academic skills and good works were influential friends.

Surprisingly, what today we might imagine to be serious misbehavior did not automatically rule out a successful church career, or at least continued employment. Problems with absenteeism and drinking seem to have been routine, and more than one priest had trouble controlling his temper when dealing with what he considered to be inferior Indians and mixed bloods. Perhaps most astonishing was the near universal existence, and acceptance by the church and the populace, of concubinage. Long-term monogamous heterosexual relations, effectively marriage, and even if these resulted in children, were not necessarily an impediment to advancing in a church career, so long as they involved mutual consent and did not generate scandal. What did attract the immediate attention of the Inquisition were homosexuality, bestiality, heterosexual promiscuity, the seduction of maidens or married women, or solicitation in the confessional. But even if charged and convicted, the delinquent priest could expect only temporary exile from the place of his misconduct or forced confinement for a time in a church retreat for "spiritual exercises." At worst, he might suffer loss of his licenses to preach.

For most members of the late colonial clergy, while not denying in some a special calling, the priesthood was a job, and potentially a good job in a world of growing population and tightening possibilities. Few offspring of the elites entered the parish clergy, but families of the tiny colonial middle class commonly hoped to place a son or two in the church, both for employment and for prestige. Where possible, families gave or willed chantries (*capellanías*) to help support members or descendants who entered the priesthood. These were annual incomes for the saying of special masses and guaranteed by liens on property. Most priests, though, gained the bulk of their livelihood from fees for services—payments made for baptisms, marriages, burials, confessions, and so forth. A table or scale set by custom and church law was supposed to determine the charges, but in fact these often were the focus of conflict and claims of overcharging and delinquency. Indian parishioners paid on a reduced scale or not at all, but the community was responsible for *servicio personal* (personal service), supplying the priest with the food, animal fodder, and firewood he required, as well as servants to staff his house.

Some parish priests combined agriculture or stock raising with their religious duties, and others, though the hierarchy frowned on these sorts of activities, engaged in commerce or trade. Priests specifically were forbidden to be tavern keepers, bakers, or butchers; to own mills or *obrajes*; to raise animals for the market; or to buy cochineal, honey, cotton, corn, blankets, or woven goods for resale. Clearly many violated these strictures, and what a priest could not do his family members sometimes did. For most priests and their parishioners such outside activities were not a serious problem, but some members of the clergy exploited their positions to take advantage of their flock.

Hopefully not typical but certainly not unique among late colonial priests was Father Ponciano Garrote Bueno, for some thirty years in charge of San Lorenzo Mazatenango, on Guatemala's Pacific coast. In addition to the usual practices of overcharging for his services, stealing money from the *cofradías*, demanding extraordinary amounts of food and personal service from his parishioners, and abusing Indians by word and with physical violence, Garrote Bueno, in cooperation with his brother Manuel, aggressively extorted land and labor from the town to develop his hacienda San Rafael. He stole the property of minors and orphans entrusted to his care and loosed cattle on the plantings of neighbors to drive them off land he wanted. Garrote Bueno badgered the *Audiencia* for *repartimiento* labor, although the governor of the province made it clear that this was not local custom, and Indian leaders protested that if required to work for the brothers "the entire town would flee into the woods." The priest must have had well-placed friends: an 1802 inventory of "Criminal cases against members of the clergy" revealed a number of priests with one or two complaints, whereas Garrote Bueno had registered forty-three and his career was not over. It would be a grave mistake to imagine that all, or even more than very few, members of the colonial clergy engaged in abuses with the imagination and on the scale of Garrote Bueno. But many did seek to supplement what they felt were inadequate incomes with extra activities, and inevitably these created at least the potential for tension and conflict with their parishioners.

The Military

Other corporate groups in the colonies shared some of the privileges or special legal status of the clergy; among these was the military. Neither Spain nor Portugal had a large presence of regular military forces in the colonies because of the costs this entailed. Much of the regular military that was present before the late eighteenth century remained isolated from the rest of colonial society, stationed in coastal forts, up the Amazon River, or on the frontiers. Few creoles were to be found in the army officer corp. The work was poorly paid, enjoyed relatively low prestige, and could be dangerous and difficult. Officers came above all from what might be called "military families," Spanish and Portuguese families that had a tradition of sending their young men into military careers. Offspring of lower-middle-class families who hoped to advance themselves but did not have the money or contacts to gain a university education also enrolled in the military.

Creoles went instead into the militia. Except for some of the coastal units experienced in repelling pirate attacks, most militia companies were a martial joke, and the Spanish regular officers assigned to train them after the

Seven Years' War were appalled at what they found. Bahia's militias were no better; when the sugar planters had to fight runaway slaves they brought in *paulista* (from São Paulo) mercenaries. For American elites, membership and rank in the militia did not so much give prestige as it displayed and reinforced status won in other areas—commerce, landowning, or mining. Being an officer had nothing to do with military talent, training, or success, but it did offer titles to those who had not gone to university, and the chance to wear flashy uniforms. To the rank-and-file militia, membership gave the *fuero militar*, the right to trial in special military courts likely to favor militia members. Control of the militia was important too to the landowning elites, because in the absence of a regular police force, the militia was the chief instrument of social control in the countryside. Though it rarely confronted a foreign enemy, and then usually with disastrous results, the militia did put down slave uprisings and peasant revolts, police worker unrest, transport taxes and Crown goods, and guarantee tranquillity on market days and during public festivities.

In the wake of the defeats of the Seven Years' War, the Crown set about reforming New World defenses. Viceroy of Peru Field Marshall Manuel de Amat y Juient, for example, surveyed the situation in that colony. Even the regular troops that garrisoned the fort at Callao were said to be useless, badly dressed, and undisciplined, "unreliable during wartime and unruly in peace."[4] Apart from some of the black and mulatto units from the coast, the militia was in complete disarray. Over the next decade the viceroy raised membership to almost 100,000 and with the distribution of medals, memberships in religious orders, and the offer of the *fuero militar* he lured *peninsulares* and creoles into the officer corp. But the militia's equipment was in poor repair and their training almost nonexistent. Only the units in Lima and on the coast were likely to respond to a call to defend the colony. When the Túpac Amaru revolt broke out in 1780, highland militia units collapsed or collaborated with the rebels; in one case the rank and file guarded the gallows while the rebels executed their officers. Militia soldiers from Lima and the coast eventually ended the immediate threat by breaking the siege of Cuzco, but it was a viceregal pardon not military prowess that finally brought the uprising to a halt.

Merchants

While there was little question about the social preeminence of upper-level Crown bureaucrats, clergy, or military officers, merchants and those engaged in commerce occupied a more ambiguous position in the colonial world. Or rather, they occupied a very wide variety of positions, ranging from street vendors through tavern keepers to retail shop owners and to the top levels of wholesale and international trade. Only the latter, for example, did Portuguese law officially recognize as *homens de negócio* (businessmen) and accord a status approaching that of a sugar mill owner. The divide for merchants was between wholesale and retail, though even the largest wholesalers were not above renting space for a shop or supplying goods to a retail store run by a relative or an employee. In both Spanish America and Brazil elite merchants overwhelmingly were peninsula born. Those who were successful in the viceregal centers, and who did not retire to Europe, tended to buy rural properties and to shunt their sons and daughters into the landowning elite. In provincial centers such as Buenos Aires or Veracruz, on the other hand, merchants also came from the peninsula, but there they more commonly made local alliances and marriages among fellow importers and trained their sons to succeed them. Perhaps in the secondary centers trade did not generate enough wealth to allow diversification, or investments in land returned too little status or income to repay the effort.

The large merchants usually hired their most trusted employees from the mother country, from among relatives or their home community. These men arrived young and began work as cashiers, agents, and supervisors, sometimes literally sleeping "on the counter" in their early years while building up contacts and experience. The most successful the merchant took into the business as associates and partners, and sometimes they married one of his daughters or even his widow. Important merchant families of Mexico City went further, not only recruiting relatives in Spain to work in their commercial enterprises but bringing over others to be trained and placed in the church, government service, and the professions, as part of efforts to broaden their social and political network.

The pursuit of profit and monopoly advantage commonly embroiled the merchants in conflict with other groups in colonial society. Wholesale traders favored limited supplies, restricted markets, and high prices, and the Crown supported this approach to facilitate tax collection and maximize the export of silver from the colonies. Not surprisingly, by the second half of the eighteenth century many of these importers were finding it increasingly difficult to compete with contraband goods introduced along miles of unguarded coastline or even through the main ports with the connivance of pliable customs officials. For at least a century peninsular industry had been unable to keep up with the manufacturing advances in England and the Low Countries, so that "Spanish" and "Portuguese" goods too often were simply items from other countries, resold in the colonies at prices inflated by markups, turnover taxes, and a cumbersome and outdated transport and marketing system. Contraband trade in the colonies exploded in the second half of the eighteenth century as the Industrial Revolution cheapened many goods, especially iron products and textiles, greatly expanding potential New World markets. Colonial merchants fought back by diversifying their areas of sales and purchases and by complementing their peninsular commerce with intercolonial links and with trade to the Philippines and Africa. They favored enforcement of trade restrictions when these benefited them, or at least disadvantaged their competitors, while at the same time they sought to evade those laws that did not work to their advantage. The lack of "patriotism" evidenced in contraband trade and tax evasion infuriated Crown agents, and their correspondence was full of disparaging remarks about the greed and shortsightedness of merchants, even as many of these officials themselves profited from bribes and illegal partnerships.

Dependent on the merchants for credit and supplies were the *hacendados*, plantation owners, and the miners who produced the raw materials for export and bought European and Asian imports. The potential for cross-purposes is evident. Traditional scholarship has focused on disputes between the (creole) producers and (peninsular) merchants as one of the major sources of elite discontent leading up to independence, but more recent work has downplayed such problems. Instead, scholars have emphasized wide areas of common interest and the awareness that the groups were not as separate or different as a schematic presentation suggests. Marriage linked merchants with landowners and mining families. Some merchants, as we have seen, also invested directly in landed estates or acquired these through their marriages. Because in the late eighteenth century rural properties typically earned rates of return well below those available in wholesale trade, these patterns suggest that wealth garnered in commerce may have been dissipated in land, partly as a hedge against the instabilities of trade but also in an effort to buy social prestige. Merchants purchased public offices and honors, sometimes to boost their business interests but also as part of a strategy of social mobility. Finally, merchants shared membership and power with the landed and mining elites in a number of boards and organizations, from religious brotherhoods and lay membership in the Inquisition to the militia, the town council, and committees set up to collect special taxes or to undertake emergency public works. As in any family, relations of cooperation and conflict ebbed and flowed but strong bonds remained.

Artisans

Below the large merchant houses that carried on the intercolonial and wholesale trades, commerce shaded off through specialized retail establishments into more humble general stores and down to taverns and petty vendors, who shared the streets with others scrambling to make a living, including artisans, unskilled day laborers, beggars, prostitutes, and criminals. The Spanish imported into the colonies the institution of artisan guilds, meant to restrict entry into the trades and to guarantee quality work. However, the quick emergence of large numbers of slave, Indian, and mixed blood craftsmen who continued to be excluded from the guilds on the grounds of race and illegitimacy greatly weakened the system. Artisans made up perhaps 10 percent of the population in late-eighteenth-century urban centers but were many fewer in the small towns and rural areas where demand could not support specialization. The largest numbers of artisans were in the less-skilled tasks, for example, shoe making, tailoring, carpentry, construction, and baking, while sword makers or book binders were rarer, and gold- and silversmiths strictly limited. If Quito painters and sculptors produced famous works of art, alongside these artists sweatshop workers assembled tens of thousands of rosaries for starvation wages in a primitive putting-out system.

New World artisans were notorious for the poor quality of their work, a result of several factors. There was a strong tendency toward self-promotion, so that a journeyman in Spain commonly called himself a master in the New World. In the early days, and later on the frontiers, no one asked too many questions, given the shortage of craftsmen. Poorly skilled, undercapitalized "masters" in turn trained generations of less able apprentices, often placed in training programs by their parents with little attention to aptitude, treated by the masters simply as cheap labor, and physically and verbally abused.

Barely literate, ignorant of simple mathematics, poorly prepared to absorb new ideas or develop improved techniques, journeymen went looking for employment. Few had the capital to set up their own establishment and instead sought employment with others, but existing workshops could only absorb a limited number. Those who did find a place were not always model employees. Much like the proto–working class in eighteenth-century Europe, colonial artisans demonstrated a distinct aversion to steady work habits. They were always ready to leave the shop for an afternoon in the tavern or a bit of gambling in the street, and many found it difficult to turn up for work on Monday ("San Lunes") after a Sunday of heavy drinking. Free artisans sometimes shared not only crafts but actual working space with slaves, and where their skill was greater, slave foremen supervised, and even chastised, free apprentices and journeymen. The poorest of the artisans and those unable to find steady employment in a workshop stationed themselves on street corners and solicited tasks from passersby. They typically lacked capital even to purchase the necessary raw materials, which the customer had to supply, and rarely did they deliver the work as or when promised.

A poor artisan with steady employment might make three pesos a week, roughly the same as an urban semi-skilled laborer and less than even the lowliest rural *vicarios*. Such an income did not support a family, and left the artisan always on the brink of being pitched into destitution by illness, injury, or a decline in demand for his skills. The latter was particularly a problem for men who worked in weaving or with iron and leather, who faced increasing competition from legitimate and, especially, contraband imports in the years after 1750. Post-independence free trade crushed wide segments of the artisan class in all but the most isolated or culturally conservative areas. Many handicraft workers now scratched out a living repairing and refurbishing imported goods.

Beggars, Slaves, and "Lepers"

Ruined artisans added to the population of free black, poor white, and mixed blood "lepers" that increasingly "infested" urban centers in the late eighteenth century. Some of these had been born in the cities and others had fled there from declining conditions in the countryside. The problems for the urban poor in finding employment were particularly acute in societies such as Brazil, where slaves dominated manual and semi-skilled tasks. Also, because so many among the free poor had themselves come from backgrounds of slavery or coerced labor, the simple definition of personal freedom might be not to work, or at least not to work as steadily or regularly as the bosses wished. The men found employment at casual day labor, in construction, in transportation, and in domestic service; the women were servants, laundresses, and street sellers. But, as with the artisans, casual employment for the urban poor became increasingly uncertain after the turn of the century as the colonies were sucked into the commercial circuit of the Industrial Revolution, with the instability this entailed.

Some found that begging paid better than other forms of work, and it was more attractive than the agricultural labor they associated with slavery or *repartimientos*. Beggars were not vagrants, who were able-bodied but refused to work, but individuals who suffered, or effectively simulated, physical or mental impediments that made it impossible for them to do other jobs. There were different categories of beggars. Some asked for alms at the doors of churches or at religious festivals, others begged at a known point and had an established clientele, others who went door to door, and some were slaves forced to beg and to turn over what they made to their masters. The church defined giving as Christian charity and the duty of all who could, but beggars did better if they had a good story or could demonstrate some particularly gruesome physical distress. Above all, they had to act in an "appropriate" manner, showing deference and humility. Groups of beggars sometimes formed loose communities, banding together for protection and occupying semi-public places at night.

If the church and society traditionally had sanctioned begging and valued charity, by the 1830s attitudes were changing. Fear and resentment at the perceived rebelliousness of the urban poor, fed by a number of post-independence uprisings, and concerns about public health gradually became the defining elements in the popular view of beggars. A new criminal code in 1830 Brazil, for example, took control of the licensing of beggars away from the church and invested it in the justices of the peace. The state began to move more aggressively to differentiate vagrants from legitimate beggars, drafting the former into the armed forces. Gathering points for beggars more and more seemed foci of disease, and by the 1860s the police were sweeping indigents from the streets and warehousing them far from the center of town. Two fundamental changes undermined the popular perception of begging as legitimate work. On the one hand, the rise of what one might call "bourgeois values" associated with the Industrial Revolution increasingly defined poverty not as a constant and an opportunity for religiously inspired giving but as moral failure. Poverty was not God's will but a sin, against God and the economy. At the same time, with export production expanding rapidly, the demand for labor was similarly growing. In Brazil this coincided with the end of the international slave trade, condemning slavery to a slow death and raising the necessity of a transition to free labor just as coffee production began to take off. These changes demanded more state and elite attention to the problems of mobilizing and controlling the free population. One tactic was to criminalize previously tolerated behaviors such as begging, closing off alternative forms of survival and forcing these men and women to seek wage work.

At the bottom of the urban social and economic pyramid were slaves, criminals, and convicts. Looking, for example, at turn-of-the-century Rio de Janeiro, what comes across vividly is the dependence on slaves for every manner of work, except white collar jobs and policing. Even in the latter case, however, it was common to use captives to hunt down escaped slaves. More generally, slaves worked at all the artisan crafts: they shaped iron, tin, copper, gold, and silver and even manufactured the shackles and chains that held their fellows; they pursued the needle trades, and an escaped slave tailor was easily identified by his deformed fingers. Slaves shut poor whites out of the shoe making business. They were barber-surgeons, experts at bloodletting and applying leaches, and if this failed other blacks buried the body. Whites and blacks alike consulted slave *feiticeiros* ("witch doctors"), who were probably at least as successful in these years as medical doctors at curing patients, and slaves were highly regarded artists and musicians.

Officially a city, even Rio de Janeiro still embraced large agricultural areas, and these, together with the near suburbs, produced food for the urban markets, an activity that depended heavily on slave labor. Along Rio's sea front and in the bay slaves fished, and further out they crewed the whaling boats. Slaves dominated all forms of transportation: they conducted the carts bringing goods to and from the port and the countryside and manned the mule trains into the interior. Slaves carried the sedan chairs of fine ladies and cripplingly heavy casks of water; where fountains were available, female slaves fetched the water for the households. The *tigres* (tigers) carried away the night waste. Singularly indicative of the qualities of slave society, slaves sometimes made small amounts of money carrying the packages, or even the umbrellas, of those passing through the streets, for no free person of quality would ever be seen carrying anything in public. Slaves quarried rock, and others worked as masons, carpenters, and painters in construction. Most of the domestic servants in Rio before 1850, both male and female, were slaves.

For slaves probably the best work in the cities was artisan handicrafts. A common pattern was to buy and train a slave and then live off renting him or her out; in other cases, a craftsman trained and replaced himself with a slave. Some slaves rented themselves, living apart and paying the master an agreed-upon sum each month. Many found in this a way to freedom. Free black and mulatto artisans generally preferred people of color as employers, but slaves wanted to work for whites because whites paid the best wages and received the best commissions. Slaves worked well enough and cheaply enough that they forced free labor out of the market. The situation only began to change after mid-century. The end of the slave trade and the demand for workers on Brazil's coffee frontier raised prices and drew slaves out of the cities, while a growing tide of European immigration made free, white workers more cheaply available.

Information on crime as an economic activity, as opposed to a means of settling interpersonal differences, remains scarce for nineteenth-century Latin America. Most urban areas had little or no regular policing, and few records were kept. The lives of the urban poor seem to have been permeated with theft and violence, but state agents gave this scant attention. Taverns and street vendor stalls served as meeting places for criminals and offered opportunities to fence stolen property or swap it for alcohol or sex. Precisely to stop such transactions, town regulations limited the number of customers in the drink shops and required these establishments be open to public view. Similarly, street vendors' stalls could not be closed off with curtains, and customers were not allowed to enter them.

Poverty and unstable employment exacerbated relations within families and between neighbors and provoked much of the interpersonal violence that peppers judicial archives. Alcohol added to these outbursts. Chiefly, these were crimes of personal violence, and often they involved women. Ironically, the female victims of physical abuse or wife beating, rape, or ritual kidnapping also suffered suspicion and close questioning from the authorities. The assumption was that the woman must have brought it on herself by the manner in which she behaved. For example, rape of a single woman outside the house might not be harshly punished, because as "unprotected property" she "deserved it." Even to report such a crime impugned family honor and for this reason it was likely to be hushed up or listed as an "attempted" rather than an accomplished fact. But there were also categories of crime that more properly fall under the category of work.

In the wars for independence and during the subsequent regional and political conflicts, all sides drafted anyone they could get their hands on. Many of these reluctant soldiers deserted at the first opportunity, sometimes taking with them their arms and always their training and experience in violence. Deserters, escaped slaves, and criminals formed bandit gangs that ravaged the post-independence countryside of Mexico, the Rio de la Plata region, and coastal Peru, among other areas. Before independence, bandits around Lima were mostly poorly armed bands of mixed bloods and impoverished whites that scarcely threatened anyone except isolated Indian peasants and the odd petty trader. This changed in the decades after 1810. The turbulence of the independence movements offered the perfect opportunity for slaves to escape, and others gained experience in arms when forcibly enlisted by competing factions. By the 1830s and 1840s the bandits around Lima were almost exclusively blacks and mulattos, well armed, much more violent than in past years, and a serious threat to commerce on the Callao road. They attacked not only travelers and mule trains but haciendas, and skirmished with the militia in the suburbs of the capital itself.

These were not social bandits. The blacks and mixed bloods robbed and killed whomever they encountered. They earned the bitter enmity of the indigenous communities, whose members eagerly cooperated with the state in finding and destroying bandit hideouts. Generally the gangs were small, with a dozen or so members, and their survival rate was rarely more than a few years, but new ones continued to pop up. Only after mid-century did the republics began to field effective urban or rural police forces able to deal with this problem.

Sometimes overlapping these bandit gangs or working in conjunction with them were smugglers and *contrabandistas*. Contraband traders imported illegal slaves and foreign or untaxed goods and carried away precious metals and diamonds or other valuable commodities such as sugar, indigo, or cochineal. This was particularly a problem in the mining areas, where the authorities singled out secular priests as among the worst offenders. Many swarmed to the new strikes in eighteenth-century Minas Gerais, where they proved particularly difficult to police because their religious status exempted them from civil justice. In 1713, 1714, 1721, 1722, 1723, 1725, 1744, and again in 1753 governors ordered them expelled from the region, with no success. At least some seem to have been guilty of a wide range of crimes in addition to smuggling, including banditry or cooperating with bandits; one was described as "living scandalously, having abandoned his religion and given himself over to all manner of vices and greatly disturbing the peace of those who live near him."[5] Others became involved in counterfeiting, a crime that directly threatened state power and greatly exercised the authorities of both empires. In gold mining areas gold dust served as money and adulteration was common: "You only had to scratch plaster from the walls to make money," went the saying from nineteenth century Goiás. For this reason, gold dust that had circulated in the interior carried a 20 to 40 percent discount when it reached the coast.

Those caught and convicted of serious crimes faced draconian punishment. The *Acordada*, Mexico's colonial rural police, for example, tried, sentenced, and shot captured bandits on the spot, and other prisoners suffered the famous *ley fuga*, "shot while trying to escape." Political offenders were exiled to penal settlements in Africa. For lesser offenses men and women received fines or time in jail, or they might be put to work at hard labor. In Brazil, for example, courts condemned prisoners "to the galleys," though this form of punishment never existed in the colony. Instead, the sentence meant that these criminals served their time at hard labor in chains. In New Spain, as we have seen, owners of textile mills and bakeries rented Indian and mixed blood convicts. The *Audiencia* sometimes sent convicted Indians to labor on the fortifications at Veracruz, effectively a death sentence because of the health conditions of the port. Convicted whites, mulattos, and mixed bloods, on the other hand, were more likely to end up at penal labor on the forts of Havana or Puerto Rico, particularly after the Seven Years War. There they joined military deserters, civilian smugglers, and defrauders of the royal tobacco monopoly sent from Spain.

During the second half of the eighteenth century the number of convict workers in Havana increased. With a growing population in Spain and a decline in the application of the death penalty, both the range of crimes punishable by penal labor and the number of prisoners sent to the New World went up. In fact, Spanish convicts sometimes waited years in peninsular ports for the military ships required to transport them to the Caribbean. Initially the state mixed wage labor, slaves, and convict workers on the Havana fortifications, but after 1770 it was possible to dispense entirely with the free workers and slaves. Prisoners judged particularly vile received sentences directing them "to the pumps" that drained the docks, arduous and killing work. Living and working conditions generally were difficult, as they were meant to be, but most of the prisoners survived, particularly as the century progressed and sentences became shorter. Between 1778 and 1782, for example, the Havana penal labor force experienced more than a 40 percent turnover. If some of these died or escaped, more were released on completion of their sentences. In Brazil the authorities also mixed free workers, convicts, and slaves on the fortifications of Rio de Janeiro, but the state never had a systematic policy for the use of penal labor in the New World. Although the Spanish state encouraged time-expired convicts to settle in the outlying areas of Cuba, and Portugal occasionally sent *degredados* to remote parts of Brazil, neither the Portuguese nor the Spanish Crowns adopted programs of "transportation" comparable to that used by England in the Caribbean and Australia.

Somewhere between slave, free, and convict were the *libertos* of Argentina and the *emancipados* of Brazil. These were Africans rescued by the British from the illegal international slave trade but who instead of being sent to Sierra Leone or Saint Helena were released in the New World, into the care of the national governments. In Argentina most of the men ended up being drafted to fight in the independence struggle and in the civil wars that racked the country for decades thereafter. Only in the 1830s did Juan Manuel de Rosas end this practice. The press ganging of free blacks, *libertos*, and slaves and their deaths from wounds and disease is one of the reasons traditionally cited to explain the dramatic decline of Buenos Aires's black population during the nineteenth century.

An 1818 agreement between Great Britain and Brazil provided that released captives were to work for the state or for a private person of "known integrity" as "apprentices" for no more than fourteen years. Of roughly 10,000 *emancipados* registered before 1850, most were auctioned to private employers who were to provide them room, board, and clothing but did not pay them wages. The Brazilian state proved exceedingly lax in looking out for the welfare of these theoretically free persons. In fact, the government doled many of them out to the politically well-connected as cheap labor; despite a legal limit of eight *emancipados* to a given employer, the Duque de Caxias in the 1860s was said to have had 23 or 24 working for him. Worse, many were illegally enslaved. Some of those who received *emancipados* falsified death certificates and sold the unfortunates into slavery, and in other cases they simply kept them at work long past the stipulated fourteen years. Because the employers had little invested in these individuals, they commonly treated them worse than slaves. Pressed by the British, the Brazilian government in 1868 reported that of the *emancipados* for which it could find records, 3,856 had died, 2,801 had been freed, and 3,410 remained unaccounted for and quite likely were still held in bondage. The fate of the *emancipados* is an almost perfect demonstration of the tendency of slave owners and the state they controlled to attempt to reproduce the essential conditions of slavery even as the system was falling apart.

Women's Work

To this point we have discussed various sorts of urban work but only occasionally have addressed roles or tasks specific to women. Women could and did do, at one time or another, almost every manner of work available in the towns and in the countryside, including such tasks as construction, sugar cane cutting, and mining which are usually thought to be "men's work." But there were certain occupations popularly and statistically associated with women. Before examining these it will be useful to make clear two aspects of gender construction in colonial Latin America. First, there was no specifically "women's history"; that is, there was no set of historical experiences consciously shared by all or most women. Race and class divided colonial women to the point that these almost entirely extinguished any sense of communality based on sex or gender. Elite white women, for example, saw female slaves chiefly as black and slaves, and Indian women as above all Indians, not as women. Similarly, poor women thought of themselves as having little in common with their betters. There was little cross-class or cross-race gender identity.

Equally fundamental was the "honor and shame" complex. The Iberian peninsula shared in a circum-Mediterranean culture that demanded the close control of women, control necessitated by the perceived inability of women to restrain their own sexuality and the danger this presented to their families and to society in general. According to this understanding of gender relations, men had "honor," that is, they were to be ready and able to defend the interests of the family. Women had "shame," by which was meant a public modesty and restraint of behavior that did not invite criticism of themselves or their family or bring into question their sexual propriety. To a greater or lesser extent all classes subscribed to "honor and shame," but elites had the most reason and were best able to fulfill its requirements. Aspirant elites used "honor and shame" to define their hopes. Marriage was about status, strategic family alliances, and the accumulation and transmission of property. Families exchanged women for social, political, and economic reasons. It follows that the children who resulted from these marriages, and who stood to inherit the family rank and property, required a clear paternity. Nothing brought more grief to elites, and to the poor caught up in their struggles, than a disputed inheritance.

Preoccupation with "purity of blood" greatly aggravated concerns about "honor and shame." Having fought through centuries of conflict with Moors and Arabs and mixing every day with a population of Jews and recent converts to Christianity, Iberian elites were always quick to assert that their ascendancy held no taint of "inferior" blood. Concerns that a man of a despised color or condition might somehow establish sexual contact with a female member of the family increased enormously in the New World, with its vast majority of Indians, blacks, and mixed bloods. Until the end of the colonial period the Spanish state forbade marriages between races, and only in 1755 did the Portuguese Crown officially allow Indian–white, but not black–white, unions. By definition, then, mixed bloods must also have been illegitimate, born out of wedlock. The mass of the New World population, most of whom bore the double burden of racial-cultural inferiority and illegitimacy, formed a constant real or implied menace to the "honor" of the elite, or would-be elite, family.

Elites

For upper-class women, work options were limited. Most hoped to *tomar estado*, to take up their rightful place in society, either through a proper marriage or by entry into a suitable convent. The more common option, and the one the Crown, if not all families, strongly preferred, was marriage. Both the Portuguese and, less aggressively, the Spanish Crowns restricted the construction of convents in the New World and discouraged sending women to cloisters in the mother country. The hope was to instead populate the colonies with tax-producing, loyal citizens. For families, marriage was at once a chance to declare, and hopefully to improve, social status and make important connections. Although some who married must have been swayed by what we today might call "love," generally this was not common precisely because there was so little opportunity among elites for contact between unmarried members of opposite sexes. Love came, if at all, after marriage. All evidence suggests most elite children of both genders shared their families' attitudes and their expectations of matrimony and were happy and proud to marry well, by the definitions of the time. This was what they expected and what they wanted, and certainly fewer of them had to be coerced into family-arranged marriages than melodramatic tales sometimes suggest.

Over time, though, attitudes did change. For example, by the second half of the eighteenth century marriage contracts and women's wills in Spanish America rarely mentioned dowries, an integral part of elite alliances a century before and a key element in traditional family pacts. Similarly, the emotional concerns of marriage choice were coming to play an increasingly important role. On several occasions in the late eighteenth and early nine-teenth centuries the Spanish Crown reiterated its hostility to marriages that breached established class or race boundaries and it reinforced the power of parents over children. But evidence from Cuba, for one example, shows that potential marriage partners sometimes found ways around such limits. When blocked by parental objections, couples now more often took direct action. In what became an established, if hardly accepted, tactic, young men and women kept apart by their families for reasons of race or class eloped and engaged in sexual relations. The next morning the girl returned to her family and the boy turned himself into the authorities. The family, of course, could prosecute for abduction and rape or seduction, but inevitably this would air the scandal, including the girl's loss of virginity, to the public. It would also be a public admission both of the inability of the family to guard its honor and of the now greatly diminished ability of the daughter to marry. Alterna-tively, the families involved might decide that marriage, even given the prior objections, would be less damaging to their reputation than hanging out their dirty linen for all to see. In many cases the couple successfully forced the parental hand, but in others they miscalculated, and the gap was such that the Crown's agents or the families felt the marriage would so violate established norms as to threaten social stability. Then, it seems, all were ruined.

For female elites who did not marry, the only alternative to a long and anomalous spinsterhood was to enter a convent. This could have advantages for everyone involved. To place a daughter or sister in a prestigious religious establishment declared and confirmed, just as did a successful marriage, elite status. Precisely for this reason getting in was difficult. Not only did a pro-spective novice have to demonstrate legitimacy and purity of blood at least equal to that required for marriage, but the family had also to provide her with a substantial dowry. Apart from status, having one or more of their female members in a convent gave a family preferential access to loans from these institutions, loans that were among the most important sources of credit in the colonies. And convents were reluctant to foreclose on the bad debts of their members' parents or relations.

For the nuns it was not a bad life, and it spared them the inconveniences of a husband. In Brazil the women commonly had two or three slaves to attend them, lived in well-appointed cells, and had access to a variety of food and sweets. Indeed, some convents were famous for the candies and pastries they sold at the gates. Sexual relations were not unknown, whether with priests or other men spirited into the building or among the women them-selves. Nuns and monks were the constant butt of salacious speculation and the object of more than one church investigation. The sisters bought and sold prop-erty through proxies, and some made personal loans and collected debts.

Spanish convents differed from those of Brazil in several ways. Whereas Brazil had only one until the eighteenth century, and the Crown kept a very tight rein on the number of women allowed to enter, in the Spanish American world there were dozens scattered over the length of the empire. Discipline seems to have been tighter in most Spanish cloisters, and the women had fewer servants, but here too they engaged in land owning and trade, and in some instances even bought and sold the cells they inhabited. Sharing the convent with the nuns might be lay sisters, women who took vows but paid smaller dowries and participated in the physical work of running the institution. Separate houses held *beatas*, poor but pious Indian and mixed blood women who lived together in groups and survived on alms or what work they could find.

Apart from the chance to serve God, one of the chief attractions of convents in the Spanish American world for some women was the chance to gain an education and to participate in a life of the mind. The most famous example of this choice was Sor Juana Inés de la Cruz of New Spain, but across the empire many intellectually curious young girls must have found tremendous relief and great joy in the life of the cloisters.

There was another unusual but not uncommon status potentially available to an elite female, that of widow. A young widow of property and good family normally came under enormous pressure to remarry quickly; her moral situation was extremely precarious, her children needed a father, and her wealth made her attractive to suitors. An older widow past her childbearing years, on the other hand, had achieved the status of "honorary" male. Her sexuality now endangered no one. Widows managed properties and businesses they built on their own or inherited from families or their husbands, engaged in local and long-distance trade, served as guardians for their children, and pursued legal cases and gave testimony in court. Although these activities sometimes required them to work through a male representative, and they suffered from a higher rate of illiteracy than men, widows and older spinsters competed successfully in the business world. Juana López de Salazar of Guadalajara, by the time that she arrived at her third marriage, for example, had become part owner of a company with a local merchant, possessed ten slaves, had donated 4,000 pesos to the Jesuits and endowed two chantries, and now provided her new husband a "dowry" of 2,000 pesos.

Other than managing property or running a store or an established business, respectable employments available to women in either colonial empire were few. As a result, women with claims to elite status, but without family or other support, often lived lives of hidden poverty and desperation. Travelers described, for example, the phenomenon of the "absent lady" in nineteenth-century São Paulo. These were white women too poor to have slaves or free servants but who because of their status could not be seen in public during the day engaging in activities such as fetching water or buying food. Instead, they went out at night. Ironically, visitors sometimes thought them prostitutes, but a knowledgeable local resident explained that "there are many women who, when seen in the streets at night, are slanderously labeled as dissolute, when in fact they are honest and virtuous and are forced to make these nocturnal excursions because they have no one who can go out during the day to buy [what] they need."[6]

Elite status was hard won and harder still to maintain, and the situation of women in these years depended very much on the success of their family in navigating the shoals of late colonial and early independent Latin America. Particularly in the turbulent first years after the break with Spain, political and economic chaos brought some wealthy families down, and it pushed others who were simply comfortable into desperation. Long-distance commerce, for example, could be very profitable, but the risks were enormous, particularly as colonial stability gave way to civil wars and competing regimes. The onset of free trade ruined artisans and traditional merchants alike: their high-priced, generally second quality goods found no market, debtors fled or were themselves destroyed, and credit dried up. Some, though by no means all, European-born bureaucrats lost their jobs. As we have seen, in Mexico City most stayed at their posts, and in Brazil many remained at least until the anti-Portuguese riots of the early 1830s. Leaders of political factions that came out on the losing side of local conflicts felt themselves lucky to escape into exile with their lives. Loyal opposition and a tolerance for dissent were not values characteristic of the new nations' politics. Some immigrant landowners and merchants survived independence only to be destroyed later by politics, as for example those in Mexico who sided with the French intervention of the 1860s. Given a dominant New World ideology of upward social mobility and economic success, there is a tendency to note the survivors of the independence period and to pass over the downward mobility and impoverishment suffered by those families not astute or lucky enough to have come out on the winning side.

In the Factory

Political and economic upheavals actually began well before independence, with the Bourbon and Pombaline reforms. In the wake of the Seven Years' War the Iberian states sought to stimulate colonial development and to bring these economies under tighter control. As one measure, the Spanish Bourbons moved to incorporate more women into wage work force: in 1753 77 percent of female workers in Mexico City were domestic servants, whereas fifty years later this percentage had fallen to 54 percent, and now 43 percent of the women who worked outside their homes were in the trades and commerce. In 1799 the Crown ordered guilds not to oppose women who wished to learn artisan trades or put barriers in the way of their employment.

Particularly significant for women seeking wage work was the overhaul of New Spain's state tobacco monopoly. Traditionally, dozens of small family workshops had produced cigars and cigarettes, either on their own or on a putting-out basis, and these were retailed by taverns, small tobacco stores, and street sellers. When the Bourbons converted the industry into a state monopoly after 1764 as part of efforts to improve revenue collection, the state gave little attention to the problems of the many farmers ruined by new production limits but did attempt to include urban tobacco retailers in the monopoly's sales network and found places in the new tobacco factories for as many as possible of the former home artisans. By the turn of the century the Mexico City factory alone employed some 5,000 workers, over half of them women. The factory was the colony's most important employer of nondomestic female wage labor and, counting the workers' families, tobacco manufacture directly affected close to 20 percent of the population of the capital.

Men rolled cigars, drove the wagons, and did the heavy lifting, but women made cigarettes. Cigarette production was subdivided in a proto-industrial fashion into a series of specialties, including tobacco classifiers; cigarette makers; wrappers and counters; and guards and supervisors. Most employees worked by *tarea* (task), a version of piecework: to earn their salary they had to produce a certain quantity or number of items each day, and if they failed their pay was docked. As they left work each evening the women received the paper needed for the next day's task, paper they were supposed to prepare at home on their own time. Instead, some sold the paper to contraband cigarette manufacturers and replaced it with poorer quality materials. To assist them with their work, or simply as a substitute for child care, women brought children or young relatives to the factory floor. A woman who one day could not work or had to leave suddenly to attend to a sick family member sold her *tarea* to one of a flock of trained but unemployed cigarette makers waiting outside the factory gates.

As this suggests, factory managers had no difficulty getting workers. Unemployment was rising in late Bourbon New Spain, and the wages the factory offered approximated those of male workers or poor artisans, much above what women could hope to earn at other forms of manual labor. To turn these women into a disciplined industrial work force was quite another task, however. As did male artisans and handicraft shop workers, women resisted the regimentation of factory labor. Some missed Mondays or others habitually arrived late, a practice the managers tried to control by shutting the factory gates promptly at eight each morning. One manager found the women "ill-bred, arrogant, restless, difficult to control, and discontented."[7] When the factory sought to cut costs in the 1790s by eliminating customary employee benefits or raising quotas, the women struck and took to the streets. However good the factory positions might be compared to other employment opportunities, most of the women were not yet socialized to the rigors and rhythms of industrial labor. Not only did they lack an industrial mind set, but they still had access to other resources, typically through extended kinship relations or links to rural villages, that allowed them some independence from the demands of the factory.

Employment for women in the Mexico City tobacco factory peaked in the early nineteenth century, after which growing political conflicts undercut not only markets and supplies but also work opportunities for men. A traveler now found the female workers much more docile, but already men had begun to push women out of what were a declining number of jobs in the factory. By mid-century census data revealed that most of the employed women in the capital were again domestic servants. Migration from the war-ravaged countryside to the cities, more men available for factory work, competition from imports, and economic disruption had severely reduced wage labor opportunities for women outside the domestic sector and greatly increased competition for the few factory jobs still available.

In the Home and in the Street

Not many of the women in nineteenth-century Latin America who needed work had the luck to get a job in a modern industry such as the tobacco factory. Most fell back instead on traditionally "female" activities. Many worked with textiles. While *obrajes* produced substantial quantities of cloth, the majority of cotton, and much wool, thread and fabric used by Latin America's population came from home production, whether for family consumption or on a putting-out basis for resale. Women and children commonly spun thread by hand, often working in groups to keep each other company; travelers remarked that the hands of the women of all classes were never idle. Both men and women wove the cloth, the women usually on back-strap looms and the men on crude foot- or hand-powered wooden looms. Other home artisans dyed and finished the cloth. Spinners and weavers rarely made enough from these activities to support themselves, but the work did provide a useful supplementary income, and in areas such as Quito it had the very real advantage of exempting them from the *mita*. Inevitably, *corregidores* and priests invaded the industry, using their power to force the Indians to spin and weave textiles for below-market wages and paying them, if at all, in goods evaluated at unrealistically high prices. The overall output of artisan textiles in the colonies was substantial: for example, Quito in the late eighteenth century shipped more than 500,000 yards of locally produced "fabrics of the land" to other parts of the empire.

But contraband and then free trade after independence made life difficult for hand spinners and home weavers. Consumers agreed that artisan-produced cotton and wool clothing outwore Manchester's manufactures but it could not match the imports' prices. The effects of these changes were enormous. The commodification of textiles stripped them of their relational component. They no longer embodied family labor or demonstrated in their colors and patterns respect for community and tradition. By removing one of women's key roles in the family, the collapse of the domestic textile industry contributed to their marginalization. Seamstresses continued to find work shaping imported or locally manufactured cloth, but competition, both among the mass of unemployed women in the cities and from imported ready-made clothing, drove prices for their labor below starvation. Other artisan activities typically associated with women, such as pottery making, the weaving of mats and hammocks, and food processing, also suffered the effects of competition from imports. Here too, rising unemployment among men prompted them now to invade what once they had disdained as "women's work."

Women who could muster modest amounts of capital sometimes opened small grocery and general merchandise stores (*pulperías*) or taverns. Larger operations owned mostly by men dominated the upper end of this retail commerce and offered a wider variety of goods and better facilities for credit than could most of the women proprietors. By contrast, women owned perhaps 10 percent of the *pulperías* and dealt in penny sales to a marginal clientele. A typical inventory might include small amounts of soap, rum, cheese, bacon, sugar, coffee, potatoes, corn flour, and candles. Government-controlled food prices meant the small shops, because they had to buy from the larger retailers and could not take advantage of wholesale prices, made money on food items only if their supplier weighed them a bit extra by accident. Otherwise, they sometimes profited from the sale of other commodities or by charging high rates of interest or by engaging in illegal activities.

Established taverns usually also belonged to men, but illegal drink shops, set up precariously by the side of the street or in residences, often were run by women: one estimate for early-nineteenth-century Mexico City put the number of legal bars at 758, as against some 850 clandestine establishments. The shops served contraband, untaxed alcohol including *aguardiente*; wine laced with alcohol; home-brewed, illegal *chicha* (fermented fruit juice); and, in Mexico, *tepache*, made from old, soured *pulque* treated with brown sugar.

Owners took clothing or other items in pawn, and a near-naked drunk sprawled on the pavement was a sure sign of an illegal tavern nearby. The authorities suspected too that these establishments received stolen goods and served as meeting places for criminals and prostitutes, and they tried repeatedly and with little success to shut them down.

The most visible form of work for poor women was street vending. Some hawked goods from trays or baskets carried on their heads, others had small stalls, and where local authorities opened public markets women were a strong presence among the buyers and sellers. Most often the women sold food. Because the urban poor rarely had cooking facilities where they lived, they had to eat at cheap restaurants and on the street. A partial list of what these vendors offered in nineteenth-century São Paulo included cornbread, corn flour cakes and rolls, meat and fish dishes, candied yams, roasted peanuts, roasted manioc and manioc biscuits, and cane juice, as well as alcohol and tobacco, both probably contraband. A Mexican street scene would not have included the manioc products but would have added roasted ears of corn, *atole*, and tortillas. On a good day female vendors could earn as much as a semi-skilled male laborer. Street sellers had unusual personal freedom for women in late colonial and early nineteenth-century Latin America, but this was possible only because society assumed that poor women and members of racially despised groups by definition had no "shame."

Least attractive to poor women but the job most available to them was domestic service. Fully one-half to two-thirds of all women in nineteenth-century Latin America who worked outside the home were servants. In areas such as Brazil, coastal Peru, or Buenos Aires, African slaves and free blacks dominated this activity, while in Mexico, Central America, and the highland areas of Peru, Ecuador, and Bolivia more often servants were young Indian girls, recruited, sometimes forcibly, from the countryside. Servants were paid little or sometimes given only room and board and commonly subjected to verbal, physical, and sexual abuse. A key distinction was between those servants who were "of the house" and those who went "into the street." The ones who lived and worked in the house were effectively part, if an inferior part, of the family, and their behavior reflected on the "honor" and public reputation of the family. By contrast, the mere fact that a servant went regularly "into the street" was self-evident proof of a lack of shame and largely vitiated any claim to protection by her employer. Whether a servant found the environment of the house protective or confining, or thought going out into the city's streets was degrading or an opportunity for personal freedom varied with the person and the specific situation.

Housework was grueling and repetitive. Worst off were the servants of poor employers, typically the youngest and least skilled of such workers, who had to do everything, often under difficult conditions and with inadequate equipment. In better-off households duties were more diverse and hierarchically ranked. High on the domestic pecking order was the cook. However, hers could be brutally hard work, starting well before sunrise and going on until after midnight, with heavy carrying, exposure to the dangers of fire and hot foods and, in the tropical lowlands, intense heat and humidity. The personal maid to the women of the house held a similarly high status in the servants' world, but, in return for a relatively light work load and perhaps cast off clothing and jewelry, these servants bore the brunt of the wrath of a frustrated or angry mistress. Employers freely admitted beating servant girls and splashing them with boiling liquids and hot wax. Other servants had more diversified duties that might include everything from setting the table, sweeping and cleaning, or tending the children to carrying out the night waste, to be dumped in the street or in barrels in the back courtyard. A very specialized task was that of the wet nurse, commonly employed by elite and even middle-class women. These women sometimes lived in the household, or a child might be boarded out for an extended period with one of them.

The life of the servants who went "into the street" was quite different from those of the house, for the world outside was a dangerous space. Urban streets were rough and poorly paved, if paved at all, and littered with human and animal waste, rotting garbage, dead animals, and the occasional human corpse. Tropical rains and the blazing sun or fog and morning chill attacked those who went out. Carts obstructed narrow passages, and robbers, drunks, and the mentally ill verbally and physically assaulted passers by. Because homes did not normally have food storage facilities safe from heat, humidity, and vermin, families shopped for food every day, and sometimes several times a day, and repeatedly had to fetch water from public fountains. Carrying the clay jugs of water or heavy packages from the market was physically exhausting. A servant sent with money for purchases or returning home with the food and other items might be targeted by robbers, and if anything but very old and ugly she certainly was the object of suggestive comments and propositions from the males she encountered. Did she see these forays into the street as freedom from the stifling restrictions of the household or did she fear for her honor and integrity? Did she flirt with the men, buy and sell a bit on the side, and trade gossip at the fountain or did she run a daily gauntlet of fear and temptation? Dangers aside, more than one elite female eagerly awaited the return of the servant girl bearing the latest gossip from a world banned to her.

Bridging the world of "street" and "house" was the laundress, who came into the house to take the family's most intimate garments and expose them to public view. A few among the elites had their own servants to do the laundry, and in other cases laundresses came and worked in the house, but it was more common for them to pick up the soiled clothing and wash and dry it at public fountains designated for this purpose. Washing was physically very demanding work that, apart from the carrying, required bending and stooping, the use of harsh soap and constant immersion in water, and heavy pounding. If some of the street children had fun at the laundresses' expense, tracking dirty footprints across the wash laid out to dry, the work had to be done again.

As the elites and the state constantly and loudly worried, some of the women who escaped the supervision of family and household did slip into suspect and even criminal behavior. The working poor tried desperately to differentiate themselves from social marginals, but crowded housing, abuses by their employers, and an unstable economy could pitch them overnight from minimal decency into abject misery and force them into illegal activities. Robbery, assault, and murder rarely involved women, except as accomplices or victims. More often poor women fell afoul of the law by receiving stolen goods, by operating an unlicensed tavern or dispensing untaxed or illegally obtained food and alcohol, or because of the practice of prostitution or witchcraft.

Public authorities in the mining areas and cities always suspected female street vendors of selling sexual services, but any "uncontrolled" woman was presumed to be an actual or potential prostitute. Prostitution as such was not illegal, although by mid-century for someone to live off the proceeds of prostitution was. Indeed, it was thought that prostitution, by diverting aggressive male sexuality from assaulting or seducing "honorable" women, played a necessary role in an "honor and shame" society. It was, a doctor explained, "the alternative least damaging to society" because without it "honorable women, the daughters of good families, and wives would necessarily become the objects of corruption."[8] But prostitution did represent uncontrolled female activity of the most startling sort.

Before the middle of the nineteenth century most prostitution was casual, a part-time activity for women who failed to make a living in other ways. So many poor seamstresses supplemented their income with prostitution, for example, that observers in both Spanish and Portuguese America assumed the two went together; in the Brazilian port of Santos swarms of these impoverished women sold themselves to visiting sailors. Authorities sometimes referred to certain localities as "brothels," but in fact these usually were simply places made available for a small price where part-time prostitutes took the soldiers, apprentices, and manual laborers that made up the bulk of their clientele. It is hard to know how common such encounters were or how many women or men were involved. Since few of the poor could afford a church wedding, almost all of them, and no matter however stable and long lasting their unions, lived in what was legally concubinage, a state the church and the authorities routinely labeled "prostitution." Not until the second of the century, however, did genuinely professional prostitutes become common.

Inhabiting the marginal world of the poor servants and artisan-prostitutes, and often linked with these in the popular imaginations, were *feiticeiras* or *hechiceras* (women who cast spells, "witches"). While in many instances— for example, in highland Mesoamerican Indian communities or where there were large numbers of African slaves—males read signs and communicated with the ancestors, almost always where contact with the supernatural was intended to provoke an active intervention in human events the role was for women. Much of an *hechicera's* work dealt with love, winning back the affections of a man who had strayed, and with childbirth, arguably the most dangerous moment in most women's lives: Arcângela, a *feiticeira* of late-eighteenth-century Minas Gerais, was popular with women because, it was said, she had made a pact with the devil to ease the birth of children. Alternatively, women sometimes turned to these specialists for abortions. Largely without power in the day-to-day world, women necessarily took an indirect approach in attempting to solve the problems central to their lives. In the turbulent environment of nineteenth-century Latin America there was a strong demand for specialists in the supernatural.

Conclusions

In colonial Spanish America wealth came from the countryside, but power was in the cities. This was not the case for Brazil, by contrast, where the *senhores de engenho* and, subsequently, the miners, exercised the predominant power. Apart from the anomalous urban civilization of eighteenth-century Minas Gerais and the capital of Salvador, towns mattered little in colonial Brazil, a situation reinforced by the Crown's refusal to sanction higher education or even a printing press in the colonies. The Spanish colonies already had universities at mid-sixteenth century and a flourishing urban culture that rivaled European cities during the seventeenth and eighteenth centuries. Here Crown bureaucrats carried on the work of running the empire while merchants brought in European goods and exported raw materials and precious metals. Retailers, professionals, and priests filled a tiny middle group. At the bottom was a growing mass of urban poor. This included Indians, but distinctly urban Indians, who less and less had contact with their communities of origin and increasingly made up a recognized element of the cities' populations, with their own marriage and residence patterns. Competing with them for work was a growing population of mixed bloods or *castas*. Indeed, the *castas* were most obvious, and most remarked upon, in the towns and cities. In the countryside they were more likely to be absorbed into one of the parent groups. In the towns, on the other hand, they increasingly formed a distinct group but one legally and socially disadvantaged. With independence legal discrimination largely ended, but wars and collapsing economies made the situation of the poor, if anything, worse. Now joining their ranks were ex-slaves, ruined artisans, demobilized soldiers, and the population uprooted from the countryside, all searching for survival. Small wonder that crime and banditry flourished in the decades after 1820 or that the elite-controlled new national states responded with coercive labor and social control systems.

Except where independence led to the abolition of slavery, and this occurred only where the institution was weak and unimportant, political change did not greatly alter Latin American patterns of work. Nor did it immediately change the situation of women. In some ways independence worsened women's conditions. Existing values of "honor and shame," "racial purity," and patriarchy continued to restrict women's opportunities. More importantly, the effect of the wars in many areas was to deplete the male population, or to draw the men away for long periods of fighting, throwing on to women the whole responsibility for supporting themselves, their children, and those not caught up in the fighting. In some areas their situation deteriorated further when the fighting ended: the effects of the wars, together with the impacts of free trade, wrecked much of the colonial economic structure and cast men out of work. This, in turn, tended to push men into areas of employment that women had dominated before, for example, the Mexico City tobacco factory. By mid-century women's chances of finding paying work other than domestic service were less than they had been a generation or two before.

Chapter 4

Export Economies, 1850–1930

T he years between the mid-nineteenth century and the Great Depres sion witnessed more change in Latin America than had any similar period since the first decades of the conquest. National elites and foreign investors increasingly restructured local economies to service the demands and opportunities of the expanding North Atlantic Industrial Revolution. Though Latin America did not entirely abandon such traditional activities as precious metal mining and the export of luxury commodities, emphasis shifted now to the large-scale production of industrial raw materials and basic food items and food substitutes and their sale to the industrializing countries.

Two changes made this possible and profitable. With industrialization, Western Europe was urbanizing. People were leaving the countryside for the cities, and this, together with population increases, made it increasingly difficult for local farmers to meet demands for food. As the real income of the urban working and middle classes rose, they had more money to spend on more and better food. Employers and the state sought to have this demand met as cheaply as possible, so as to keep down wages and costs. Domestic agriculture responded with mechanization and the use of natural and chemical fertilizers, but this was not enough. Consumers more and more found their food imported from abroad: wheat and beef from Argentina, sugar from Cuba, coffee from Brazil, Colombia, and Central America, and tropical fruits from the Caribbean.

Tying producers and markets together were the new railroad and steamship lines that expanded rapidly after mid-century: for example, local and foreign capital laid more than 65,000 miles of railroad track in Latin America during the half-century after 1860. Ocean freight rates dropped 50 to 80 percent in the same period. Whereas as late as the 1830s or 1840s primitive land transportation restricted noncoastal Latin American exports to such high value per weight items as silver and natural dyes, by the 1880s railroads and screw steamers moved tons of wheat, coal, meat, and natural fertilizers from ports as distant as Valparaíso, Chile, and Callao, Peru, to Europe. By the first decade of the next century Europeans and North Americans could slice Jamaican and Colombian bananas into their breakfast cereal. It was a massive change and it affected everyone: in distant parts of rural Mexico, for example, local peasant revolts accompanied the arrival of the railroad. The new lines dramatically increased land values and prompted the forcible removal of Indians and peasants to make way for market agriculture. A new generation of Liberal dictatorships augmented and used state power on an unprecedented scale to develop land and labor conditions favorable to export production.

Changes in exports prompted new work relations. African slavery remained profitable in Brazil and Cuba after 1850, but even here elites increasingly perceived it as an impediment to the expansion of liberal capitalism and a retrograde system that reflected unfavorably on the country and on them. Planters gradually gave it up, substituting for it wherever feasible coercive contract labor. In those areas where a substantial indigenous population survived, the possibilities offered for new export production sometimes prompted the revival or the extension of systems of forced wage labor largely abandoned since the past century. More broadly, though, the trend after mid-century was toward a freeing of labor, in the countryside and in the towns. Swelling national populations, augmented in some areas by foreign immigration, meant that more and more the rural and urban poor did not have access to enough land or other resources to assure their survival. They needed wage work. Landowners gradually dispensed with expensive and cumbersome coercive mechanisms to opt instead for cheaper and more flexible free labor. By the turn of the century various new ideological and political currents were beginning to circulate in the urban areas, urging workers there to organize and even to strike in pursuit of new economic and political objectives.

Mines and Agriculture

Until well past mid-century most European countries maintained mercantilist policies that protected domestic agriculture. Not until the 1830s did even England, the chief proponent of free trade, do away with the "corn laws," reducing or eliminating barriers to the import of foreign foodstuffs. Instead, the first reaction of the industrializing countries to the increased demand for food was to attempt to raise levels of domestic production. The small-scale and irregular land area characteristic of much of European farming limited the possibilities for mechanization; the application of natural and chemical fertilizers to raise output and rebuild the soil was more promising. The traditional method used to recover soil fertility was crop or field rotation, dating back to the medieval "three field" system. However, this required that large areas be left idle for extended periods or planted only in ground cover while the soil recuperated. Now urban growth encroached on agricultural land, and new food requirements made it harder to leave land unused, and then only for shorter periods. The solution was to apply more fertilizer than had been possible using the traditional farm animal by-products and agricultural waste. In the mid-nineteenth century this meant guano.

Guano is a natural fertilizer rich in ammonium nitrate. It results from the weathering over centuries of the droppings of millions of birds that fed on sea fish. Guano could be found in many places, but the best known deposits were on the Chincha Islands off the coast of Peru. Here a notorious guano trade developed. Commercial excavation of guano for export got underway on the islands in the 1840s when a series of government contracts leased exploitation rights to local and foreign entrepreneurs. The immediate problem was a shortage of labor. The islands were dry, uninhabited, and uninviting, and the work was backbreaking, unpleasant, and dangerous. Workers shoveled daily quotas of four or five tons of guano into wheelbarrows, pushed these to the edge of the cliffs, and dumped the material down long canvass chutes to the waiting ships. The process released noxious ammonia gas and huge amounts of choking dust, and if this were not enough, foremen verbally and physically abused the men to force the pace. Not surprisingly, there were few free workers in the guano diggings. Instead, early contractors turned to convicts and recaptured army deserters leased from the government and slaves purchased or rented from nearby coastal plantations. But slaves were expensive, and convicts and deserters offered neither a promising nor plentiful source of workers.

Exports began to expand dramatically only after 1849 with the introduction of Chinese contract labor. Most of these workers came from the south of China, recruited into the "coolie" trade by contractors in Macao from among the millions of Chinese displaced by war and social conflict. In theory, the labor contracts that brought these men to Peru were agreements struck freely and by mutual consent, but as in most such cases the traffic involved considerable deceit, and even coercion, on one side and much simple ignorance on the other. Contracts ran anywhere from three to eight years, and the workers were required to repay their transport costs, as well as any other debts they ran up, out of their salaries. On the island the men suffered conditions close to those of a penal colony, and the Peruvian government made little effort to police the contracts or to ensure the workers' rights, limited as they might be. Men unable to meet their quotas were flogged or imprisoned, and those that could not work because of illness or injury saw their debts mount. The foremen and some of the time-expired Chinese ran stores, drink shops, and gambling houses and sold opium. If the drug dulled the pains of physical labor, addiction drove the men deeper into debt and postponed the day they could hope to escape the islands.

British sea captains loading guano reported "revolting atrocities" and "unparalleled brutality" in the treatment of the indentured workers. The Chinese sometimes responded to an intolerable situation by committing suicide, throwing themselves off cliffs or ingesting huge quantities of opium. Only in the second half of the 1850s when the London antislavery societies took an interest in what was going on on the islands did conditions begin to improve.

The situation of workers in the nitrate mines to the south of Peru in Chile's Atacama Desert were better but still difficult. This area constituted the only commercially available source for sodium nitrate, and as guano deposits gave out in the 1870s and 1880s sodium nitrate became more important to commercial fertilizer production. It was also the basis of the modern explosives industry. In the extraordinarily dry, hot, and hostile environment of the Atacama, nitrates occurred in the form of caliche, deposits of ore three to ten feet below the surface and scattered across the desert. The key worker, and among the best paid, was the *barretero*, who found the caliche, excavated preliminary holes, and then blasted away the desert surface to produce a series of trenches. This was dangerous work. Often, he, or one of the small boys who actually went down into the holes to set the charges, suffered injury or death. After a successful blast the miners moved in to break up the caliche, load it into wheel barrows, and take it back to the processing mill.

Mills were located adjacent to deposits, and owners moved these from one site to another to take advantage of new finds or better quality ores. Machines crushed the ore and dissolved it in water, and as the mixture dried the sodium nitrate crystallized out. The process of nitrate extraction was technologically primitive and labor intensive, from the breaking up of the ore to the final loading on to railroad cars for transport to a coastal port. Workers suffered the effects of heat, lack of water, dust, poisonous fumes, and from the dangers of explosives and poorly maintained machinery with few safeguards. Because of fluctuations in world markets and because local deposits could run out without warning, producers found it more profitable to rely on large numbers of workers rather than investing in more efficient but expensive machinery. Workers could be hired or fired as production cycles changed, but capital costs stayed fixed.

Despite the dangers and hardships, men clamored for the work. The California Gold Rush, the War of the Pacific, and a civil war in the early 1890s whipsawed Chile's economy with violent fluctuations in prices and in demand for the country's agricultural exports. As land prices in the central valley mounted after 1850, owners raised rents and increased the demands on their *inquilinos*, or resident workers. The rural population was increasing and, as a result, wages for day labor were falling. Travelers described roads full of families displaced from estates or from small holdings and looking for employment, even if only in return for food. To an impoverished population already largely cut loose from the land, migration to the North was not unattractive, particularly as wages there were much better than in the South, even counting the higher cost of living. In the nitrate fields a man with luck could save money, unthinkable for farm laborers. When nitrate employment collapsed, as it did periodically with cycles of oversupply, the government provided free transportation back to the central valley.

In contrast to the situation on the guano islands, nitrate workers overwhelmingly were nationals, while the owners of the mines and mills generally were not. Foreign entrepreneurs controlled not only production but shipping and marketing facilities as well and sought repeatedly to form cartels and monopolies. This clear juxtapositioning of local labor with foreign monopolists made it relatively easy for the workers in the nitrate area to mobilize "nationalism," a force much easier to grasp than "class consciousness," in support of their claims and protests. Actually, the nitrate workers had an unusual variety of means available to them to attempt to improve their situation. The most obvious was physical mobility. The Chilean state was the least inclined of the late-nineteenth-century Latin American governments to support the use of extra-economic coercion to control labor. Employers tried, using *fichas* (script) and debts at the company store in efforts to immobilize their workers. None of this was very effective. There were too many competing employment opportunities. Even aided by state-subsidized transportation, the mine owners never managed to flood the northern labor market to the point of turning conditions of labor supply and demand entirely to their favor. Workers readily left their jobs, sometimes two or three or more times a year, often decamping in wage disputes or over safety conditions, but also because they heard the food was better at another mine or because of a girlfriend or simply because other miners were leaving.

This sort of mobility was at best an individual solution, however, and it did not address the underlying structural problems for labor rooted in the nature of the industry itself. To attack these required cooperation and concerted action. Not surprisingly, nitrate workers were among the first in Chile to organize to press their demands against employers. They set up *mancomunales*, regional organizations that brought together skilled and unskilled workers. *Mancomunales* combined many of the characteristics of mutual aid societies, of proto-unions called *resistencias*, and of workers' educational circles. These organizations used drama and propaganda to attack the ideological hegemony of elite-dominated culture and to raise awareness among the workers of themselves as a group with common concerns. *Mancomunales* were responsible for some of the earliest strikes in Chile, including the infamous confrontation at Iquique in 1907 that resulted in the worst massacre in Chilean labor history.

But by attempting to include workers at various levels of skill and consciousness, and with members spread over a wide area, the *mancomunales* lost the intimacy and solidarity of the shop floor. Most succumbed to state repression in the first decade of the new century. Less ambitious were the older mutual aid societies still being organized by the workers to help with such crises as injury and death. By the early twentieth century, however, both *mancomunales* and mutual aid societies were taking a back seat to the more overtly political activities of groups such as socialists, anarchists, and syndicalists and to the unions and political parties these ideological tendencies promoted. The state responded to these activities with pitiless repression, setting off two decades of conflict only resolved, and then incompletely, in the 1920s.

Gauchos and Immigrants

Although mining continued to be important in some areas, and developed into new exports such as Bolivian tin and Colombian coal, the economies of most Latin American countries remained, as publicists never tired of repeating, "essentially agricultural." Latin America from the colonial period had exported agricultural products, notably sugar, indigo, cacao, and tobacco. In the late eighteenth century large-scale shipments of cattle hides and then meat began to be added to the list. For the previous two hundred years cattle ranching on the Argentine pampas had involved little more than the hunting of wild animals, descendants of cattle released from failed colonies or those that had escaped from Spanish settlements and that multiplied at fantastic rates on the virgin grasslands. Essentially they were a free good for anyone with a horse and a knife. There existed no commercial markets to speak of in the area and little overseas communications before the creation of the Viceroyalty of the Rio Plata in 1776. In this environment, the *gaucho* developed and flourished. He was a mixed blood, fiercely independent cowboy who owed his allegiance and his work to no one but himself or to the occasional war lord (*caudillo*) that won his respect.

During the late eighteenth and early nineteenth centuries the situation for the cattle and the cowboy underwent rapid change. In part this was because more shipping opened the way to supply salt beef to Brazil's slave population and because creation of large citizen armies during the Napoleonic Wars greatly increased demand for leather. The growth of Buenos Aires offered too an urban market for fresh meat. To take advantage of these new opportunities entrepreneurs began to organize commercial haciendas, or *estancias*, on the plains around Buenos Aires. These properties required an increased and more dependable supply of labor than traditionally available from the gaucho. With labor costs estimated at 80 percent of hacienda expenses, these workers would also need to be cheap. Some owners turned to African slaves, but generally this was uneconomic. Whereas the labor needs of cattle ranching were seasonal, slaves had to be fed, clothed, and housed year round.

An alternative was to harness the gaucho to the needs of the export economy. Generally he was uninterested in regimented, wage-earning work on someone else's property, and his free way with what were now other people's cattle frustrated those attempting to improve the quality of the pampa's herds. The state and the landowning elites attacked the labor problem by criminalizing the gaucho's free life, labeling him a "vagrant" and trying to force him on to the hacienda. As early as 1804 rural men were ordered to carry "working papers," which had to be signed by an employer every two months. Without these a lower-class male was by definition a vagrant and subject to forced labor on public works. In 1822 the newly independent state introduced internal passports, documents required to move from one district to another. Those caught without the proper papers faced conscription into the military. Deserters and men fleeing impressment flooded the more remote parts of the countryside and fled to the frontier; others turned to crime when they could not produce the papers necessary to obtain legitimate work.

Unable or unwilling to imagine any way of incorporating the rural population into wage labor except through violence and repression, both the Unitarians and the Federalists repeated vagrancy and impressment laws over the next half-century, standardizing these in the Rural Code of 1865. This law provided that workers were to have written contracts with clearly specified conditions, but they also might be required to remain at work on a property even beyond their agreed upon time if the employer needed them. To seek work outside their county of residence lower-class men had to secure the permission of the justice of the peace, a local official who handled all worker–employer disputes and who notoriously was under the thumb of the large landowners. As one result, there were so many complaints against the abuses of the justices that in 1867 the state simply refused to receive any more! The rural poor also fought back with evasion and with cattle rustling, often in collaboration with renegade members of the elite who disposed of the stolen hides and animals for them. But after 1880 the railroad, the repeating rifle, and the Conquest of the Desert worked together to seal the gauchos' fate.

Ultimately, though, it was the farmer at least as much as the justice of the peace and barbed wire that displaced the gaucho from the plains around Buenos Aires. Shortly after independence landowners near the city discovered the possibilities of sheep raising, chiefly for wool for European rug mills. The availability of wool attracted railroads, and these, in turn, made commercial agriculture viable for the first time in the interior of the province. Even more than cattle or sheep raising, agriculture required an expanded labor force. In the 1860s, when the country's seemingly interminable civil and foreign wars finally ended, however, the population of the republic was still quite small. To resolve similar labor shortages, Peru and Cuba imported contract workers, and Mexico and Guatemala stepped up exploitation of their indigenous populations; Brazil brought in large numbers of African slaves. Argentina turned instead to European immigrants.

Many Latin American countries hoped to attract such immigrants in the second half of the nineteenth century. They anticipated that an influx of Europeans would provide not only needed workers but "unclog the nations' arteries," "bleach out" the local population, and raise the nation's moral and cultural levels. Most of the republics were disappointed, not only because they failed to attract many immigrants, but because those who did come generally did not have the impact anticipated. In countries where there already were dense indigenous or mixed blood populations, low wages and harsh working conditions frightened immigrants off. The few who arrived tended either to join the elites in exploiting the local population along already established lines or "went native" themselves, as did, for example, some of unreconciled Confederates who fled to British Honduras and Brazil after the Civil War. Despite slavery and a large but unevenly distributed mixed blood population, Brazil managed to attract large numbers of Europeans late in the century, but only to a few areas. Of all the countries in nineteenth-century Latin America, Argentina was most identified with mass European immigration, and was the country in which these immigrants most obviously affected work relations.

Argentina had much to attract Europe's poor. One advantage was the calendar. Well into the twentieth century large-scale commercial farming of staple grains such as wheat, rye, and barley depended heavily on manual labor. Problems of cost and maintenance kept machinery at a disadvantage on the pampas. At harvest time, gangs of men and women worked their way across the plains cutting, binding, and loading crops aided only by a few horse-drawn reapers and carts. These gangs were made up largely of immigrants, who labored seasonally in the countryside and then retreated to urban areas or went back to Europe during the off seasons. Argentina benefited from being in the southern hemisphere, so that migrants, "swallows" the Argentines called them, could work the harvests in Europe and North America and then move south during the slack times. Most of the migrant workers came from southern Europe, particularly Spain and Italy, though after the turn of the century the flow from central Europe picked up. Inexpensive and rapid steamship travel made such long-distance shifts possible, the more so because Argentina's exports of hides, meat, and wheat demanded many more vessels than did its modest merchandise imports. The ship owners were happy to offer cheap passage to the workers. The "swallows" came and went, but over time many stayed, perhaps two-thirds, and most of these ended up after a time in Buenos Aires, a city that in 1914 was 60 to 70 percent foreign born, as against perhaps 30 percent for New York in the same year.

Little free or inexpensive land was available on the pampas, and there was no Argentine equivalent of the United States Homestead Act. Although the state, working with several international groups, developed colonies of small and medium-sized immigrant farmers up river in Corrientes and Santa Fé provinces, and some of the British-owned railroads sold modest plots along their rights of way, large properties dominated the pampas. The immigrant had scant hope of buying land there, but the large owner could do little without labor. Even where the *estanciero* (large landowner) only raised cattle, new demands from the European markets required a quality of meat beyond that available from "creole" animals and free range. What developed on the pampas was a system of tenant farming with advantages for both immigrant and the landowner, though it rewarded them unequally. An agricultural journal described how it worked: "The land is first divided into fenced pastures of four to five thousand acres and then subdivided into surveyed numbered lots of five hundred acres each without intervening wire. These lots are rented on a three-year contract . . . to Italian farmers who bring their own equipment and supplies [to cultivate wheat] and agree at the end of the period to leave the land sown with alfalfa, the seed being supplied by the owner."[1] An immigrant without the capital that such arrangements required could start out instead as a share cropper. Tenant contracts and share cropping allowed the landowner to expand his improved pasture at little or no cost and sometimes to participate in the profits of grain farming.

It was a difficult life for the renters and tenants. The worst of the pampas was the isolation, aggravated by impermanence. Leasing patterns guaranteed that the farmers would be separated from one another by distance and by bad or nonexistent roads. Condemned to move on in a few years, the tenant was loath to waste time or money improving his housing conditions or sanitary facilities, and with the constant turnover among the rural population there was no chance to develop a sense of community or to foster local institutions. The small farmer colonies had clubs, singing and patriotic societies, and sewing circles, but on the pampas there was only the country store (*pulpería*) or the small town. The store, really a tavern, offered the opportunity to drink, and perhaps to become embroiled in one of the knife fights for which they were infamous. The towns had a bit more, a general store, a railroad station, a school, and perhaps a doctor or a church. But work and poor roads made visits to even these unpromising hamlets rare.

Tenants and sharecroppers had scant hope of upward mobility through agriculture. Rarely could they afford to buy land, and, in any event, success on the pampas required capital and a scale of operation few immigrants could hope to achieve. For those able to string together a couple of good years or who managed to acquire a small store or a business in one of the country towns, the dream was to move to Buenos Aires. Those who failed also washed up in Buenos Aires.

Coffee: Landowners and Workers

Argentina's reliance on the two export crops of wheat and beef gave it a relatively favorable position in late-nineteenth-century Latin America, where most national economies lived or died on the fortunes of a single item. Typical of these was coffee, one of the region's most pervasive new exports after mid-century. Coffee went from a luxury in the 1780s to a necessity by the 1880s and every morning it jump-started millions of European and North American workers. Demand for coffee was so great that production expanded constantly over the course of the century, yet, apart from one or two momentary breaks, prices stayed firm or rose. Coffee was unusual too in that, unlike sugar, for example, it supported a wide variety of production schemes, from small family farms to huge slave labor plantations, all of which could be made to operate profitably.

Much of the best coffee came from Central America. Throughout the colonial period the isthmus's elites had sought a product that would bring them sustained and stable prosperity. Cacao, silver mining, indigo, and, after independence, cochineal fueled regional booms, but the effects typically were limited to small areas, and the industries soon collapsed. By the mid-nineteenth century coffee appeared to offer the long-sought-after vehicle needed to integrate local economies into the expanding network of world trade. Nicaragua remained a marginal producer, as did Honduras, but Costa Rica, El Salvador, and Guatemala all became major growers and exporters of high-quality coffees in the half-century after 1840.

The Central American republics shared Argentina's problem of a surfeit of suitable land but a shortage of available labor. While Costa Rica was simply sparsely populated, the difficulty confronted by El Salvador and Guatemala's would-be growers was not, strictly speaking, a small population but instead one uninterested in working on the coffee estates. The largely indigenous populations lived in corporate communities in the countryside that owned or had access to enough land to satisfy their needs. They were not so much averse to wage labor as they had limited uses for cash, and when they needed money they had ways to earn it more attractive than labor on the coffee *fincas* (estates).

The area of Guatemala most promising for coffee in the 1870s and early 1880s was the Pacific piedmont. However, most of the country's indigenous population did not live here, however, but in the adjacent highlands. Not only had they scant interest in going down to work in the newly developing coffee zone, the Indians greatly, and rightly, feared the diseases of the hot country. During the colonial period the Crown had specifically forbidden the forced removal of highland residents to the lowlands because of health considerations. The Liberal regimes that came to power after 1871 had fewer scruples, and the eager planters had none. But Guatemala was relatively a large country with a huge predominance of Indians, and the state was not powerful enough to mount the sort of direct assault on community resources that marked the transition to coffee, in neighboring El Salvador, for example. Elites feared that if pressed too hard the Maya might rise up in the sort of "caste war" that racked parts of southern Mexico for much of the nineteenth century and that had seemed possible in Guatemala during the Carrera insurrection of the 1830s. There were other, better ways rooted in centuries of established custom.

Unlike central Mexico, in Guatemala coerced wage labor (*repartimientos* or, in the nineteenth century, *mandamientos*) had not died out during the colonial period. It was still used in the province right up to the early nineteenth century, for agriculture, for carrying, and to build a new capital city after the disastrous earthquake of 1773. The practice faded in the last years of the colony and the first decades of independence, in part because the chaos of civil war and rebellion weakened the state's hold on the countryside and also because the ravaged economy had no need of large numbers of workers. In 1876 the new export-oriented Liberals dusted off and relegislated the old colonial system of forced wage labor: departmental governors, the president ordered, "were to provide to the owners of *fincas* who ask[ed] for labor the number of workers they need [from the Indian towns], be it fifty or a hundred, according to the importance of the enterprise."[2] Those who wanted *mandamiento* labor applied to the governor and paid the workers' wages and travel costs in advance. The indigenous officials of the villages were responsible for mobilizing the men, and sometimes women, and seeing to it that they went to the coffee estates on time.

Mandamientos did extract labor from a reluctant population and the practice persisted until the 1920s, but the drafts shared many of the disadvantages of the old *repartimientos*. Because the groups turned over frequently it was difficult to select or train workers to raise the productivity of the enterprise; employers lost money if the men fell ill, died, or ran away; and the drafted Indians typically worked slowly and resentfully and required constant supervision. In fact, the main utility of *mandamientos* may have been as a coercive mechanism to force the highland Indians into another form of bound labor, debt peonage.

Debt peonage in late-nineteenth-century Guatemala was not the result of accident or individual choice as in some other areas, but instead was underpinned by very specific state coercive policy. According to Guatemala's 1894 labor law, almost the only way an adult male Indian could escape being drafted into *mandamientos* was to be able to prove with his *libreta*, or work book, that he owed a debt to an export plantation, a debt he was bound to pay off with his personal labor. Each year tens of thousands of Indians reluctantly left their highland villages to work for two to four months on lowland and piedmont estates. They cleaned the groves of weeds and picked the harvest, paying down debts they had taken on as wage advances. The Indians encountered appalling conditions on the plantations: verbal and physical abuse, inadequate food and housing, polluted water, disease, and long hours.

Whatever their debts, though, and however much the state and the employers pressed, the inhabitants of the highland refused to go down to the *fincas* each year unless they received additional wage advances. Since to be free of debt simply made them liable for *mandamientos*, the Indians not only stayed in debt but sought to drive these debts up, extracting as much money as possible from the often exasperated employers. If they were particularly unhappy with conditions on one estate, they could and did run away, abandoning their debts. Other *fincas* were glad to have them, and gave them new advances, no questions asked, or they could cross the border and work on the coffee estates of Soconusco. Most, though, simply returned to their home villages where labor agents had no trouble finding them, but there was little the agents could do but try to convince them to return to the *finca*. The day-to-day power of employers or even the state in the highlands actually was quite limited. The Indians could not overturn a coercive system or evade it entirely, but by identifying and pressing on its weak points they could force employers to negotiate for at least marginally better conditions or more advances.

Even in their worst situation, *mandamiento* or indebted workers were not chattel slaves, the legal property of others to be bought and sold at will. Indeed, most of the ex-Spanish colonies abolished slavery soon after independence. Brazil, by contrast, began commercial production of coffee early in the century using African slave labor. Slavery had nothing specifically to do with coffee; rather the growers were simply perpetuating a system that had characterized all of Brazil's major cash crops since the sixteenth century. But the so-called "South Atlantic system" of slavery and plantation agriculture that for almost three hundred years had been at the heart of the production of New World tropical exports was dying, largely due to the efforts of Great Britain.

The British from late in the eighteen century had been seeking to end the international slave trade. As one of the last major offenders, Brazil repeatedly promised to stop the import of Africans. In 1826 the emperor signed a treaty to this effect, but the state made no serious effort to enforce the agreement, and Brazilians largely ignored it. Pressures continued to mount, however, and now not just from England but from many of Brazil's other European trading partners and investors, and even from some of the local elites who more and more found the traffic retrograde and an embarrassment to a modern nation. The practical problem for the export economy was that Brazil's slaves commonly had a work life of only seven to ten years and never achieved a net positive rate of reproduction. For Brazil the end of the slave trade meant the end, if gradually, of slavery.

When the Brazilian government in 1850 signed yet another treaty ending the trade and now moved to enforce it, coffee planters began to give serious attention to other sources of labor. One temporary expedient was to bring slaves to the coffee frontier from less prosperous parts of Brazil, and over the next several decades tens of thousands of slaves traveled south on coastal steamers or were marched overland from the decadent sugar areas of the Northeast. This was at best a stop gap measure, and the planters reluctantly began to turn an eye to the nation's growing free population as a possible source of labor. This presented several difficulties. Parroting racist prejudices imported from Europe, oddly inappropriate for a generally rather dark-skinned elite, planters complained of the "laziness" of the free mixed bloods and mulattos, of their reluctance to, in effect, work like slaves. For the poor, of course, not working, or at least not working at the sorts of activities that slaves did, was the very essence of freedom, what set them apart from slaves. They were not eager to forgo this for the wages and conditions planters offered. Government efforts to restrict access to land as means of generating a pool of available workers or to enforce debt labor contracts had uneven success.

If slavery was doomed and the local free population was not only racially inferior but depressingly intractable, there was the alternative of European immigration. Early efforts in the 1850s failed. The Europeans, chiefly Swiss and Germans, arrived burdened with heavy debts from the costs of their transportation and the equipment and supplies needed to set them up as tenants and sharecroppers. Most soon despaired of ever paying off these obligations. For their part, the employers tended to treat the immigrants like slaves, prompting confrontations and threats of diplomatic intervention. Many of the immigrants soon fled to the cities or back to Europe. These early failures temporarily dampened interest on both sides, but the problem of "labor scarcity," of which the planters and their press never tired of complaining, continued and got worse, with slaves aging and internal reservoirs drying up. The solution appeared in the 1880s with, on the one hand, the growing availability of immigrants from southern Europe and, on the other, the decision of the provincial government of São Paulo to subsidize immigrant passages. The system that developed used tax revenues to import large numbers of workers, depressing wages and working conditions for the immigrants and the local population alike. It was an ingenious scheme and it worked.

Immigrant families arriving on government-paid tickets were put up in a hostel in São Paulo. There coffee growers contracted them to work as *colonos* on their estates. Conditions and forms of pay varied between properties. This was not entirely accidental, as it made it difficult to compare conditions, but a more or less standardized *colono* work pattern soon emerged. Each family was given care of a certain number coffee bushes, 2,000–5,000, depending on the amount of labor it could field. The family pruned the plants and kept them free of weeds and in return received a fixed sum per bush. Usually they were allowed to plant food crops between the coffee trees for their own subsistence or for cash sale. *Colonos* also had the use of a house, rent free, and could raise small animals or cultivate a garden patch in the area around it. Aided by seasonal labor, the *colonos* worked the harvest too, earning a piece rate based on the number of pounds they picked. And there might be miscellaneous day labor for wages available on the estate or on a neighboring property. The more ambitious among the *colonos* could take on a *contrato de formação*, preparing, nurturing, and transplanting coffee seedlings. Thus, families derived their income from a variety of monetary and nonmonetary sources.

What struck every observer of the São Paulo's coffee region in the late nineteenth century was the intense mobility of the *colonos*. By the consent of both parties contracts rarely exceeded a year. This allowed landowners to quickly dispense with unsatisfactory workers, but it put the estates in a buzz of uncertainty at the end of each harvest as employers and *colonos* calculated their situation and shopped for a better one. *Colonos'* concerns were not just money but also living conditions and relations with the estate owners. Complaints about abuses from employers that were still accustomed to slavery reached such a point that shortly after the turn of the century the Italian government briefly banned emigration to Brazil. Nevertheless, there were advantages and opportunities for the workers in the system. The basic food and housing guarantees cushioned families against downturns in the market or layoffs, and there were possibilities for capital accumulation and upward social and economic mobility, particularly in such riskier ventures as the *contratos de formação*. As one result, by 1905 21 percent of the landowners in western São Paulo were immigrants, and by 1920 that proportion was almost one-third of the landowners in the entire state. Others moved to the cities to open a business or take up a trade or to seek work in one of a growing number of factories.

Brazilian plantations grew coffee on a massive scale, but labor shortages led to hurried and unselective harvesting and a low-quality product: the "Brazilian method" of harvesting notoriously involved spreading cloths on the ground and beating the branches with sticks. Guatemalan planters, by contrast, were able to manage both large-scale production and selective harvesting because of the great numbers of indigenous workers made available by coerced labor. Some of the other producers in Central America and the Caribbean won a reputation for high-quality coffee based, instead, on the family farm. Puerto Rico and Costa Rica, for example, began with small units and family labor and maintained this structure well into the twentieth century. Already by the 1830s Costa Rica was exporting coffee through the Pacific coast port of Punta Arenas, coffee grown on small homesteads in the high central valley and transported initially to the coast on muleback. Almost alone in Central America Costa Rica had entered the nineteenth century with neither a substantial indigenous or mixed blood population available to be coerced nor an appreciable number of African slaves. This was not the result of any particular aversion to forced labor but instead of a colonial poverty rooted in the failure to develop a profitable export crop. When coffee arrived to fill this gap, Costa Rica had little choice but to develop it as a small-scale enterprise. Coffee rewards close attention, and Costa Rican families picked each bean only as it ripened, in a process that could last six months. The difference in quality and consistency that came with this sort of care, as opposed to Brazilian methods, was notable, and was accentuated by processing.

Initially each Costa Rican grower cleaned his own coffee, pounding away the outer pulp and inner layer of *pergamino* (parchment) with a mortar and pestle. This resulted in broken beans and debris mixed in with the coffee and an acidity and bitterness in the final product. As European markets became more demanding, processors throughout Central America adopted the "wet" method of preparing coffee. The new technology had quite different results in Guatemala and Costa Rica, and these showed the limits of family coffee production. Wet processing utilized an elaborate set of tanks and machinery that required large quantities of coffee to work efficiently and to justify the capital costs involved. Guatemalan estates with a hundred or two hundred hectares planted in coffee supplied this, and by controlling processing growers not only captured additional value but guaranteed the quality of their product.

For Costa Rican producers the situation was quite different. The relatively small harvest of each property could not support the costs of a wet processing installation, and as the market more and more required higher-quality coffee, growers lost control of this stage of production. Instead, a separate group of processors, some of whom were growers as well, set up the necessary equipment and bought, processed, and sold coffee supplied by the small farms. Given the expense of such an installation and, more importantly, the costs of transporting raw coffee, each processing mill soon exercised an effective monopsony in a given region and could set the prices at which it purchased coffee more or less at will. By financing small farmers and foreclosing when these failed, processors could also gain control of more land and expand their own production. In the early twentieth century, and despite Costa Rica's national myth of classless equality, a clear hierarchy had begun to emerge: a small oligarchy of processor-producers, a less well off stratum of large producers that did not have processing mills, small growers precariously holding on, and an increasing number of landless or almost landless rural dwellers forced to seek wage work on others' properties. Whereas in Brazil and Guatemala coffee growers were able to profit from state intervention to drive down costs, Costa Rican family farms increasingly had no choice but to exploit themselves for the profit of the processors.

State and Community

The pull of the market and the effects of increased integration to the world industrial economy were felt not just by export producers and their labor force, but also by the much larger part of the population that worked in peasant agriculture and the local food producing sector. For indigenous communities, and for much of Latin America's rural lower classes generally, the early years of the nineteenth century in many areas had been something of a golden age. The widespread if temporary collapse of export economies reduced demand for labor and land, and national elites, preoccupied with independence and post-independence politics, largely left the rural poor alone, except for those unfortunate enough to be drafted into one of the competing armies. This changed after mid-century as new, development-oriented Liberal governments came to power in one country after another. Peasant populations from northern Mexico to southern Chile and Argentina found their lands invaded and themselves subjected to harsh labor regimes. Some rebelled and all resisted when and where they could. However, the Liberal states created new governmental structures and deployed new repressive technologies funded by export profits to impose "peace" on the countryside, a "peace" that was as good for domestic and foreign investors as it was hard on the rural inhabitants, and harder still to evade.

State control of the countryside rested increasingly on newly professionalized armies and on new rural police forces such as the National Guard in El Salvador and the provincial polices of Brazil, and the famous, or infamous, Rurales of Mexico. The rank and file of the armies were press ganged and brutally treated and few of the poor sought this sort of work, but the new police agencies did offer employment opportunities for the rural and urban lower classes. The Rurales, for example, were formed initially under Benito Juárez in 1861, and numbered some 1,000 in the mid-1870s and more than 2,000 by the turn of the century. They patrolled chiefly those areas of concern to foreign investors. Shortly before the Revolution, for example, 80 percent were stationed in small detachments at factories and mines to repress labor discontent and break up attempts to organize. The Rurales were notorious for continuing the tradition of the *ley fuga*, applying it now not only to captured bandits but to political opponents of the dictator Porfirio Díaz and to labor and peasant activists. Although popular mythology had it that the Rurales were chiefly ex-bandits recruited into the police for their gun fighting skills, in fact most of the enlistees came from peasant and artisan backgrounds. The pay was not much better than that of a common laborer, and the turnover was high: after 1900 only about 13 percent completed their four- or five-year enlistment, and almost none re-upped. A few, on the other hand, made a specialty of enlisting, deserting and selling their equipment, and then reenlisting again under another name. This was not difficult because the corp made no background checks and took everyone physically capable. The Rurales, far from elite work, was simply another job, and apparently not a job that encouraged many to make a career of it. Like the army, the Rurales were useful for shooting workers or poorly armed peasants, and they served Díaz's purpose of projecting an image of state control for foreign businessmen, but they collapsed when real fighting broke out in the Revolution.

The difficulties that rural population faced in the late nineteenth century were not, however, entirely the result of outside demands for land and labor or even state repression. A fundamental problem was the growth of their numbers. Latin America's population increased dramatically from the second half of the nineteenth century:

Populations of Latin American Countries (in thousands)[3]

Country	1860	1880	1900	1910	1920	1930
Argentina		2,457	4,452	6,615	8,861	11,896
Brazil	8,418	11,748	17,894	22,216	27,404	33,568
Peru		500	3,000	4,000	4,828	5,651
Colombia			3,894	4,807	6,089	7,425
Venezuela			2,445	2,596	2,818	3,118
Mexico	7,500	10,000	13,607	15,160	14,409	16,553

Apart from foreign immigration in a few areas, the exact reasons for these increases remain unclear. The first of the growth predates turn-of-the-century medical and public health advances, and available evidence is quite against linking these increases in most cases to improvements in diet or work regime. It is worth remembering, too, that even with this growth it was only in the twentieth century that Latin America regained the number of inhabitants it had had four hundred years before when the Spanish arrived. Still, growth caused problems. After three centuries of land loss and degradation of the environment, accelerated now by the expansion of haciendas and plantations to take advantage of the export boom, many communities did not have the resources available to support larger populations or even sustain the ones they already had.

Although some communities responded to population increases by planting colonies in previously uninhabited areas and on the frontiers, and some families moved to town, more widespread was temporary migration in search of wage work. Indians and mixed bloods from Peru's sierra, for example, increasingly signed up for labor on cotton and sugar plantations along the coast. Although this labor recruitment lacked the spur of *mandamientos*, it depended too on wage advances and debts. Earlier in the century residents of the highlands had resisted going to the coast for the same reasons as had Guatemala's indigenous population. The state was not powerful enough to force them, and the owners of large properties in the highlands would certainly have fought the loss of their workers to a more dynamic part of the economy. Coastal entrepreneurs had turned instead to black slaves and Chinese contract labor, and then to Chinese and mixed blood free workers.

When the trade in Chinese "coolies" to Peru ended in the mid-1870s, there remained the question of what would become of the thousands of Chinese that still survived. Few could afford to repatriate themselves, and landowners and the state did everything possible to instead keep them in the local labor pool. The War of the Pacific in the 1870s devastated coastal plantations. Some of the Chinese workers joined the invaders in looting and burning properties and then fled to Lima, but in the aftermath of the war most returned to agricultural work. Chinese labor contractors put gangs together and made agreements with plantations to supply workers at so much a head. The contractors also ran stores that supplied the men with tools, food, alcohol, and opium, and they lent them money, binding the workers in a web of credit that operated largely outside the review of Peruvian law. By the 1890s the system was breaking down, however. The men were aging and not being replaced by new levies from China and, as a result, labor productivity was declining. Recruitment of some 30,000 Japanese around the turn of the century proved only a temporary expedient.

As railroads penetrated the mountains adjacent to the coastal plantations and population pressures mounted in the sierra's villages, employers now found that they could recruit indigenous and mixed blood workers there with modest wage advances. Temporary migration offered the villagers a chance to earn money to supplement what they could make at home and allowed them to continue as part of a community from which poverty might otherwise have forced them out. This reminds us that, apart from a few extreme cases such as Guatemala or Yucatan, indebted labor in nineteenth- and early-twentieth-century Latin America functioned only when and where the workers saw in it some advantage for themselves. Even the new Liberal states after mid-century could not coerce all of the countryside all of the time, and they did not attempt to. Though these governments sometimes visited exemplary violence on communities that too actively resisted state or landowner demands, had the rural population refused to work the export economy would have collapsed. Everyone understood this. Far from being unilaterally imposed upon the rural poor, then, the relationships involved in debt labor were almost always, and continually, negotiated and renegotiated. Of course, to say that bargaining occurred is not to suggest that the parties bargained from positions of equal strength or to deny that the poor negotiated because centuries of exploitation had stripped them of the resources necessary to maintain their independence. But in the situation in which they found themselves they struggled to get the best they could. To ignore this, to see them simply as tragic victims, is to deny them agency, to deny them the right to make their own history, if under disadvantageous conditions. That is not the way they saw it.

An alternative to seasonal migration, though a sharper break with the community, was to go to live as part of the resident work force on a large property. We have encountered *colonos*, *arrendatarios*, and *inquilinos* on colonial haciendas and plantations. Traditional literature has painted these as the most oppressed of all rural workers, without homes or property of their own, bound by pitiless "debt slavery," and surviving at the whim of the owner. This was certainly not true in most areas by the second half of the nineteenth century. Rather, established renters and permanent workers generally held a privileged position in the turbulent new economic environment, and they knew this and resisted change. Particularly, they resisted being forced off the property and into the category of *jornaleros*, or free day laborers.

It was day laborers that aspired to the situation of *inquilino* or *colonos*. Permanent workers typically enjoyed free housing, more and better rations, and credit at the hacienda store or in town. Up to mid-century, at least, the work demands upon them generally were not great. A similar economic and status distinction might exist too, for example, between *arrendatarios*, those who paid a fixed rent, had some control over what they grew, and enjoyed better credit conditions, and sharecroppers, who were required to produce what the landowner demanded. In addition to serving as the basic agricultural labor force, the resident workers, together with tenants, renters, and sharecroppers, nearby smallholders and other hangers-on (*paniaguados* or *criados*) made up as well the core of owner's personalist clientele. It was from among these men that he recruited armed retainers to fight his land and political battles.

Changes in the world economy after mid-century altered the situation of permanent workers, and not for the better. As market possibilities expanded and land values rose, owners began to see new commercial opportunities for their properties. The effects on their workers were two. On the one hand, employers began to increase the amount of work required from both renters and resident laborers. A study of census returns for Chilean *inquilinos*, for example, shows a tendency toward larger and more complex families, as permanent workers and renters took in relatives or kept children at home to help meet new work demands. Average family size rose too because children who in the past would have married and formed their own nuclear families on another part of the hacienda no longer had access to land.

Struggling to avoid being pitched into the mass of landless poor, resident workers, tenants, and smallholders not only worked more and longer hours, but they migrated to look for other employment during the off season. Women were left to run the households: by the 1860s areas of central Chile had 120 women for every man and 40 percent of the households were female headed at least part of the year. Well before the end of the century, then, the status of a resident worker no longer, to the extent that it ever had, necessarily or primarily suggested coercion. Rather, debts indicated a favored status. Owners reacted to new market opportunities by reducing the more privileged and independent renters to sharecroppers, converting sharecroppers and other tenants to day labor and increasing demands on them, and expelling those no longer necessary or who resisted. As much as possible, export producers ridded themselves of debts and resident workers and relied more and more on a growing rural proletariat and semi-proletariat. By the 1930s even a work environment as coercive as Guatemala's had replaced debts with "vagrancy" laws, and in the 1940s abolished even these.

Gathering

Before leaving the realm of indebted labor, we should touch briefly on gathering, a commercial activity from the earliest colonial period but one that boomed in the late nineteenth century. In the sixteenth century the Portuguese had sent Indians out to find and harvest natural products such as cinnamon, rubber, and herbs and spices, the *drogas do sertão*. The earliest exploitation of cacao and cochineal in Spanish America also depended on harvesting wild plants. Probably the longest running, large-scale gathering industry in Latin America was that of *yerba mate*, a bitter tea favored as a beverage in Argentina, Paraguay, and southern Brazil. Although the Jesuits raised *mate* for a time as a plantation crop in their missions on the Brazil–Rio de la Plata frontier, after the expulsion of the order in 1767 these fields reverted to nature and gathering again predominated. Prime regions for this were northern Paraguay and southern Mato Grosso (Brazil).

The harvesting of *yerba* began in Asunción, where a merchant financed a gathering contractor, providing him with money, tools, and food and supplies. The contractor, in turn, hired thirty or forty workers, advancing them money and credit to tide their families over while they were away. Once a scout had located a likely area the main work force arrived, transporting their equipment by boat, cart, and mule train. Because aggressive harvesting commonly killed bushes, expeditions had to press further and further into the forest, confronting disease, wild animals, dangerous rivers, and hostile Indians. At their central camp the workers built a rather elaborate drying and processing structure and then fanned out into the surrounding area to cut the leaves. The men received credit against their debts for the *yerba* they brought in. After the leaves were toasted to drive out moisture, the men sewed them into hide-wrapped bundles weighing some two hundred pounds and manhandled these onto ox carts to be taken to the nearest river outlet. It was dangerous, back-breaking work, and not a few of the men ended the season with little to show after they had paid what they owed. But nothing bound them to the trade or forced them to go into debt. As was the case with the loggers or chicle gatherers who followed similarly arduous forest trades, these men were, on the whole, relatively well paid for the time and place and took pride in their abilities and the courage and physical strength the work required.

More notorious was the rubber gathering industry in the Amazon basin. Here the circuit began and ended in the city of Belém do Pará at the mouth of the Amazon River. Natural rubber had been known for centuries, chiefly as a novelty, but the spread of vulcanization, a process perfected in 1839 that allowed rubber to retain its flexibility in cold weather, opened vast new commercial possibilities. The popularization of bicycles and then automobiles at the turn of the century stimulated demand. Until the second decade of the twentieth century, when the Dutch managed to form successful plantations in their East India colonies, rubber had to be gathered in the wild, and almost all of it came from the Amazon basin.

Belém merchants, backed by international trading houses, advanced money and goods to middlemen (*aviadores*), usually small merchants in upriver towns. These in turn used credit to recruit rubber tappers from among local *caboclos*, descendants of Indians and Europeans. Traditionally the *caboclos* and their families had lived by fishing, subsistence gardening, and occasionally gold mining on the tributaries of the Amazon. Because rubber trees were found scattered widely in the forest, it took considerable local knowledge and skill to locate and tap the trees, process the sap, and bring it out. Although the pyramid of credit that rested on the tappers' backs was certainly burdensome, and few got rich, gathering did offer them access to consumer goods they had never imagined before. Given the open expanses of the forest and rivers, it plainly would have been impossible to force the *caboclos* to continue rubber tapping against their will.

The horrific labor conditions popularly associated with rubber tapping, and broadcast in European and North American newspapers in early twentieth century, involved not the *caboclos* but other groups of workers. The rubber boom lured thousands of Brazilians into the Amazon from the impoverished states of the Northeast, particularly after the great drought of the 1877–80. For most this proved a disaster. Without local knowledge, and deeply in debt for transportation and supplies by the time they started work, these men were dependent upon the *aviadores* for survival. Instead of having them gather rubber on their own, for which they lacked the experience or knowledge, the supply merchants used these men to service established circuits of trees. Many succumbed to the hazards of the rain forest or to alcohol or fell in knife or gun fights in the camps and small towns. Their wives and daughters, even if they escaped having to work off the dead men's debts, had little alternative to the slave-like conditions of domestic service. The pretty ones ended up in brothels.

Toward the headwaters of the Amazon, particularly in the areas controlled by Colombia, Peru, and, before the Acre War in 1902–3, Bolivia, the rubber boom engulfed whole Indian societies, groups protected until then by isolation and a lack of any resource that interested Europeans or Brazilians. This all came apart now. Adventurers flooded in. Sometimes they forced the Indians to gather the rubber, and in other instances they simply appropriated the women and killed the men, doing the rubber tapping themselves. *Aviadores* controlled vast areas almost entirely innocent of state presence, except when the merchants called in the army to put down resistance. In many areas slavery effectively reigned. Reacting to this the British in 1910 sent consul Roger Casement to investigate conditions on the Putamayo tributary of the Amazon. There he found the "murders of girls, beheadings of Indians and shooting them after they had rotted from flogging."[4] Those who survived were left with shattered cultures and bodies racked with venereal disease and alcoholism when the boom receded after World War I.

The End of Slavery

By the middle of the nineteenth century forced and free wage labor were common in Latin American, but in several areas African slavery persisted. The peak decade for slave shipments to Brazil was the 1840s, and slavery continued to be important in the export economy into the 1880s. In only one country, however, did planters create a major slave-based economy almost from scratch in the nineteenth century. This was Cuba. Technically, of course, Cuba was not a country but a colony of Spain, but the enfeebled condition of the mother country gave Cuba's Spanish and creole elites considerable leeway in developing their own local policies. The island had dozed through much of the colonial period with an economy based on subsistence agriculture and the provisioning of the treasure fleets. The capture of Havana by the British in 1761 and the Haitian Revolution in the 1790s radically altered this. The brief British occupation showed the commercial possibilities for Cuba of a more open economy, and the Haitian Revolution destroyed what had been the world's most important exporter of sugar. Cuba now stepped in to fill the gap: by the early 1830s the island was producing some 70,000 tons each year, roughly the output of Jamaica; by 1840 Cuba's exports were up to 161,000 tons, and in 1870 700,000 tons were harvested, over 40 percent of the world's output.

Because of mounting pressure against the international slave trade, the Africans brought to Cuba in the nineteenth century were expensive. Because they were expensive, ownership was concentrated in a few hands. The vast capital requirements of modern sugar production, evident in the huge *centrales* (central processing mills) that came to dominate the countryside, accentuated the trend toward concentration. At mid-century less than 10 percent of the free population owned slaves, but, unlike some of the other Caribbean islands and parts of Brazil, this did not mean a few whites in a sea of Africans. By the 1860s half of the island's population was European or European-descended creoles, and the prostrate Spanish economy continued to encourage emigration. These whites and some 400,000 slaves shared the island with more than 200,000 freedmen and free mixed bloods. Most whites and people of color did not own slaves and survived in the towns by artisan work and day labor and in the countryside by cattle raising, tobacco farming, and food production. By contrast, 80 percent of the slaves belonged to a small number of wealthy owners who, increasingly in cooperation with foreign capital, employed most of them on large sugar plantations.

Where slavery had developed gradually, and where there were repeated cycles of boom and collapse, as, for example, in Brazil's Northeast or in the Old South of the United States, elements of a human relationship commonly developed between masters and slaves. Or at least the cost of a slave relative to what he or she could produce encouraged moderate treatment and efforts to prolong his or her work life. On the export frontier, by contrast—whether in Mississippi, Cuba, or São Paulo—a booming economy rewarded maximum production brought to market as quickly as possible. If this destroyed the slaves in the process, the profits would pay for more. Brutal work regimes, inadequate housing and diet, high mortality rates, and a very skewed ratio of male to female slaves characterize such regimes. Cuba was no exception. Rapid expansion of the slave force in the early and mid-nineteenth century made it one of predominantly young men, most of whom had been torn from Africa only a short time before and were in no way reconciled to their situation. They resisted in all the ways they could imagine. The owners, in turn, struggled to contain this population with exhausting work regimes and violent punishments intended to terrorize and intimidate. Flogging was common and sanctioned by the 1842 slave code, as were stocks, shackles, chains, and incarceration. The law limited the work day to sixteen hours but planters routinely ignored this, and during the harvest slaves might have only a few hours' sleep a night.

Cuban slavery and the slave trade that supplied it hid for a half century behind the cloak of the United States South, but the outcome of the U.S. Civil War, as well as a Cuban independence uprising in the 1870s that disorganized large areas of the rural economy and freed many slaves, forecast the imminent end of the system. As did most slave owners, Cuban planters responded by staging a delaying action while seeking to create a replacement labor regime that as closely as possible approximated slavery. The government freed slaves over age 60 as well as those born after 1868, but the latter were to remain under the "tutelage" of their mothers' master until they reached age 18. The 1880s witnessed introduction of the *patronato* system: all slaves were now freed but had to continue work for their former masters as "apprentices" in return for a nominal wage.

As Cuban slavery collapsed, planters searched desperately for replacement workers. Prisoners and army deserters supplied only a few, and efforts to use white colonists from the Canary Islands failed, for the same reasons that Brazil's early immigration schemes had failed. Sugar growers bought several thousand captured Maya rebels from the governor of Yucatan, but the real solution appeared in the now familiar form of Chinese indentured labor. Between 1847 and 1874 Cuba imported approximately 125,000 Chinese contract laborers, more even than Peru. Employers paid the recruiters a fee of 125 pesos a head, plus any money advanced to the workers. According to their contracts, the men and women—about 20 percent were women— were to work for eight years at 4 pesos a month for men and 3 pesos for women, plus food and housing, clothing, and medical care. By comparison, unskilled day laborers in Cuba at this time earned up to 25 pesos a month, but without the other benefits.

Most of the Chinese labored on the sugar estates in gangs headed up by Chinese foremen, and they were subject to essentially the same corporal punishments as slaves, in fact if not according to the law. Contract Chinese workers traded among planters for 340–425 pesos apiece, whereas slaves sold for 500–600 pesos. Those workers that survived their initial term were required either to recontract themselves or leave the island, but in fact many seem to have slipped into petty commerce and free wage labor. Since the contracts did not provide for paid repatriation, and few of the Chinese could have saved the necessary amount from their meager wages to return home, probably few ever saw their homeland again. By the late 1870s Cuban plantations employed one of the most diverse labor forces in the history of New World plantation agriculture: African slaves, Maya convicts, Chinese indentured laborers, and free workers drawn for the local mixed blood and freedmen population, as well as from poor creoles and Spanish immigrants, many of the latter time-expired soldiers who saw no possibilities if they returned to Spain.

The Origins of Industrial Labor

Even as export production of raw materials and food expanded, urbanization, population growth, and improved communications were laying the groundwork for new forms of industry and commerce. Despite admitted exceptions such as Chile's nitrates, most of Latin America's international commerce was routed through a limited number of ports closely linked to the national capitals: Buenos Aires in Argentina, Santiago–Valparaíso in Chile, Lima–Callao in Peru, São Paulo–Santos and Rio de Janeiro in Brazil, Mexico City–Veracruz in Mexico, and Cuba's Havana. These centers attracted and concentrated government spending and much foreign investment. As one result, larger and more sophisticated local consumer markets developed, markets that increased the demand not only for imports but for more and better quality domestic manufactures as well. Prior to the 1930s, though, there was little conscious effort by Latin American governments to encourage domestic manufacturing or to attempt to stimulate so-called "import substitution industrialization." A broad consensus agreed on the superiority of industrial imports over local products and on the fruitlessness of attempting to promote "artificial" industries in the face of import competition. But export downturns, such as that of the 1890s, and world events that cut off imports, especially World War I, made some expansion of domestic manufacturing logical.

To understand how industrial labor came to be constituted in this context, it is necessary first to understand how industry was divided in turn-of-the-century Latin America. Most domestic production of consumer goods remained in the hands of artisans and small-scale shops. These were factories in name only, employing a handful of workers and little or no machinery, and producing goods such as shoes or soap or construction materials or cheap ready-made clothing for the low end of the market. The capitalization of such enterprises was low, output limited, economies of scale typically nonexistent, and division of labor elemental. They differed little if at all from colonial *obrajes*. Profits depended on cheap labor and monopoly or near monopoly of the market, allowing the sale of second-rate goods at artificially high prices. Not surprisingly, consumers tended to avoid such products when they could, not simply out of ideological confusion and a "colonized" mentality but because imports were a better value.

With limited capital, or forced to pay exorbitant rates for borrowed money, and without a market broad enough to easily absorb amortization costs, domestic producers could not afford the modern technology or machinery necessary to raise productivity and make their goods more competitive. Wages in these shops were low, though not as low as those in the countryside, and conditions sometimes difficult, but the pace was human. The workplace was usually near home and workers often could take time off when they needed it; they had a personal relationship with their employer, who commonly labored at the next bench. If they had lost their status as independent artisans, they still carried the necessary skills in their hands and eyes, owned their own tools, and recognized only a limited social distance between themselves and the boss. Separated one from another in myriad small shops and enmeshed in personal relations with their employers, these workers had no sense of themselves as a "working class." To the extent that they espoused an ideology beyond traditional paternalism and hierarchy, it was likely to be an individualistic anarchism, as effective as police spies in dividing and weakening worker solidarity.

Contraband imports during the late colonial period and the onslaughts of free trade in the early years of independence ruined much domestic thread and textile production, driving antiquated *obrajes* out of business. By the last quarter of the century, however, foreign and domestic entrepreneurs were setting up textile mills to compete with imports. Using often outdated and cast-off imported machinery to produce cheap, low-quality fabrics, these factories made a profit because of the poor wages they paid the women and children that dominated their labor force. Women were favored not only because of their superior fine motor skills but because they were thought to be more docile than men and unlikely to organize or to resist employers' demands. Textile and clothing production also was sometimes broken down into simple tasks and farmed out as piecework at home. A 1906 Argentine study showed, for example, that 99 percent of the labor force in the clothing industry was female. While many of these workers found employment with the few large companies, two-thirds actually worked at home, for wages or rates lower even than those paid in the factories. But these circumstances were better than what domestic service offered and had the advantages of being safer for female virtue and more easily combined with the women's socially defined chief roles of wife and mother.

Although textiles continued to be important, the branch of industry that expanded most dramatically during these years was the processing of agricultural and mineral products for export. Governments welcomed such activities because they added value and increased tax revenues, while exporters favored local preparation because it allowed them use cheap labor while reducing the bulk and weight of the exports, lowering shipping costs. Archetypical were the meat-packing plants of Buenos Aires. Although there was some export of live animals from Argentina in the nineteenth century, distances and problems with disease favored the sale of processed meat products. Early on this was salted beef, but the market was limited. Only late in the century, when the steamship and artificial refrigeration made possible the shipment of frozen and then chilled beef, did Argentina become a major supplier of meat to Europe.

Foreign companies such as Swift and Armour opened large processing plants in the suburbs of Buenos Aires, employing a work force that mixed European immigrants, chiefly for unskilled or semi-skilled tasks, with a smaller number of native-born Argentines, who handled the more skilled butchering jobs. Owners imported the latest techniques from the United States, creating, as one writer put it, a "continuous, mechanical disassembly line." Technological marvels these may have been, but for the men the work was brutal and filthy: "Often it happens that animals with tumors and boils full of pus come down the line. . . . Then pus spurts out on your face [and] touches your mouth and eyes."[5]

Obeying the new logic of Taylorism, packing-house owners broke down the activities on the line into ever simpler tasks, to replace skilled men and women with unskilled, cheaper labor, and to speed up the process. In the early twentieth century 10 to 25 percent of these workers were women, and they made up 50 percent of some divisions, such as trimming, where fine motor skills again were at a premium. But the mills were damp, bloody, violent places, the very antithesis of the home environment and nurturing roles society assigned to women, and women sought employment there only with the greatest reluctance. Divisions within the labor force by nationality and gender, and the widespread use of company spies and blacklists, hampered efforts to organize, and a ready supply of government-protected scabs made it hard to strike. When the workers did go out, their demands were simple: clean drinking water, wash-up facilities, and company-supplied uniforms; a stop to verbal and physical abuse by supervisors and to the use of fines to discipline workers; and an end to the constant "speed-up." They met with little success.

Whether they labored in the textile mills or in the meat packing plants, women in early-twentieth-century Latin American almost universally defined their wage work as "helping." That is, because established gender roles placed their proper activities in the home, anything outside this was deviant. Yet the majority of poor and working-class families, immigrant and locally born, could not survive on what the man made, if indeed there was a male head of household. But for women to enter the wage labor force not only took jobs from men but threatened male status and the whole structure of gender dominance, thus the need to see female wage work as temporary, as "helping" the family, an appropriate role for women. Of course, for many families this income was in fact vital. For others, the definition of what was necessary changed over time, whether food or better housing or school supplies, as the fortunes of the family changed. This explains the combination of high turnover among female workers in the factories with the fact that many women stayed at the same jobs for years: poverty or upwardly mobile ambitions kept some women at wage work for extended periods, where others, whether because of new economic conditions or pressure from society and their families, entered and left the labor force. Even those who enjoyed their work rarely saw it as a desirable option or thought of it in terms of a career or a form of self-realization.

Compared to textile operatives or meat packers, workers linked to transportation, in particular the men who labored on the railroads and in the ports, had better luck during these years at developing self-conscious, job-based identities and in struggling collectively to improve their situation. Transport workers were particularly important to the national economy, and because their skills made them difficult to replace on short notice, they enjoyed leverage denied others. Railroad engineers in Argentina, for example, formed La Fraternidad (The Fraternity) in 1887 and struck repeatedly and with some success for better wages and conditions. The employment of unsympathetic foreigners in supervisory positions, particularly on the British-owned railroads, however, and a plentiful supply of cheap labor for the unskilled tasks hindered broader organizing efforts in the industry. Finally, a series of labor defeats after World War I prompted the formation in 1922 of the Unión Ferroviaria (Union of Railway Workers), for all of those not eligible for La Fraternidad. Together these organizations could and did shut the railroads down. The Radical Civic Union governments that ran the country from the mid-teens through the 1920s sometimes sided with the railroad workers, or at least took a neutral stance, particularly when the job actions were against a foreign-owned line. As a result, the railroad workers managed some victories, even as organizing efforts in other industries succumbed to post-1918 repression and unemployment.

Railroad workers owed their strength not just to their importance in the economy but also to the development of an "occupational community." The irregular schedules of their working lives and a strong sense of themselves as a labor aristocracy led them to interact chiefly with each other, on and off the job. They lived in the same areas, participated together in mutual aid societies and cooperatives, and sought railroad employment for their sons. Thus, the sanctions available to enforce a strike went well beyond the shop floor, encompassing all aspects of the workers' daily lives. Although their wages were not particularly high, by the early 1930s railroad workers did benefit from pensions and protection against layoffs, and they had guarantees against the worst sorts of workplace abuse common to Argentine industry at the time.

For urban labor, then, and not just for railroad workers, the construction of consciousness and solidarity took place not only on the job, but also in neighborhoods and through participation in class- and work-based institutions. Latin America workers, as in early industrial North America and Europe, tried to live within walking distance of their employment. Few could afford public transport even when this became available, and because hiring commonly took place on a day-by-day basis, they needed ready access to the work sites. Most lived crowded together in *conventillos* or, in Portuguese, *cortiços*. Although some of these were purposely built, the majority were large, old houses in the center of the city that elites had abandoned as they moved to newer, tonier districts. Speculators bought the houses and divided them into one-room apartments for working families. In other cases housing was jury-rigged from scrap wood and tin where space could be found: "in the backyard of a bakery and sugar refinery on a piece of muddy, infected ground . . . was a low shack covered with zinc, like many others in the neighborhood. A group of workers lived in it, eating kitchen scraps from the same filthy plate as the bakery cat and the rats of the area. When one fell sick with yellow fever, they brought him out into the yard, where he died and waited decomposing for the funeral cart."[6]

For the poor these conditions made the "home" a place to sleep or perhaps to work, but other functions commonly associated with it, such as eating or relaxing, took place in the street. If such forced and constant proximity sometimes induced conflict, it also prompted a sharing of experiences, information, and resources, and it facilitated an awareness of a common predicament. Poor women, in particular, found it almost impossible to survive except as a joint effort. Thus when reforming governments late in the century began to knock down the *conventillos* and *cortiços* in the name of public health and safety, the residents resisted, not the least because "urban renewal" in this manner made no provisions for affordable housing to replace what they lost. Instead, the poor now were dispersed, whether to the *favelas* (hilltop slums) of Rio de Janeiro or to the bleak workers' suburbs of Buenos Aires or Santiago, where they had to depend on expensive and unreliable public transport to get them to their jobs. Isolating the workers, and the poor in general, by taking them out of downtown and making them subject to transportation links easily controlled by the government facilitated state control.

Given Latin America's dependence on exports and imports, ports were central to the success of the commercial economy. During the first decades of the twentieth century, for example, two-thirds of Brazil's coffee shipments went through the *paulista* port of Santos. The foreign-owned Companhia Docas that ran the port facilities there hired stevedores to load and unload the ships on a daily, or sometimes twice daily, basis, using the "shape up" or *parede* (wall) system. Gang bosses selected men one at a time from a crowd clamoring for work at the dock gates. Good workers and those with experience were more likely to be taken on than novices, but the very availability of the unskilled depressed wages and dampened the chances of seasoned men to bargain for better wages or conditions. Once through the "wall," the stevedores worked in small groups of six to twelve and were paid as a unit on a piece rate basis, spurring cooperation. The contrast between the extreme individuality of the "wall" and the common experience of the loading group provided the men a lesson in both their own vulnerability, which they hardly needed, and the possibilities of strength and success through unity.

Stevedores shared the harbor with other laborers, including those doing construction and repair, warehouse men, and the cart drivers who transported cargo to and from the ships. Work in the warehouses required physical strength, agility, and stamina, for the normal day was 14 or 15 hours. The carters threaded their way through crowded streets ten hours a day, exposed to rain and sun. Because of its often-noted abolitionist history, Santos had a large black population by the 1890s, but support for abolition was not the same thing as an absence of racism, and the ex-slaves found themselves relegated to marginal work or even used as strike breakers. As part of their drive to rationalize and cheapen port labor, the employers successfully played upon national and ethnic differences to divide the workers one against the other, and early efforts to organize found these barriers hard to overcome.

Not all of those who labored in the expanding cities of turn-of-the-century Latin America were artisans or part of the proletarian poor, of course. Jobs in retail sales and in offices—white collar employment—grew as well. By the nature of their work, these *empleados* had to present themselves as *gente decente* (respectable folks), neatly dressed and socially above those who labored with their hands. But low pay, long hours, the high cost of the proper clothing and a "respectable" address, and an absolute dependence on the whims of their employers left them constantly on the edge of ruin and torn with anxieties. Employment demanded a secondary education, but the tasks themselves were generally undifferentiated and did not require special skills or training beyond literacy. Hiring depended on personal contacts, and continued employment depended upon complete subservience to the boss. Sexual exploitation of female employees was not unknown, and clerks sometimes had to kick back part of their pay to supervisors in order to keep their jobs. As one writer explained, "the effort to approach the ranks of the aristocracy and differentiate themselves from the mass of workers and artisans . . . condemned them to a lifestyle and to social rituals in their dress and appearance that were constantly beyond their objective possibilities."[7] Under these social and financial pressures, the beginnings of class or group consciousness emerged. This was not a revolutionary consciousness, of course, and white collar workers generally shunned contact with industrial or rural labor and avoided the new ideologies that agitated the lower orders.

In the wake of World War I, the effects of inflation and the examples of a teachers' strike in Chile and a successful action by textile workers and stevedores in Callao prompted Lima's white collar employees to go on strike for the first time early in 1919. They claimed to be the true victims of inflation, "forced by fate" and by "needs greater than the working class" to live beyond their means. Over the next several years they gained various pieces of protective legislation, including notice before firing, compensation for years served, and injury and illness insurance, but these improved their situation only marginally. In some ways they harmed it. This sort of collective action convinced many employers that their clerks and sales persons were ungrateful and as such had forfeited traditional rights. Unfortunately for the *empleados*, if they had lost a presumptive right to paternalistic care, they were not yet adequately organized to sustain effective bargaining to improve their situation or to protect their jobs, and the state had yet to construct the social "safety net" characteristic of European industrial nations.

Apart from the anxiously aspirant white collar employees, though not always very far apart, were those who worked at crime and commercial vice. Criminal activities expanded and professionalized around the turn of the century. Particularly in the coastal cities of the Atlantic seaboard the more lucrative aspects of organized crime fell into the hands of immigrants, and they linked these up with criminal syndicates in Europe and North America. Activities included gambling, drug trafficking, extortion, systematic theft in the ports, and sex work. Female prostitution, for example, which fifty years before had been mostly a casual, part-time activity of poor women, now was organized and rationalized by the criminals and the state and turned into big business. Latin America governments, imitating European and North American models, began to legislate the registration and medical inspection of prostitutes and to require that their work be restricted to licensed brothels or to specific "zones of tolerance." This was meant both to control the spread of venereal disease and to repress the criminal elements and disruptive behavior thought to characterize the bars and hostels where prostitutes sought their clients.

In Mexico, Central America, and Peru, and apart from the women in the few establishments that catered to elites, prostitutes came chiefly from among the local mixed blood and mulatto populations. In Atlantic ports such as Buenos Aires and, to a lesser extent, Rio de Janeiro, on the other hand, foreigners dominated the work. Particularly evident were Jews from Central Europe: 75 percent of the registered prostitutes in 1900 Buenos Aires were foreigners, and most of these were Jews. Similarly, Central European Jews, *caftans* the Brazilians called them, dominated the illegal pimping and trafficking of women in turn-of-the-century Rio de Janeiro and Buenos Aires. The collapse of Central European economies in these years, together with European anti-Semitic restrictions, drove many poor Jewish women into prostitution, unfortunately reinforcing Latin American anti-Semitic stereotypes. Despite the predominance of foreigners in the traffic and contradicting the often lurid headlines of the time, there was scant evidence of genuine "white slavery," the coercion or deception of innocent European women for prostitution in Latin America. Investigations by consuls and social service agencies showed that overwhelmingly the women knew what they were getting into. This itself, of course, condemns the societies, both European and Latin American, that offered poor women no better opportunities.

Ideologies, Unions, and Parties

As Latin American cities grew and diversified and pressures mounted to resolve the social and economic problems that plagued them, various groups and ideologies came forward to offer solutions and to compete for the attention and allegiance of the urban population. Best known of these, apart from traditional nationalism, paternalism, and the ideas of the church, were anarchism, syndicalism and anarcho-syndicalism, socialism, and revolutionary socialism or communism. Immigrants and intellectuals imported these ideologies and political organizations from Europe, but each tendency adapted itself to local environments. Anarchism broadly anticipated a rising consciousness among workers based on self-education and the laboring experience, a consciousness that at some moment in the future would explode into a general work stoppage, bringing down the capitalist state. Anarchism was profoundly political, but its adherents eschewed parties or participation in the existing political system. In Latin America anarchism became particularly the ideology of artisans and craftsmen, a reaction to the collapse of their economic and social situation. Here the enemy could not be their employer, for most were self-employed. It was, instead, the "state," in the service of international capital. Buenos Aires and Santos competed with each other for the honor of being the "Barcelona of Latin America"; tendencies and factions proliferated, and publications multiplied. Anarchist-led general strikes racked major Latin American cities, particularly Buenos Aires, in the first two decades of the new century. For all of this, the number of adherents was never large, and anarchism eventually fell victim to its own distrust of organization and to government repression.

Syndicalism also rejected politics, focusing instead on direct bargaining with employers. Anarcho-syndicalism expanded this, carrying direct action into the streets, with strikes, boycotts, and sabotage. As they developed in Latin America, syndicalism and anarcho-syndicalism fought for greater control of the workplace. They sought to increase worker consciousness and power by organizing unions that focused not just on broad ideologies but that also pursued and won concrete day-to-day gains for workers. The result was that for all the radical rhetoric, syndicalist and anarcho-syndicalist goals were more reformist than revolutionary: clearly defined job categories and pay scales, better wages, safer conditions, and shorter work days. This reduced the sense of threat they posed to employers and the state.

In Argentina anarcho-syndicalists took control of the main labor organization, the General Confederation of Workers (CGT) in 1915. Spearheaded by port workers and aided by the sometimes neutral or even mildly pro-labor stance of the Radical Civic Union (UCR) government, the confederation won a series of victories in Buenos Aires. For a Latin American state to be anything other than reflexively repressive of attempts to organize labor was highly unusual. Argentina was different because of a 1912 law that enacted universal male suffrage, the most immediate result of which was the election in 1916 of a UCR government under Hipólito Yrigoyen. The Radicals' need to keep the working-class vote, together with a pragmatic anarcho-syndicalist CGT leadership ready to cooperate with the state when it served the unions' purposes, promoted government intervention in labor disputes during the last years of the war that more than once favored the workers.

Even the Radicals, however, were not yet willing to grant broad legitimacy to labor or to consistently recognize its right to organize or bargain collectively. At most the government pressed employers to honor the agreements they had made with workers and to limit the more egregious use of violence and strike breakers. Under these circumstances, labor's wartime gains proved short-lived. Postwar inflation and unemployment promoted another round of worker–employer confrontations and renewed conflict, culminating in the infamous "Tragic Week" in January 1919. A strike by metal workers led to escalating police attacks, and then to the unleashing on working-class residential districts of bands of right-wing vigilantes, the Liga Patriótica, made up of the offspring of the elites together with thugs employed by factory and ship owners. In the wake of this violence the state did not immediately abandon the workers' interests, as many have supposed. But continued reactionary attacks by employers and their allies in the government, together with an economic downturn in 1920–21 and squabbling among various labor groups, soon crippled the unions. The anarcho-syndicalists had mistakenly interpreted the short-term political expediency of the UCR for a more permanent state commitment to neutrality and fair treatment in labor–capital conflicts.

Part of the reason that the state acted aggressively against labor in the 1920s, and this was the case in much of Latin America, was the Russian Revolution. Socialist ideas, activists, and parties had existed in Latin America from at least the late nineteenth century, but generally these did not prosper.

Attempts at electoral politics were frustrated by both the small size and internal divisions of the industrial proletariat and by a political system that allowed the socialists scant space. In the rare instances where these candidates won election, national assemblies commonly refused to seat them. Socialist newspapers were banned or heavily censored and the police regularly sacked and torched their headquarters and jailed, exiled, or deported their leaders. The Bolshevik triumph reinvigorated the revolutionary wing of the socialists, however, and in country after country during the late teens and 1920s these split off to form Communist parties. Most remained tiny and subject to ferocious if intermittent repression, and the parties tended to devote at least as much energy to internal factional struggles as to popular agitation.

More seriously, their evident dependence of Communist parties on the dictates of Moscow and the International greatly weakened their position among increasingly nationalist Latin American working classes. Ill-starred insurrections in El Salvador and Brazil in the early 1930s, the International's demand that Latin American workers cooperate in popular front governments with a local "bourgeoisie" that for decades had cracked their heads, and the Soviets' alliance with Hitler undermined popular confidence in the party. A political line that interpreted Latin America's situation as "feudal" and therefore not yet ready for revolution drove off many would-be adherents who hoped for rapid change. The Communist Party before World War II served as a convenient excuse for police crackdowns on labor and social activists, but in most Latin American countries it had little significant role in organizing workers or in leading the struggle to improve their situation.

Ironically, in the one case where genuine revolution did engulf a country before 1930, urban labor played an unimportant role. Simply in terms of numbers, this was probably inevitable. The Mexican Revolution was above all an uprising of peasants and rural workers bent on gaining access to land or improving their conditions on the haciendas and in the mines. What support they found in the cities came chiefly from the ruined artisans, adherents of a largely impotent anarchism. Despite the bloody repression of strikes such as those at Cananea and Rio Blanco in the years before 1910, the regime of Porfirio Díaz generally was more tolerant of demands by industrial workers than it was of those from the countryside. Mexico's minuscule industrial proletariat adhered not primarily to socialism or anarchism but instead made reformist demands. That is, they sought to improve their situation within the capitalist system, not to destroy that system. Urban labor generally supported Madero against rural unrest, and the members of Mexico City's Casa del Obrero Mundial (House of the World Worker) aligned themselves with Venustiano Carranza against the more radical Zapata and Villa. Once in power Carranza repaid this support by closing the Casa, and he greeted the pro-labor articles of the 1917 Constitution by not enforcing them. The economy, in any event, was in collapse in the last years of the decade, and labor was in no position to pressure the state or employers. In the 1920s and 1930s labor did gain strength but only as part of a bargain with a semi-authoritarian state that more often than not used the workers for its own interests.

Conclusions

The second half of the nineteenth century witnessed a remarkable increase in Latin America's integration into the world capitalist economy. Under the prevailing tenets of free trade, Latin America's role in this developing world division of labor was to supply raw materials and food for North Atlantic industry and for the consumption of the industrial working class and urban elites. Latin America also served as a market for Europe and, increasingly, North America's industrial exports. Though this latter role is often overlooked, for much of the century Latin America absorbed as much of England's exports as, for example, did all of Asia. But it was as a supplier of industrial raw materials and cheap food that Latin America was most evident. This had important effects on the region. Perhaps the best known of these is the way in which the rise of capitalism and political democracy in Europe had prompted the imposition or spread of retrograde, coerced labor systems on Latin America, including not just African slavery, but forced wage labor and debt peonage and the import of contract laborers. Moreover, European technology such as the railroad, the telegraph, and the repeating rifle allowed new Liberal regimes to impose an unprecedented level of control on the countryside after mid-century that facilitated coercive labor recruitment and limited the possibilities of even free labor to organize or to protest conditions.

There were wide regional variations in the timing and impacts of this incorporation process. In some cases—for example, Argentina and Brazil—new crops and new opportunities provoked large-scale international migrations that fundamentally altered population patterns. In others, such as Peru and Guatemala, new exports instead provoked massive internal migrations and the forced inclusion of much of the population in the wage sector. When, as for example with Peruvian guano or Chilean nitrates or Brazilian sugar, the exhaustion of resources or a changing technology or simply more efficient competition caused a local economy to collapse, it left isolated and impoverished areas that had once been prosperous and closely integrated into the world economy. This was particularly damaging where export production had destroyed or heavily damaged the local natural resource base or a pre-existing economy, leaving devastation in its wake.

Generally, Latin American urban labor had little success at organizing or in attempting to define or defend rights before 1930, and such efforts had no impact whatsoever on the countryside. Population growth, the volatility of the economy, and the immigration policies of some governments meant that by the early twentieth century, and in direct contrast to the previous three centuries, labor surpluses flooded many employment markets. This was aggravated in the 1920s as modern communications accelerated migration from the countryside to the cities. An oversupply of workers depressed wages and made strikes and bargaining almost impossible for all but the most skilled of the urban labor elites. Ethnic and cultural divisions further weakened efforts at working-class solidarity and allowed employers and the state to play upon a growing nationalist consciousness. Occasionally governments took a neutral stance, or even intervened to favor the workers, as, for example, when local labor struck a foreign-owned company such as the British railroads in Argentina. More commonly, though, Latin American Liberal regimes beat and shot workers in the interest of a "good business climate," and of attracting foreign investment.

The very volatility of these boom and bust economies, however, meant that on the upswings not only did the demand for workers increase, temporarily pushing up wages, but opportunities opened for individual social and economic mobility through job promotions or by shifting to work as petty entrepreneurs. Such mobility tended to validate the system and to reinforce reliance on individual initiative rather than cooperation. Coupled with often ferocious police repression and with worker organizations that sometimes were more interested in fighting among themselves than in advancing worker rights or improving working conditions, it is not to be wondered that early unions found it slow going.

Chapter 5

Work in Modern Latin America

T he effects of the Great Depression on the economies of Latin America were vastly uneven, depending on a particular region's main crops or products and on government policy. Central America provided a dramatic example of the first variable: in those areas dependent on bananas, local economies collapsed, whereas where coffee predominated growers continued to enjoy a relatively steady demand, if at reduced prices. In terms of policy, perhaps the most notorious example of state intervention was the Roca–Runciman Treaty of 1933, drawn up between Argentina and Great Britain: in return for guaranteed access to British markets for their wheat and meat, the Argentines abdicated any effort to protect domestic manufacturing from British imports. Ironically, Argentine industry grew nevertheless and by the early 1940s contributed more to the gross domestic product than did agriculture. Argentina was not alone.

The years from the Great Depression to the end of the twentieth century were marked by intense urbanization and industrialization in many areas of Latin America. Even the agricultural export sector was dominated more and more by large, highly capitalized "factories in the field," while food production for the domestic market remained mostly in the hands of impoverished peasants and small farmers squeezed by a declining resource base. Families expelled from the countryside by these changes fled to the urban areas, and adding to this population was a spiraling birthrate, the result of improved medical care and public health measures. Many of the cities' new inhabitants found work, if rarely prosperity, in industries that grew up to provide cheap goods for local consumers. Urban workers, and would-be workers, sought solutions to their poverty and to their political and social marginalization not chiefly in radical schemes, but in the multiclass politics of populism and in "bread-and-butter" unions. As the political sophistication of this population grew in the 1960s and 1970s and their demands escalated, military regimes intervened in country after country, in the name of "national security" and to assuage the fears of foreign capital and domestic elites. But the military proved no more able than civilian politicians to handle the growing problems, aggravated in the 1970s and 1980s by the world oil crises and falling commodity prices. The collapse of domestic industry, together with new tariff policies in the 1990s, threw thousands out of work. Many who only just had begun to claw their way out of poverty fell back into misery, dependent now on a Hobbesian "informal" economy.

Migrants, Industry, and Politics

The depression and the Second World War provided tremendous, if unanticipated and unsought, stimuli for import substitution industrialization in Latin America. Local manufactures replaced items the countries previously had imported but which falling export returns now made it impossible to buy or which changes in wartime priorities took out of circulation. Typical of such goods were inexpensive textiles, processed food and beverages, soap and paint, shoes, and agricultural tools. The potential or real advantages for Latin America of local industrialization included reduced expenditure of foreign exchange, diversification of the local economy against the vicissitudes of monocrop dependence, and new employment opportunities. Industrialization also brought, the argument went, new technology and "modern" values and ideas. But it was not without problems. The relatively small size and very limited buying power of most Latin American national populations meant that factories produced for tiny markets, raising unit costs and condemning consumers to higher prices and to generally poorer-quality products than the imports to which they were accustomed: Bolivian miners in the 1960s, for example, remembered a past when they had been able to buy sturdy English woolens in the company store, instead of shoddy local textiles. Such market limitations facilitated monopoly, which in turn encouraged corruption and contraband, undercutting government revenues. Domestic manufacture of consumer goods depended too on the import of foreign capital equipment, and sometimes raw materials and energy such as coal and oil, potentially aggravating rather than alleviating balance-of-payment problems.

Linked to industrialization, though not entirely dependent upon it, was urbanization. Latin America's cities grew rapidly in the twentieth century:

Latin American Cities[1] (in thousands)

City	1900	1930	1960	1990
Buenos Aires	664	2,149	2,967	2,960
Lima	130	281	1,262	5,706
Santiago	256	696	1,169	4,385
Bogota	100	235	813	4,921
Rio de Janeiro	811	1,469	3,307	5,473
Mexico City	345	1,961	2,832	8,235

Unlike the years around the turn of the century, however, this was largely the result of internal not international, migration. At the same time that depression and war cut off the flood of Europeans to the New World, the changing situation in much of Latin America's countryside and in the small towns accelerated the flow of people to the larger cities, and particularly to the national capitals. In terms of push factors, most important were the effects of the intersection of a rapidly growing rural population, a population that after 1945 began to benefit from some of the century's public health advances, and the continued spread of capitalist export agriculture. Cattle, for example, replaced peasants on the Pacific coast of Central America, and capital-intensive sugar production began to take over from relatively labor-intensive coffee in the uplands of São Paulo. More and more the countryside suffered what economists euphemistically labeled "unabsorbed labor capacity." Some rural families went to the frontier, to the Peruvian or Brazilian Amazon or to Mexico's or Ecuador's Pacific lowlands or to the Guanacaste peninsula of Costa Rica, but more often they headed for the cities. Urban life offered more than simply *movimiento* (action). Even the marginally employed could hope for education and rudimentary health care for themselves and their children, and in the cities there was the hope, fitfully realized, of getting ahead economically and socially. Together with the descendants of European immigrants, who were citizens as most of their parents had not been, migration from the rural areas "nationalized" the urban mass population of Brazil and Argentina, and filled new slums across the continent.

Though they were in the city, not all of these migrants were necessarily yet of the city. They brought with them traditional rural ideas of deference, hierarchy, and paternalism, values perhaps ill suited to the push and shove of the new metropolis. To the enormous frustration of activists who sought to draw these new city dwellers into unions and political parties that stressed horizontal class allegiances and solidarities, the recent arrivals tended instead to seek traditional and familiar vertical relationships with a powerful patron, typical of those between landowners and laborers. For this reason, factory owners, for example, commonly preferred recent immigrants from the less developed parts of the countryside. Many of those seeking work came recommended by others already employed in the plant or with letters from local notables in their home communities, and once they got a job they felt the need live up to these recommendations by cooperating with management. They were what one writer has called the "boss's people," and they often formed the core of pro-company, or "yellow," unions that opposed serious efforts at organizing or bargaining.

These were relationships of immense inequality and often brutal exploitation but also of not unbridgeable social distance. They offered the workers some security in return for patterns of behavior they understood. Migrants could sometimes replicate part of their rural experience in small artisan workshops, or on construction or labor gangs, or in primitive mills that survived because of tariff protection, but as more and more of them found work in modern factories or in huge meat packing and metal working plants ruled by the assembly line and Taylorism, old values applied less and less. Factory owners driven by capitalist rationality did not want the cost or the bother of personal involvement in the lives of their employees, had this even been possible with hundreds or thousands of workers. For their part, the workers found the social and economic distance between themselves and the owners increasing. If they sometimes made good money, at least compared to rural wages, the migrants nevertheless too often found themselves adrift in a world that seemed without solid morals or predictable behavior.

A working class cut loose from its familiar moorings, an economy turned upside down by world depression and war, and a national elite faced with the collapse of its traditional sources of wealth made the 1930s and early 1940s a turbulent period in Latin America. States cut services and employers cut wages, seeking to transfer to the poor as much of the cost of the economic disruption as possible. Workers, particularly in the cities, fought back with protests, strikes, and violence. Government responses varied: for example, simple repression in Argentina, Bolivia, or Central America; partial political inclusion of the urban population in Chile's Popular Front government; and incipient populism, a social and political phenomenon that would dominate much of Latin America for the next half-century, in Brazil and Peru.

The key element in populism was the charismatic leader who sought to replicate on a mass scale traditional hierarchical and personalist relations. His message rejected the necessity or inevitability of class conflict and substituted instead a call for cross-class cooperation under his direction. For the recently enfranchised urban poor he was a new but still a familiar figure who offered not only attention to their concerns but active incorporation into the body politic through their vote. To the elites he promised to defuse class tensions and integrate the urban masses without radical changes, and for the incipient middle classes he provided power and jobs, in the party and in an expanding state bureaucracy. Populism was primarily an urban phenomenon that depended on mass communications and the expansion of the political franchise. Even movements such as Víctor Raúl Haya de la Torre's American Popular Revolutionary Alliance (APRA) in Peru that gained strength in the countryside did so only after being driven from the cities by the intervention of the armed forces. Indeed, most populist leaders made few appeals to the rural population and specifically avoided addressing agrarian problems so as not to arouse the wrath of traditional elites. In Peru, for example, the military, not APRA, carried out land reform.

A number of politicians labeled "populist" gained power in Latin America during the years from the 1930s to the 1960s, and central to their success were urban workers and organized labor. Independent labor leaders and intellectuals in these years frequently, and loudly, despaired of the urban masses for their "false consciousness," their willingness to buy into populist programs rather than support class-based revolutionary parties and policies. Yet for all of his disingenuousness, the populist did pay attention to the urban lower classes and did deliver real benefits to them, something traditional elites had no interest in doing and ideologically driven fringe political groups could not do.

Brazil's Getúlio Vargas perhaps only fit the classic populist model after his election to the presidency in 1950, but the policies he enacted during the 1930s and 1940s epitomized for many populist labor relations. Those fragments of organized labor that had survived the repression of the 1920s played almost no role in bringing Vargas to power in 1930. Nevertheless, he quickly understood that times had changed and that in order to retain power he would need to address concerns beyond those of the old state political machines and regional bosses. Vargas saw urban workers as one among several groups, including also the *tenentes* (military reformers), the traditional military, and the organized political left and right, that he could play off against each other for his own purposes. This is why, even in the absence of effective pressure from below, Vargas created a new Ministry of Labor and pushed through provisions for government-administered pensions and disability insurance, as well as regulations on night, female, and child labor. These reforms were written into the 1934 Constitution, expanded under the authoritarian Estado Novo after 1937, and consolidated in the 1940s. Helpfully, some of the less sophisticated among the elites failed to understand the advantages to them of a state-directed labor system and opposed Vargas, raising his standing and the credibility of his policies with workers and the urban poor.

Brazil's 1943 Consolidation of Labor Law (CLT) spelled out a system of corporatist labor relations that has endured, if not without challenge, into the

1990s and has inspired widespread imitation. In a dramatic innovation, the state now not only allowed but encouraged unions to organize, but only those unions that the Ministry of Labor recognized and only those that the state could control, or at least limit. For each employment category there could be only one union local per municipality, the one local recognized by the state. These unions were "to collaborate with the public authorities in the development of social solidarity."[2] Their main task was to deliver to their members services such as medical and dental care, vacation facilities, and, eventually, retirement benefits. An *imposto sindical* (union tax), consisting of one day's pay, required of all workers not just union members, funded authorized union activities. The Ministry of Labor controlled collection and distribution of these monies, guaranteeing that they would not be used for unapproved activities, such as a strike fund. Strikes, in any event, now were illegal and in theory unnecessary because all labor–employer disputes were to go through an elaborate network of labor courts.

Union members elected their leaders, but the state could intervene in any union and force a change of directors, with the effect that many locals and federations came to be dominated by collaborationist *pelegos*, petty bosses who looked mostly to their own interests. Although workers were aware of the benefits available through the unions, many refused to join because of their disillusionment and disgust with corruption and boss rule. Or they affiliated just long enough to get union support for a complaint before the labor courts and then dropped out. At the same time that the state manipulated recognized unions, it cooperated with *pelegos* to crush independent organizations or rebellious currents within established unions.

When Vargas returned to power in 1950 he quickly found himself forced to test the limits of the system he had created. The effects of the Korean War disorganized the world economy, and markets for raw materials were erratic and prices depressed by the arrival of new African and Asian producers. Import substitution industrialization had saturated available local markets, high prices and mediocre quality made exports by these industries difficult, and producers and consumers alike were dependent on expensive credit, fueling inflation. Crisis loomed in 1954. In the absence of anything substantial to offer labor, Vargas ratcheted up his language of confrontation and elevated radicals in his government. But, confronted with growing rightist and military pressures linked to internal problems and to the international Cold War, Vargas refused to fall back on the working class and the urban masses that had voted for him or to attempt to arm or lead them for a genuinely revolutionary struggle. Instead, he chose a dramatic exit, committing suicide. By definition populists were not revolutionaries, whatever their rhetoric, and when confronted with a definitive political crisis in every instance they abandoned their supporters.

Only a year after Vargas's defeat, Juan Perón, president of Argentina and probably Latin America's best known practitioner of populists politics, also fell from power. Perón had come to office via the military, but he was far from the stereotypical Latin American military dictator. Even more so than Vargas, Perón's power rested in his relationship with labor. During the 1930s Argentina's conservative-military government crushed most of the labor organizations that had survived the 1920s. Though perhaps a third of the industrial work force still belonged to a union, the main confederation, the General Confederation of Workers (CGT), was split and ineffective, and real wages declined. At the same time, with imports reduced as a result of the depression, industrialization expanded, and the numbers of plants and workers increased by 50 percent. Conditions for workers were difficult. Employers routinely ignored the limited existing labor legislation, and the courts almost universally sided with capital. Simultaneously, the composition of Buenos Aires's population was changing, with a drop-off in the arrival of Italians and Spaniards and the inflow each year of thousands of *cabecitas negras* (dark-skinned mixed bloods) from the pampas and the far interior. Straight from the countryside, these new urban dwellers shunned unions and looked instead for a leader in whom they could trust and who would improve the precarious and hard conditions of their lives.

A military coup in 1943 produced such a leader. Colonel Juan Perón was not an important participant in these events, but he sided with the winners and as a reward was given the directorship of the relatively unimportant National Labor Department (later Ministry). Perón systematically built up the Ministry and with it his own political position, and he actively courted labor support. He pushed through legislation that expanded the social security system, froze rents, and provided for a thirteenth-month bonus, and he intervened directly in labor disputes to force recognition of unions and collective bargaining and to favor those unions that supported him. By 1945 workers were marching under the banner "In defense of the benefits received from the Minister of Labor."[3] When Perón's too evident political ambition led to a falling out with his military peers and to his arrest, organized labor turned out by the tens of thousands and marched to downtown Buenos Aires, demanding and gaining his release. For the next decade Perón-allied unions and confederations marked October 17, "The Day of Loyalty," with huge rallies. In 1946 Perón won the presidency. His support came from a populist cross-class alliance that included white collar workers, small and large industrialists, and those attracted to his nationalist position; but above all Perón depended on labor.

Labor was even more dependent on Perón. Indeed, the second half of the 1940s was something of a golden age for Argentine industrial workers, or at least those in the more advanced sectors that belonged to Peronist unions. The state followed a conscious policy of income transfer: wages and salaries in this period rose from 45.2 percent of the national income to 56.7 percent, and the unskilled, overwhelmingly recent migrants from the interior, benefited relatively most of all. The state set up agencies that bought wheat and beef from Argentine rural producers at controlled prices and then sold these abroad to war-ravaged Europe at what the market would bear, using the difference to subsidize programs for urban workers. Rural landowners accepted this expropriation in part because the political environment was clearly against them, but also, and despite the workers' gains, because they still were doing well. The government made no serious effort to enforce the rural minimum wage law, and Perón never addressed land reform.

In the cities Perón, aided by his wife Eva, worked aggressively to bring all labor within the fold of a Peronist Party and to eradicate independent union activity or political opposition. During 1951, for example, he drafted contentious railroad strikers into the army and put others under martial law. The Peronists intervened in obstreperous locals, replacing independent leaders with party loyalists, and dominated the CGT. Control of these organizations became increasingly bureaucratized in the hands of party and union hacks. Corruption, racketeering, and labor violence flourished. Corruption aside, labor clearly gained during Perón's first presidency, but the workers owed this to Perón personally and not to their own militancy or organized action.

Peronism was able to temporarily improve the situation of the urban working classes through a relatively painless transfer policy that demanded, and made, no fundamental changes in the country's economic structure or distribution of power. After 1950, however, Europe's recovery began to reduce the market for Argentina's products. Subsidized U.S. agricultural exports and PL 480 sales drove world prices down, while the Korean War and its resulting inflation raised the cost of finished goods. Decades of predatory growing and grazing techniques and a lack of capital reinvestment crippled Argentina's export agriculture, denying Perón the surplus he needed to maintain urban support. Faced with a declining economy, growing internal dissent, and the dictator's own increasingly bizarre behavior, the military stepped in and overthrew Perón in 1955. As the coup loomed, workers approached Perón to ask for arms to defend the government and their gains. Perón refused. He preferred going into exile, with the hope of an eventual return, to any serious effort to defend his government's reforms. Peronism had begun with the workers, and after 1955 whatever white collar or elite support it had garnered evaporated. This left Peronism again a working-class movement, but one that elite fraud and military repression denied any legitimate chance of achieving political power through elections.

The most successful of the depression-bred first-generation populists was Mexico's Lázaro Cárdenas, president from 1934 to 1940, and the reformist conscience of the Revolution until his death in 1970. Labor, and the working class in general, enjoyed a relatively strong political position in Mexico during the 1920s and 1930s, the result of worker participation in the Revolution and the remarkable 1917 Constitution. From Álvaro Obregón (1920–24) on, Mexico's new political leaders saw labor as one element in a political coalition they intended to construct in support of the revolutionary state, an element to be won over with concessions but also to be disciplined if it strayed from the official line. The first vehicle for this was CROM, the Mexican Regional Labor Confederation headed up by a young Luis Morones. Organized in 1918, CROM quickly allied itself with the national political leadership, putting state success first, the economic well-being of the CROM leadership second, and the welfare of the workers a distant third, and this only so long as it did not interfere with the first two priorities. CROM quickly became a byword for corruption, for deals with employers, and for union thuggery, going so far as to supply strike breakers to defeat actions called by independent unions. Under President Plutarco Elías Calles (1924–28) Morones became Minister of Labor, but by the end of the decade his and CROM's power were weakening, undercut by presidents that saw Morones as a possible rival.

Not until 1931 did the Mexican federal government pass the general regulations necessary to enable the labor sections of the 1917 Constitution, though individual states could legislate local labor relations and some had. A few state governments, Tabasco and Yucatan most famously, were radical in their advocacy of labor rights, but more often regulations favored capital. The 1931 National Federal Labor Law now outlined a national corporatist labor system not unlike that being assembled at the same time in Brazil. The law recognized unions, set a minimum wage for urban and rural labor, and provided a complex set of measures regulating collective bargaining. The federal government could declare a strike illegal and use force to end it, and it could require both parties in a labor dispute to submit to the binding arbitration of a government board. Workers were not to be summarily dismissed from their jobs because of union activity or for going on strike. The law did not require a closed shop, but workers who did not belong to the union or who had been expelled from it had no such protection, giving the union leadership considerable power to keep the rank and file in line. Employers collected workers' dues and handed these over to the union leadership, making bottom-up challenges difficult.

In 1933 Calles picked Cárdenas to be yet another of his presidential stand-ins but quickly found himself out maneuvered and exiled. Cárdenas then set about restructuring popular organizations, bringing these together under his control to support his vision of a centralized, reformist state. In common with the New Deal during these same years, Cárdenas's administration accepted that labor needed and deserved special attention because of its fragmented condition and because of a long history of state bias. Prolonged strikes and stoppages, however, could not be tolerated because they wasted resources the country needed to develop. Workers could initiate labor actions, but if these threatened serious disruption to the rest of the economy the state might step in to force a resolution. Independent labor activity, particularly activity that ignored or flouted government mandates, would be dealt with severely. Not until the 1940s did the federal government issue the infamous "Law of Social Dissolution," making it a crime to engage in any activity, including organizing independent unions or engaging in unapproved strikes, that threatened to "dissolve" Mexican society. But Cárdenas and the Party of the Mexican Revolution (PRM) (after 1946 the Party of the Institutionalized Revolution, PRI) made it clear in the 1930s that they intended to keep a tight rein on labor and to use it for what they defined as the good of the state, not necessarily that of labor itself.

This became clear during the most famous labor action of the 1930s in Mexico, the strike against foreign petroleum companies that led to the nationalization of that industry. Mexico's revolutionary governments since the 1920s had disputed concessions granted foreign companies during the *porfiriato.* By the early 1930s Mexican petroleum workers were infuriated that though they were more productive than those just across the border in Texas, they received lower wages. Mexicans fretted too about the decapitalization of the fields as oil companies shifted their investments to the Middle East and Venezuela, where politics was less troublesome. In response, the oil workers, aided by the new Confederation of Mexican Workers (CTM), formed a union, and in May of 1936 went on strike for higher wages. A government-appointed commission found in their favor, and the state demanded that the companies improve wages and conditions. Unwisely, the foreign companies went public with the dispute, taking out newspaper advertisements attacking Cárdenas and not too secretly lobbying for U.S. government intervention. This enraged Mexicans and provoked the nationalization of the oil fields in 1938, an act almost unprecedented anywhere in the world up to that time.

For the union and the oil workers nationalization turned out to be less than a complete victory. The government deemed a brief experiment with worker management to have failed and took over control of the industry, setting up a state-run company. With production now under government control, pay raises or improvements in conditions were not easy for the workers to obtain. Instead, the government used the petroleum workers' union to keep industry costs down, to help provide cheap energy for national development. The union hierarchy prospered, even as the once elite oil workers saw their wages fall relative to the cost of living. In general, CTM unions served primarily the interests of the state and only secondarily those of their members. Where these did not conflict, labor could and did make gains, even after 1940 when the governments tended to favor business and capital accumulation over labor rights.

Independent unions and labor confederations were allowed to operate in Mexico, if for no other reason than to show that the system was indeed democratic. The government watched their activities closely, however, and brutally reined in any organization or leader that threatened to disrupt the smooth functioning of the system. An occasional example sufficed. Best known was the fate of the railroad workers, whose unions from the 1920s had maintained a status apart from the official federations. Their central role in the economy and the difficulty of replacing these skilled workers with strike breakers gave them power few other labor groups shared. In the late 1940s the government finally succeeded in imposing a collaborationist, or *charro*, leadership on the main union, but in the 1950s the rank and file went out on strike anyway, protesting a 40 percent drop in real wages and unsafe working conditions on the undercapitalized state-owned lines. A modest initial victory was encouraging, and the workers, faced with continued state recalcitrance, followed this up with a general strike. The government declared the strike illegal, turned out the army to force the workers back onto the trains at gun point, and arrested thousands. The leaders received sentences of up to sixteen years in jail under the Law of Social Dissolution.

Despite state control and the occasional brutalities, populist politics did produce genuine improvements for labor. These governments recognized unions, and urban workers joined them at rates well above those of the United States. The more advanced sectors of industrial labor gained the right to bargain collectively and to strike, if with limitations, and workers benefited too from a range of social and labor programs, even though these were typically poorly funded and erratically enforced. These were real gains, and to deny them or to criticize the workers for accepting and celebrating them, out of some leftist repugnance with "reformism," ignores the difficult realities of the workers' day-to-day lives. Worse, it is elitism of the most insidious sort. Of course, populist unionism in Latin America was essentially a top-down phenomenon, dependent on the intervention of charismatic leaders and state bureaucracies. It often suffered a corrupt and coopted leadership that repressed activism and discouraged the rank and file from taking an active role in union affairs. Members learned that the unions could not defend them, only the state could. The state generally did so only under the conditions that economic and political elites allowed and only so far as this advanced the interests of these elites, not necessarily those of the workers.

Automobile Workers

No industry embodied the promise and problems of Latin American industrialization and of organized labor more than automobile production. Although dealers had assembled automobiles in various countries since the 1920s, it was not until the 1950s that automobile and truck manufacture could properly be described as an industry, and then only in Argentina, Brazil, and Mexico. During the 1960s a growing prosperity in the middle class, fueled in part by repressive state policies that redistributed income upward, increased the market for automobiles. Nationalist regimes sometimes put up protective tariffs and increased domestic content requirements, causing ripple effects through the rest of the economy. Nevertheless, the industry found it difficult to escape import substitution's problems and limits. Low incomes and uneven distribution of wealth ultimately restricted the demand for automobiles, as did the very high price of credit. Too many manufacturers and too many models raised unit costs and lowered efficiency. Even where domestic content laws resulted in greater local value added, manufacturers still had to import key tools and technology from abroad and pay licensing and patent fees to multinationals. This sent money overseas and ate up foreign exchange. Worse, the spread of automobiles meant huge increases in the demand for petroleum products: by the late 1960s even Mexico was no longer self-sufficient. Energy imports soaked up more foreign exchange, diverting funds that might otherwise have been used to import capital equipment or technology to develop other sectors of the economy.

Such problems not withstanding, automobile production and sales expanded dramatically in the 1960s and 1970s, and the workers in the automobile industry were a privileged proletarian elite. Analysts of Latin American labor have argued that whereas port and railroad workers took the lead in organizing and striking in the 1920s and 1930s, after World War II it was the workers in the metal and electrical industries that played this role, and first among the metal workers were those in the automobile plants. Their consciousness and willingness to strike were high for several reasons. Initially the industry paid good wages to attract skilled workers, but under the anti-labor policies of military and conservative governments of the 1960s and 1970s and as a result of deskilling in the plants, wages fell in real and relative terms. By the end of the 1970s mechanization of the assembly process meant that 70 percent of the work force was either semi- or unskilled, greatly reducing the workers' bargaining leverage and their income. Turnover in labor was high because of seasonal layoffs and because employers purposefully "rotated" the work force, firing those with seniority or those who could not keep up with the demanding pace of the assembly line. During the 1960s prices of automobiles fell by as much as 25 percent, opening new markets but cutting unit profits, and manufactures sought to regain these profits by speeding up production: output per worker doubled during the decade.

In May of 1969, Argentina's *cordobazo* gave notice of the role that metal workers, and automobile workers in particular, would play in national labor politics over the next decade. A series of short-lived military and civilian governments had alternated power in Argentina since the ousting of Perón. None found the formula to stabilize the economy or control inflation, and none were able to come to terms with the major industrial unions still dominated by Peronist partisans. Nevertheless, foreign capital found the business climate attractive, as multinationals bought up and rationalized the domestic industrial plant developed before 1955. The country's automobile industry more than quadrupled in output and benefited from new investments, new companies, and new models. With militant Peronists and left-wing labor activists forced underground, organized labor was divided between the accommodationist, or "Vandor" (named for the head of the powerful metal workers union), wing of Peronist unionism and a number of small and isolated unions, some of which were independent while others were "yellow" or company unions subservient to the bosses.

In Cordoba's automobile industry the most important group of organized labor was the Motor Mechanic's Union (SMATA). This union had not participated in Peronist politics and did not belong to the Peronist-dominated CGT. Instead, SMATA associated itself with the sort of "soft" or "bread-and-butter" unionism promoted by the American Institute of Free Labor Development. The AIFLD was an offshoot of the United States's AFL-CIO and funded by the CIA and the U.S. State Department to combat leftist labor in Latin America. The Frondizi government in the early 1960s had returned bargaining and labor agreements to individual plants, rather than permit the industrywide contracts characteristic of the years before 1955. The expectation was that this would fragment ↲ labor and disarm the Peronist confederations. What the state and employers missed, however, was the spread of factory floor, or internal, commissions. These were semi-secret small groups set up among rank-and-file union members in the plants that sought to organize on the job and that were hostile to both the government and their own accommodationist leaders. Plant level bargaining gave these commissions a concrete, visible target for their organizing and for worker anger, an anger disarmed at the national level by repression and by the exclusion of the Peronist party from politics.

When industrial conditions in Cordoba deteriorated after 1966, prompting mass layoffs and firings and attempts to increase productivity by cutting back on traditional rights, the automobile workers erupted in a series of strikes and plant occupations. Large segments of Cordoba's population, shaken by a declining economic situation and continuing political violence, joined them in what became known as the *cordobazo*, an urban uprising in 1969 that at one point occupied some 150 blocks of the downtown. In Buenos Aires automobile workers were but one group in a large industrial labor force and had remained largely under the control of the more accommodationist Peronists. In Cordoba, by contrast, the auto workers were by far the most important factor in the urban labor force, and the lack of integration of SMATA into the CGT at the national level allowed the local in Cordoba an autonomy unimaginable in a mainstream Peronist union. The military repressed the Cordoba outbreak, but over the following years agitation continued and escalated throughout the country, forcing the military to give power back to Perón.

Perón's triumphant return touched off a struggle for control of the Peronist labor movement, a struggle made dramatically clear by a gun fight that broke out among competing factions even before the leader left the airport. In exile he had promised everything to everyone, embracing union racketeers and urban guerillas alike. Now, if he had any hope of governing he had to choose, and each of the various factions meant to bring him down on their side. Although the workers accepted for the moment a "social pact" that limited wage increases, they began immediately to press other demands. Again, auto workers led the way. Their efforts met with some initial successes—for example, the end to a speedup at a General Motors plant—but it quickly became apparent that Perón's only real interest in labor was in recentralizing it under his control to further his political ambitions. A new "Law of Professional Organizations" put into effect in 1973 increased the power of the union bureaucracies at the cost of plant autonomy. In an important symbolic move, the government crushed the Cordoba branch of SMATA, intervening in the union and arresting the leadership. But when the economy collapsed in 1974, in part as a result of the world oil crisis, even accomodationist labor leaders had to take up rank-and-file demands. As a result, the union leadership "got the worst of two worlds: weakening the government of which it was the centerpiece without reestablishing its credibility with its membership."[4] When the military again seized power in 1976, the auto workers, with all Argentines, descended into the violence and squalor of the Dirty War.

Brazil had been under uninterrupted military rule since 1964, though this never resulted in the level of brutalities that the Argentines suffered. With Getúlio Vargas's suicide in 1954 not a few Brazilians imagined that the country had seen the end of populism and its tendency to encourage the expectations of the urban masses. In fact, though, death canonized Vargas, and for another decade Vargas-legacy populists won the presidency. Juscelino Kubitschek built Brasília and defied the International Monetary Fund, to the considerable pleasure of most Brazilians, but left an economy in ruins suffering an accelerating inflation rate. After the surprise resignation of Jânio Quadros, João Goulart, Vargas's Minister of Labor in the early 1950s, became president in 1962. The early 1960s witnessed a high level of union activity as workers struck repeatedly, in attempts to ward off the effects of spiraling inflation and in "political" strikes intended to support or oppose government policies.

By contrast, the years following the 1964 military coup are often rather euphemistically referred to as a period of "labor peace." Apart from brief and easily repressed outbreaks in 1968 at automobile plants in Contagem (Minas Gerais) and Osasco (São Paulo), organized labor was hardly visible at all. In part, of course, this was the result of simple repression. The government purged the unions, intervening in 67 percent of the confederations, 42 percent of the federations, and 19 percent of the locals, and activists were arrested, tortured, and killed or exiled. Strikes became almost impossible, falling from 302 in 1964 to 1 in 1970 and none the following year. The government reinstated *pelegos* and invited in the AIFLD to train a non-confrontational labor leadership. Real wages declined, for many workers by almost 50 percent between 1965 and 1973.

The relative quiet of Brazilian labor was the result of more than simply threatened or real violence. In the late 1960s and early 1970s the economy went through a period of unparalleled expansion known as the "Brazilian Miracle," with growth rates consistently above 10 percent a year. If wages generally failed to keep pace with inflation, economic growth broadened employment opportunities and offered many the possibility of moving up in job categories. Construction work in São Paulo and migration to the new Amazon frontier soaked up some of the society's poorest.

But for the auto workers this was not a good period, as inflation narrowed the wage differentials they previously had enjoyed over other industrial workers. In response, the Metal Workers' Union of São Paulo sought to expand its membership to be better able to oppose these tendencies, and the leadership revived the factory commissions that had been successful at shop floor organizing during the 1930s and 1940s. Then in 1977 an International Monetary Fund mission monitoring Brazil's economy for foreign investors revealed what long had been suspected: Minister of Finance Delfim Neto had used a figure he knew to be well below the actual rate of inflation when making 1973–74 wage adjustments. This fraud, in turn, undercut all subsequent adjustments. Anger now exploded among the workers, who demanded *reposição salarial*, a 34 percent increase to help make up for past losses, instead of the 20 percent the government had decreed. Broader demands included revision of the corporatist union structure, an end to obligatory dues, and the right to free and direct bargaining with the owners without intervention by the labor courts. Led by the metal workers of São Paulo's industrial neighborhoods, labor boycotted the official salary negotiations, and between May of 1978 and March of 1979 carried out a series of strikes and plant occupations.

By the late 1970s the military was following a course of democratization and a gradual return to civilian rule and was loath to deploy the full force of repression against the workers. Instead, it sought a more subtle way to end these confrontations. With a combination of threats and promises the government convinced a number of union locals in the interior of the state to agree to a compromise, and in the capital the government intervened in key unions and deposed elected leaders in favor of *pelegos*. Demoralized, the metal workers settled but demanded and won the return of their more militant leadership. The outcome was a strategic if not a tactical victory for the workers because they had forced the companies and the state to accept face-to-face negotiations, bypassing the corporatist labor court system. Nevertheless, the government effectively ignored this. When Congress rewrote the constitution in 1988 as one of the final steps in the return to civilian rule, the new document included the familiar unitary, state-recognized unions, the *imposto sindical*, and the arbitration system.

In fact, the late 1980s was a turning point for Brazilian unionism, made clear in the changing situation of the main labor confederation, the Central Único dos Trabalhadores (CUT). Growing out of the struggles in the late 1970s and early 1980s the CUT was founded in 1983 as part of a "new unionism" intended to free workers of CLT corporatism. Beyond this, from 1983 to 1988 the CUT, lead by the combative metal workers of São Paulo, was at the center of the struggle for *diretas já* (direct elections), an end to military dictatorship or pseudo-civilian governments picked to please the military, and a return to genuine democracy.

The first free elections in 1989 brought to power a government committed to neoliberalism in a populist guise. Confronted with this unexpected result of its struggle to reestablish civilian rule, the CUT, and labor in general, split. One part, Força Sindical, a confederation cobbled together of many small unions, typically from the interior and with relatively unsophisticated leadership, allied itself with the government. Another more radical faction, Articulação Sindical, took control of the CUT in 1991. But seeing no viable alternative, this group also broadly accepted the triumph of neoliberalism while still seeking to defend workers' rights and the welfare state, rooted in

Vargas's 1930s corporatism. Ironically, the "New Unionism" of the early 1980s turned to the CLT in the 1990s to attempt to protect the workers. Put on the defensive, the CUT leadership was forced to concede a central role for foreign capital in the economy and to accept the need for "efficiency," that is, mass firings, to rationalize domestic industry. In only one of many ironies, unions now lobbied for a tax cut for the automobile manufacturers, to broaden the market and keep their jobs. The CUT advocated "participation" rather than confrontation, proposing, for example, "sectoral chambers" that would involve the state, employers, and workers in the discussion of reforms. Generally the state and the factory owners ignored such ideas, and by the mid-1990s the CUT was reeling under the blows of the Plano Real and the popularity of President Fernando Henrique Cardoso.

The experience of Mexico's automobile workers differed markedly from that of either Brazil or Argentina. On the one hand, although the unions operated in a corporatist structure not altogether unlike Brazil or Perón's Argentina, they enjoyed considerably more autonomy, so long as they did not challenge the PRI or threaten the smooth working of the economy. Bargaining was direct, and labor conflicts went to the arbitration boards and the courts only when negotiations failed. Mexican unions never suffered the widespread repression characteristic of Brazil after 1964 or the violence of Argentina in the late 1970s. Instead, the state kept the unions, and labor in general, under control with real benefits and imaginative cooptation. Only occasionally did the PRI resort to exemplary violence, such as the repression of the railroad strike or the 1968 Tlatelolco massacre. The CTM after 1940 worked closely with the state and employers, allowing itself only an occasional display of independence intended to impress its members. Few were fooled. *Charro* leaders continued to dominate most locals, doling out favors and enforcing discipline.

In the automobile industry, however, the dispersal of the assembly plants to various parts of the country, together with a tendency to recruit workers from among regional populations, created opportunities for some locals to develop apart from central CTM tutelage. Echoing the experience in Argentina and Brazil, shop floor organizing below the level of the coopted leadership grew in importance in the 1960s and 1970s. The foci of protests were the familiar ones of wages, union democracy, and job security. This later was of particular importance in Mexico because of the rights to employment stability assured long-term workers under the 1917 Constitution and subsequent labor laws. Employers tried to evade this obligation by hiring large numbers of temporary workers when production was on the upturn and firing them when it slacked off, effectively churning the work force so that no one could claim the benefits of long-term employment. Despite the CTM's well-deserved reputation for "yellow" unionism, researchers working on the automobile industry have found wide variations in the independence or cooptation of local CTM leaders and in their willingness to struggle for workers' rights. These differences seem to have more to do with immediate work environment and the specific historical situation of each plant than any simple equation that labels all CTM unions as *charro* and all independent unions as tireless defenders of workers' welfare.

Indians and Miners

One of the first activities taken up by the Spanish in the New World had been mining, but the industry underwent major changes during the nineteenth century. Most obviously, much of the activity shifted from precious metals to the production of raw materials for industry. Although silver mining continued, massive discoveries in the western United States and the shift of North Atlantic countries to the gold standard eliminated marginal silver operations and directed entrepreneurial interests to other possibilities. Nowhere was this more evident than in Bolivia (colonial Upper Peru). By the late nineteenth century the wealth of Potosí was less than that of the tin mines around nearby Oruro, soon among the world's most important suppliers. In 1877 many of the small mines in the area were consolidated into the Cia. Minera de Oruro, and foreign capital, first from Chile and then from Europe, reorganized and rationalized the industry.

The first workers in the tin mines were Indian peasants fleeing the brutal poverty and serf-like conditions of highland haciendas or the narrow horizons of traditional communities. The men labored in independent gangs under the leadership of a *pirkiñero*, a specialist in finding tin ore. Conditions were hellish: "The men crawled to their work places on their hands and knees. We didn't have helmets. We lived like pigs. They didn't want the workers to live like human beings; they didn't want civilized people."[5] Pay depended on the tin content of the ore they extracted, so instead of building systematic shafts and adits, the miners followed the twists and turns of the vein, with only haphazard attention to supports and exposed to the constant possibility of a collapse. On the surface female *palliris* sorted the ore by quality before sending it for refining. Companies commonly paid workers in a scrip redeemable only at the company store, and because of the isolated situation of many of the mines the companies also provided what limited social services the miners enjoyed. Even government reports noted the abysmal state of housing and sanitary facilities, as well as the effects of overcrowding and disease. Efforts by the workers to organize or to protest for better pay or conditions were met by armed violence from the mine guards, the police, and the army. The years between 1910 and 1949 witnessed an almost uninterrupted history of violent repression and a succession of mine massacres.

In 1952 a popular uprising led by the tin miners and dissident soldiers overturned the government and brought to power the National Revolutionary Movement (MNR), a political alliance more populist than its name implies but one nevertheless committed to basic change. The new regime nationalized the tin mines and carried out land reform that effectively destroyed most traditional highland haciendas. More remarkably, the MNR set up a system of co-governance in which it shared state power with the Bolivian Workers' Confederation (COB), dominated by the miners' union. This alliance lasted only a few years, and in truth the workers never had more than a partial veto power over state policy, and the MNR quickly began to build up peasant groups as a counterweight to the mine workers, but the situation nevertheless was a remarkable turnabout. Even as they lost power, the miners remained an important element in national politics at least until the 1964 military coup.

In the early 1960s the government began to borrow abroad to recapitalize and modernize the mines. The changes had wide ranging effects on the miners' lives. For example, pneumatically operated mechanical drills replaced the old hand drilling. While this might appear to be to the men's advantage, the reality was something else. The drill weighed as much as the man who handled it and had to be held above and in front of the operator for long periods, causing enormous stress on the body. Vibrations from the drill so numbed workers that they failed to notice even cuts and injuries from falling rocks. The workers chewed coca, to dull pain and because they believed that it cut down on the absorption into their lungs of the smoke and silicates stirred up by drilling and blasting, but they also knew that prolonged use of the drug threatened an encounter with the demons of the mines. New safety masks clogged up and replacement filters were not available, and because protective glasses fogged up and the operator could not take his hands off the machine to clean them, they were of little use. There are no latrines in the mines, and the only water available was in the tubing for the drill. Technology served the machine, not the worker. Finally, the impact of new technologies was uneven: workers might receive an upgraded machine but find that there were no replacement parts available, or one segment of a process might be mechanized and not the others, leading to bottlenecks, failures, and frustrations. Managers attributed any failure to meet assigned quotas to "lazy" and "backward" Indian workers.

Worst of all, mechanization brought unemployment. One of the requirements for the foreign recapitalization loans in the 1960s was a reduction in the admittedly bloated work force, and over the decade thousands of miners were fired. This resulted in no savings of labor costs, however, because the government continued to use the state mining company as a source of patronage, adding relatively highly paid but useless bureaucrats to the staff even as it let miners go.

Particularly hard hit by the employment cuts were women. Though not a numerically significant part of the total work force, women lost almost all their places when the mines shifted to a new refining process that dispensed with the ore sorters. Most of these women were desperately poor widows of miners, and after some pressure they won the right to pick through abandoned slag heaps for ore that might now be valuable with the more efficient processing techniques. Broadly, though, the concerns of women received little attention from either the government or the unions. Subject to the "double day" typical of poor women in industrial economies, female mine workers found it difficult to participate in union affairs, and when they tried the men gave them little attention. One remembered that as soon as she rose to speak at a union congress the men began to talk among themselves and ignored her.

Behavior of this sort by the men was the product of both ideology and guilt. Machismo determined "The man at work, the woman in the home." Unfortunately, men's salaries that had supported a family in the 1940s no longer did so in the 1970s, and even overtime and working seven days a week just kept the families at subsistence. Men, and this was hardly unique to the miners, took out on women what they felt to be their own failures, denying women opportunities and abusing them verbally and physically. The unions showed little interest in women's problems and ignored altogether the contribution women's cooperatives and housewives' associations made to weathering strikes or simply to sustaining the family. Widows and orphans in particular needed opportunities to work, opportunities denied them by state policies and by the indifference or discrimination of male workers.

Mining is a particularly gendered form of work in most societies. This manifests itself at two levels. On the one hand, recent research on Chilean copper mining, for example, shows that men framed their relationship to the mine in gender terms, depicting it as a "threatening, consuming and vengeful female presence."[6] The men penetrate the mine, but it envelopes, drains, and consumes them. In response, the miners stress their strength and physical abilities, qualities that translate into both competition between mining gangs to produce the greatest output and also into resistance to the demands of supervisors and to the requirements of company culture. Above ground the men stressed a rough masculinity, fueling a world of drinking, gambling, domestic abuse, and sexual relations outside of marriage. Miners could be distinguished from "ordinary" men by their flashy clothing, free spending, and macho assertiveness; their heroes were those that successfully flouted the law and the company, for example, bootleggers. Many of the women drawn to the mining camps were similarly deviant, coming not to marry but to earn money in the bars and illegal brothels. This translated into an unruly and conflict-laden working and home environment. Efforts by employers, the state, and unions during the 1930s and 1940s to convince miners of the advantages of "bourgeois domesticity" or "proletarian morality" had scant success.

The "Informal" Sector

Urban residents, particularly women, unable to find employment in factories or shops commonly sought survival in the "informal" or "tertiary" sector: petty commerce, home handicrafts, domestic work, and crime. A study of one large Latin American city in 1960s, for example, found that while only 7.1 percent of the women had steady employment in the regular wage sector, 16.8 percent worked as servants and 14.5 percent were involved in small-scale commerce. As Latin American economies deteriorated in the 1970s and 1980s, more and more men and women found themselves cast into the informal economy.

According to some analysts this is not necessarily a bad thing. The Peruvian economist Hernán de Soto received favorable publicity, especially among North American conservatives, for championing the informal sector. Freed of state bureaucracy and controls, he posited, small-scale enterprises in poor areas flourished and demonstrated that free markets and market competition worked. This, of course, ran directly counter to decades of arguments that said that only with government protection and subsidies, or even with state ownership, could Latin American industry develop. Prosperity and modernization would come, it was now argued, from the privatization of state-owned enterprises, a lifting of controls and restrictions, the breaking of union power to protect workers' jobs and wages, and the freeing up of international flows of trade and capital. Except for the reduced role of government, the formula was not much different from that which the International Monetary Fund had touted for decades. However, it ignored the reality that where the informal sector had genuinely prospered this was due in large part to state assistance in areas such as credit, training, and marketing. But in the 1980s the market-driven approach now christened neoliberalism triumphed in international aid circles and among many Latin American economic and political elites. In Bolivia the government called its version, with no apparent irony, the "New Economic Plan."

Burdened by debt, racked by hyperinflation, with its exports in crisis and its politics and society corrupted to the core by cocaine money, Bolivia in the mid-1980s was a disaster. The left and the unions were in disarray and the COB had lost most of its influence. In 1985 the miners' old ally the MNR returned to power but now as a rightist coalition bent on a market overhaul of the economy. When the COB called a general strike to protest austerity measures, the government declared a state of siege and cut employment rolls of the state-owned mining companies from 30,000 to 7,000. Over the next several years the MNR continued to press the unions, which found it harder and harder to respond effectively or even to survive. Long-established protective labor legislation was swept aside, and enterprise after enterprise shut its doors, putting workers on the street.

State policy and the deteriorating economic situation worked together to disaggregate Bolivian social and economic life. The solidarity of the mine or the factory gave way to a scramble of street vendors and petty hustlers one against another. Numbers of "businesses" multiplied even as earnings plummeted, so that by the early 1990s incomes were roughly two-thirds of what they had been in 1987. Buying a pack of cigarettes and reselling these one at a time or hawking combs and pencils off a tray or guarding cars are not capitalist enterprises but simple subsistence, or more commonly sub-subsistence, activities. Artisans lacked the capital to acquire tools or raw materials and suffered ruinous competition as a constant stream of the newly unemployed entered the labor market, and from finished goods smuggled in from outside the country. This was not capitalism but an economy of lawlessness and strife, ruled by contraband and by drug money.

As the work environment deteriorated, people tended to fall back for support on their families and neighbors. One of the problems that undermined workers' efforts to resist state and employer pressures was the very number and variety of groups and protests that appeared after 1985. Not just trade unions but women's groups, indigenous organizations, neighborhood associations, cooperatives, and a multitude of other interest and pressure groups filled the streets day after day, weakening the impact of each protest. More importantly, the struggle for day-to-day survival occupied so much time and energy that it allowed scant space for social interaction or political involvement. All was competition. People had no time or thought for the well-being of others or for larger political or social problems. Agriculture was collapsing, undercut by illegal imports and by food aid from the United States. Rural survivors fled to the towns. By the early 1990s half the population of Bolivia was in the cities, and one-third of the households were female-headed, as men sought seasonal work elsewhere or simply deserted their families.

A study of Mexico City in the 1970s found similar conditions. Because agricultural modernization displaced women faster than men and because industrial jobs opened for women more slowly, many found their only recourse was street vending or domestic service. Some of the street sellers were Indian women from the rural areas who made short trips to the city to hawk agricultural products and handicrafts. More typically, though, the vendors were older women already established in the city and with children, and perhaps a husband, who made it difficult for them to fit the narrow confines of domestic work. On a good day they could earn more than their male companions, most of whom did casual construction labor. Street vending had the tremendous advantage, too, that it allowed the women to keep their children with them, and it was work that could be picked up and dropped on short notice, something their primary roles as wives and mothers demanded. Though they suffered ferocious competition among themselves and harassment by shop owners and the police, most preferred street vending to the other forms of low-wage work because of the personal freedom it gave them and because of the chance occasionally to make more money.

The main problem street vendors faced, apart from competition, was hostile intervention by the state. In the mid-1980s, for example, the Mexico City government began a crackdown on street vendors to win political support among small business owners and to collect taxes to help shore up municipal revenues. No new vendor licenses would be issued, and authorities attempted to herd street sellers into approved zones or markets. These efforts failed, and by 1993 the number of vendors on the streets of the capital had doubled to some 200,000. To protect themselves and advance their interests the street sellers organized into dozens of associations. Though they continued to compete fiercely among themselves for space and facilities, the vendors found that they could cooperate to deal with the state. They soon discovered that their best approach was not confrontation but instead to seek powerful patrons within the political structure to advocate for them. The multiplicity of bureaucratic agencies in the government, as well as splits within the PRI, and the recent rise of relatively successful opposition parties, all anxious to build up client bases, gave the vendors multiple points of entry into the system and various axes of leverage. While none of this alleviated the misery that had driven these men and women into the streets to survive, it did indicate that even at this level, and in an environment of limited democracy, people could sometimes extract concessions, if not justice, from the state.

"Muchachas" and Maquiladoras

Though poor young women in Latin America might dream of becoming successful street vendors or factory operatives, most of those employed outside of the home have always done domestic work. In recent years there has been a growing tendency for servants to live out and work on a daily basis, but traditionally most servants in nonslave societies have been young women recruited from the countryside to live with families. Particularly in middle- and lower-middle-class households where social boundaries might be less clear and a servant's duties more diversified, these women could occupy a liminal situation. On the one hand, their employers sometimes treated them, and encouraged them to think of themselves, as "part of the family," sharing the wife's most intimate secrets and encouraged to study or otherwise im- prove themselves. Of course, they were not children but, at best, dependents. Whereas the real children grew and moved on, the servant, unless she mar- ried and left, remained forever a *muchacha* (girl). Even partial incorporation demanded near absolute submission, manifested not uncommonly in sexual use by the men of the family. For women who could accept the social values of dependence and paternalism, the security of guaranteed room and board and a small cash wage might be attractive, or at least their best option. Those who adapted and learned to identify with new urban values commonly felt that they had improved themselves beyond their compatriots just arriving from the countryside and even their own families. At any rural festival it was easy to spot girls visiting from their town jobs by their short skirts, high heels, conspicuous makeup, and sophisticated mannerisms. But, the personal costs were high. Most young women hoped that domestic work would be only a short-term expedient to help relieve economic pressure on their fami- lies or a stepping stone to better employment in the cities or to marriage.

A study of female servants in Santiago, Chile, during the 1970s and 1980s found that because most of these women came from the countryside, the chief factor affecting supply was the condition of the rural economy. Be- tween the 1930s and the 1960s half the female jobs in agriculture disap- peared, while the rural population overall more than doubled. The result was a tremendous "underutilization" of labor and a strong push for out-migration. The early 1970s land reforms of Unidad Popular temporarily slowed this rural exodus, but with the post-1973 counter-reform huge numbers fled the countryside, only to discover that an impoverished Santiago had few jobs to offer them, even in domestic service. Not until the end of the decade and in the early 1980s as the economy turned around did the demand for servants improve. Some families now had better incomes and could again afford do- mestic help, while in other cases middle-class women were entering or reen- tering the work force and needed someone to take care of the house. Ironically, as the economy rebounded the number of women available for domestic work declined. Because for most women domestic work was a last resort, the supply of servants tended to be counter-cyclical, expanding when the economy fell and tightening as the situation improved and other types of work became available.

A lucky few among Latin America's female workers do find work that is better paid and higher status that domestic work or street vending. Generally this is no longer in such traditional industries as textiles or food processing, where mechanization continues to eliminate jobs and unemployed men displace women. Rather, in the 1970s and 1980s a pool of dexterous and docile young women trained from birth to obey males became increasingly attractive to multinational companies fleeing the unions and environmental controls of North America and Europe. Mexico was particularly well situated to benefit from these so-called "runaway shops," though in recent years new plants, or reorganized old industries, have sprung up from Central America to Chile to take advantage of this cheap labor. One area that expanded rapidly was the production of high-value agricultural products for export, including flowers, wine, specialty vegetables, and fruit. Both Colombia and Guatemala, for example, developed huge trades in cut flowers.

In Mexico, U.S. companies established plants to process winter vegetables and fruits for the North American market. Typical was the strawberry packing industry, where most of the labor was female. Overwhelmingly these were single women between the ages of 15 and 24 who had never worked before and still lived with their parents. About 80 percent of the workers destemmed strawberries on a piecework basis, while the rest sorted and boxed the fruit and were paid by the hour. An exceptional destemmer could earn more than the hourly workers, but most of the women saw a transfer to a job paid by the hour as a promotion, because it involved less stress and more stability. While wages for the packing-house workers remained well below national legal minimums, the money was nevertheless more than could be had in other local factories or at shop work or in agricultural labor.

A potential problem for the women was the seasonality of work in the strawberry plant, which commonly left them unemployed for months each year. Yet three-quarters of them did not seek other employment during the down time. These women probably would not have entered the wage labor force at all had not the increasingly respectable work in the packing plants been available. The income they earned was important to their families not so much for survival but because it allowed them to buy otherwise unaffordable consumer goods.

Although some of the young women remarked that they enjoyed being at the factory more than staying home in the villages, they were very clear that the purpose of employment was not self-realization through work. Self-realization, and the chance of a better life, would come through marriage and motherhood. Factory labor had become a stage or a rite of passage in a girl's life, a step on the way to her real goals. It is not surprising, then, that apart for some new measure of self-confidence, work in the packing plants did not lead the young women to challenge traditional values nor did it fundamentally alter the situation of women in the local society. Sadly, the factories accepted few workers from among older women, those widowed or abandoned or who had families to support and who needed the work. Children caused problems, and young women were thought to be more pliable. Finally, and paralleling the experiences of many of Mexico's male workers, the plants had employee unions, to which about half of the women belonged, but these were firmly in the employers' camp and did little to improve wages or workplace conditions.

More important than agriculture in recent years in employing cheap female labor for export production have been the so-called *maquiladoras*. These are plants that assemble parts and semi-finished pieces shipped from the United States for reexport back across the border. The 1984 Caribbean Basin Initiative spread these plants to Central America and the Caribbean, but the first and still the most visible *maquiladoras* remain along the U.S.–Mexico border, where in some cases conveyor belts directly link "sister" plants on opposite sides of the frontier. From the 1940s to the early 1960s Mexico each year sent tens of thousands of temporary male workers to the United States under the *bracero* program, chiefly for agricultural labor. When the program ended in December 1964, the Mexican government already had begun to cast about for alternative ways to soak up unemployment in the North. What caught its attention were recent changes in U.S. tariff regulations that allowed the export of partially finished goods from the United States to be processed by overseas labor and then reimported, paying taxes only on the "value added," which, with low wages, was minimal.

In 1965 Mexico created its Border Industrialization Program, meant to attract processing and finishing plants to the country's northern states. The results were not exactly what the government had anticipated. Over the next decade the *maquiladoras*, as these plants came to be known, generated more than 80,000 jobs, but high birthrates and massive migration nevertheless doubled the unemployment rate in the border towns. And the jobs created were not for the male refugees from the terminated *bracero* program but for young women. Figures placed the labor force in the *maquiladoras* during the 1970s and 1980s at 85 to 90 percent female. Electronics and domestic goods industries preferred younger, better educated girls at slightly higher wages, while the apparel factories employed older, less well educated women and paid them less. Low as the wages were, these were the best paying jobs on the Mexican side of the border and fantastically above what could be earned in the small towns of the interior, from where most of the women came. They could make more at illegal work across the frontier, but this was perceived as more dangerous and not something most families would want a young girl to do.

As with the strawberry workers, the women of the *maquiladoras* sought work for the income it promised and not for personal liberation or fulfillment, and they continued to see their best hope for a better future in marriage. Once married, few thought they would continue work and few did, and they did not return to wage employment after their children grew up, unless forced to do so by widowhood or desertion. What set them apart from the women in the strawberry packing plants was the importance of the money they earned. For fully half of the workers in the border factories their wages made up half or more of their family's income, and 20 percent of the women headed up their own households. The majority of the men in *maquiladora* households, by contrast, were under- or unemployed. Thus, for these women work was not about a new TV or a couch but food on the table.

In this light, it is perhaps startling how little their experiences changed the outlook or perspective of female *maquiladora* workers. Differential employment opportunities did generate or exacerbate generational and gender tensions in some households, but overwhelmingly the young workers brought their wages home and turned the money over to their mother or father, and they continued to take direction from their families. Work, then, even in a modern industrial setting, did not immediately undermine traditional values. The young women saw their time in the *maquiladoras* not as a career or as the first step in upwardly mobile employment, but as a stage in their lives, and hopefully a brief one, on the way to marriage and a family.

Given a high turnover in the work force and a lack of long-term commitment among the workers to wage labor, even those unions not collaborating with employers found it hard to organize or mobilize the women in the *maquiladoras*. Like the female Bolivian miners, the *maquiladora* workers suffered too from the "double day," for as wives, mothers, or daughters they found domestic chores waiting for them when they got home. Few had the time or energy for involvement in union affairs, and if they tried to participate the men commonly refused to take them seriously or actively opposed them as a threat to male control. Even male union activists anxious to work with the women tended to see labor problems in class rather than gender terms and to have only a limited idea of the specific problems the women faced.

Of course, attitudes and situations can change. After a slowing of growth and even some dismissals in the early 1980s, Mexican *maquiladora* employment rebounded strongly in the second half of the decade and the early 1990s, spurred by the North American Free Trade Association (NAFTA). The numbers in the sector doubled between 1988 and 1996, and today more than 3,000 *maquiladoras* employ 500,000 to 900,000 workers. In effect, what occurred in these years was the "maquilazation" of much of the Mexican national economy, with 27 percent of manufacturing workers today employed in *maquiladoras*, as against 7 percent in 1985. With this expansion there have come changes in the work force. Although women still predominated, in the 1990s they made up only about 60 percent of *maquiladora* labor. High unemployment among men has changed the definition of "women's work." Nor are the female workers the uniformly young, "daughters of family" they were in the 1970s. With experience and the maturing of the labor force women *maquiladora* operators are now more likely to be married, with children, and as many as one-third head their own households. And they are less likely than before to accept the dictates of the men in their lives. In October of 1997 female *maquiladora* workers at a Hyundai Motors feeder plant in Tijuana voted for the first time to join a union independent of the CTM, one that might seriously work for their benefit.

Similar challenges to gender relations are occurring in other parts of the region, for example among the populations of the Spanish-speaking islands in the Caribbean. A particularly dramatic example is Puerto Rican low-wage export industry. Female workers predominate, but fully three-quarters are over age thirty and two-thirds are married. When queried, most felt that wage work gave them more "rights" in their marriages and more independence. Rights at home, however, did not necessarily translate into militancy in the work place, and in Puerto Rico unionization of the labor force has dropped from 20 percent in 1970 to 6 percent in 1988 as the sugar industry declined. The International Lady Garment Workers' Union (ILGWU) constantly urged caution on the women, fearing that labor demands would prompt employers to move yet more apparel jobs offshore. Where this has occurred, in what observers label the "race for the bottom"—that is, to the lowest possible wages and costs—many of the earlier patterns have reappeared: by the early 1990s, for example, there were some 400 *maquiladoras* in Guatemala City, employing tens of thousands of mostly young women. The familiar complaints of long hours, dangerous conditions, and verbal and physical, including sexual, abuse were commonplace. In Guatemala, however, the usual response to attempted unionization was not cooptation or harassment but murder, or the plants simply packed up and left: "swallow industries" the Guatemalans called them. Of thirteen unions active in the early 1990s only three remained by 1996. Under such conditions one now finds *sub-maquiladoras*, small shops subcontracting to the larger plants and characterized by even worse conditions.

Organizing the Countryside

Despite the growing flood of migrants to the cities, the majority of Latin America's population after World War II continued to live in the countryside and small towns and to make its living from agriculture and stock raising. For most of the century any effort to organize these rural workers and peasants was either illegal or impossible in practical terms. The decades of the 1930s and 1940s generally witnessed either conservative civilian or military governments that brooked no organized opposition or populists who won cooperation, or at least tolerance, from landed elites by promising to keep their hands off the countryside. Where the state was ambivalent about rural organizing, large landowners and local power brokers deployed their own legal and extra-legal measures to keep workers and tenants under control. The poor could see little alternative to the existing system. Most were dependent for their livelihood on the landholders or on the owners of the mills and the low technology artisan shops that constituted the only alternatives to agricultural labor in rural areas. Even those who had their own small parcels of land needed the credit and transport services supplied by local intermediaries linked to the elites. Rural inhabitants tended to live either dispersed over the countryside, making contacts and coordination difficult, or clustered on the haciendas or villages, under the watchful eye of the landowners' representatives and agents of the state. The pre–Liberation Theology church made it clear too to the rural poor that God had put the powerful in place for his own inscrutable reasons and they were not to be challenged. Only the spread of buses and trucks in the 1950s and the diffusion of radio, and particularly in the 1960s the appearance of cheap transistor radios, began to break down rural isolation. Without positive state action to guarantee popular democracy and limit the power of local elites, however, such growing awareness only provoked frustration for many, typically manifested in migration to the cities. For decades the most aware and active of those in the countryside responded to the limits and oppressions of their lives by leaving.

It is important in this context to understand the difference between rural workers and peasants. This may seem obvious, but it entirely escaped early 1960s theorists of the Cuban Revolution who interpreted events on the island as a "peasant" uprising and as a result encouraged doomed *foco* guerrilla movements across the continent. Twenty years later the distinction caused problems for the Sandinistas in Nicaragua. Even before the overthrow of Somoza, the Sandinistas had constituted the Association of Rural Workers (ATC) as one of several popular organizations meant to give the movement institutionalized support. Despite its name, the ATC welcomed, and indeed recruited, both rural workers and peasants, and such policies led to difficulties. Workers and peasants typically want different things: rural workers tend to have much the same goals as urban workers, that is, higher wages, better working conditions, job stability, and opportunities for upward economic and social mobility for themselves and their children. By contrast, peasants want land, and unless they are part of an established tradition of communal ownership, they want that land as individual private property. Once they get it they tend to lose interest in any broader "revolution" and, indeed, often become fearful that further social or political change might threaten their property. While it took the Sandinistas some time to work this out, the United States clearly intended that the land reform it imposed upon El Salvador in the early 1980s should create thousands of small rural proprietors who, it was hoped, would oppose the left and force an end to the civil war.

Probably the best-known efforts to organize tenants and rural workers in postwar Latin America were those in Brazil. Communists and Catholic church activists battled for souls and votes in rural São Paulo during the 1950s, but it was the Peasant Leagues that received the most attention. Although during a brief period of legality from 1945 to 1947 the Brazilian Communist Party had organized hundreds of such leagues in the countryside, these had little life of their own, and most disappeared in the post-1947 repression. The first of a new generation of leagues appeared in 1955 on the Engenho Galiléia, near Recife (Pernambuco), calling itself rather grandly "The Agricultural Society of Planters and Cattle Ranchers of Pernambuco." The members were tenants, peasants, and small holders rather than workers, because, it was feared, workers could be too easily manipulated by their employers. The group's demands focused on the abolition of *cambão* (the obligatory labor that tenants owed landowners), provision of written contracts, stable tenure, and, more broadly, land reform. The league took the form of a civic association rather than a union because existing laws effectively forbade unions in the countryside. Members established contacts with reform-minded politicians in the nearby capital, the best known of whom was Francisco Julião. Recife's commercial elites had already broken the power of the state's traditional oligarchy and were open to the idea of the modernization of agriculture and the rationalization of the rural work relations. Julião quickly put himself at the head up the leagues, which spread to other properties in Pernambuco and then beyond the state's boundaries.

News of the Cuban Revolution greatly stimulated organizing activity in the Brazilian countryside. At work were both leftist groups seeking radical change and the Catholic Church hoping to head off revolution by sponsoring controlled modernization. The turning point came with the new Rural Labor Law of 1963 that legalized unions in the countryside. President João Goulart hoped that bringing tenants and rural workers into the existing corporatist labor system would mobilize their support for his regime. Unions were now more attractive than leagues because they had the right to strike, which civic associations did not, and unions benefited from the obligatory *imposto sindical*, guaranteeing them greater resources than those available to the leagues. Organizing in rural areas exploded, though it is likely that many who joined one group or the other had little idea of the differences between leagues and unions or a clear understanding of the ideological positions of those competing for their attention. In a still largely traditional society the church had a tremendous advantage. By one estimate, in early 1964 the leagues and unions in Pernambuco had enrolled approximately 280,000 members: 200,000 in church-run organizations, 50,000 in leftist groups, and 30,000 in the original leagues.

Apart from the growing hostility of the police and local military commanders, Pernambuco's swelling rural organizations faced several difficulties. Generally the tenants and workers in the countryside did not have a tradition of sustained cooperation. They joined organizations to satisfy their immediate concerns and then left when these were met, or they became frustrated and left. This was the experience of the first league at Engenho Galiléia. Once the members gained control of the property and divided it into individual plots, they fell immediately into conflict among themselves and with the laborers they hired. Here too property tended to turn league and union supporters into petty landlords fearful of reform and hostile to the demands of the less fortunate. In addition, while the 1963 labor law authorized rural unions, it also imposed the standard CLT restriction of only one union per municipality, pitching organizing groups into fierce competition for government recognition.

Sensing the futility of such conflict, various factions of the left met in November 1963 to form the Confederation of Workers in Agriculture (CONTAG). The new confederation was well funded and enjoyed strong government support but remained firmly under the control of *pelegos* anxious to cooperate with the Goulart government. CONTAG excluded the church organizations, and it ignored the original leagues linked to Julião, which, in any event, were badly divided by 1963–64 and marginalized everywhere except Pernambuco. The 1964 coup smashed the leagues and replaced any remaining union activists with collaborationists. The military of Recife became notorious even within the context of post-1964 Brazil for the ferocity with which it arrested and tortured "dissidents." Yet the new national government did not destroy unions. Across Brazil unions were allowed, and even encouraged, to continue to function, though now carefully removed from politics. Only in Brazil of all the military dictatorships of these years did trade union membership actually grow. The new regime saw unions as useful vehicles for national development, and as mechanisms for delivering social services to workers, particularly in rural areas where the population had not up until this time benefited from such attention.

Then, in 1979, and parallel to what was happening among the metal workers in São Paulo, some of the rural unions of Pernambuco began to take on a new role. They transformed themselves into vehicles to struggle not only for a better economic situation but for the broader project of social and political democratization. During the 1970s the government had encouraged the modernization of the sugar industry as part of the national motor vehicle alcohol program. As sugar production expanded and rationalized, however, it displaced many *moradores*, traditional resident workers who lived on the *fazendas*, and it encroached too on the lands of small holders, hastening proletarianization of the rural population. When the military eased its control in the late 1970s and moved toward civilian rule, Pernambuco's rural unions pressed for a democratic opening. Although land reform still figured prominently in union rhetoric, most members were in fact accustomed now to wage labor. Their leaders argued not so much for radical change as for enforcement of existing labor laws. Thus, while the CUT and New Unionism in the South fought during the early and mid-1980s to free workers from the corporatist restrictions of the CLT, the sugar workers of Pernambuco were struggling to be admitted to the system and to participate in the benefits it promised. Put another way, simple enforcement of the existing law would have effected a revolution in the rural Northeast, something the landowners understood and resisted.

Rural organizations during the 1960s in the Andean areas of Peru and Bolivia also reflected the differing interests of workers as against those of peasants and tenants, but here the two groups tended to be geographically separated. Most of the full-time rural wage workers in Peru were found on the coast, employed by large, relatively modern cotton and sugar plantations. Although technically illegal until the 1950s, unions, or attempts to organize unions, had existed in the area from the early part of the century. By the 1930s many of the workers had allied themselves with Haya de la Torre's APRA. APRA pursued a "bread and butter" strategy, pressing for better wages and conditions but eschewing land reform or fundamental social or economic change. APRA also paid scant attention to the situation of the thousands of seasonal workers that came down from the highlands each year for the harvest. Given the high capitalization of production and the relatively small size of the permanent labor force, employers could afford to improve the conditions of resident workers even as they ignored those of the migrants. By the 1960s full-time workers on the coastal plantations were among the best paid in Peru, with wages 20 percent above the national average.

Mobilization among the highland peasantry, on the other hand, came first in Bolivia, a product of the 1952 Revolution. Most of Bolivia and Peru's peasants lived under some variation of a *pongo* system: typically they owed the landowner several days a week labor in return for the use of a small plot on which they cultivated food and cash crops. The miners and the urban population precipitated the 1952 victory of the MNR, but the government soon turned its attention to the countryside, sanctioning rural *sindicatos* (peasant/tenant organizations) and carrying out one of the most thoroughgoing land reforms ever attempted in Latin America. Labor rent was abolished, and university students and organizers from among the miners fanned out through the countryside, helping to set up *sindicatos* and to prepare land claims. As we encountered in other areas, however, once the peasants received their parcels they largely lost interest in further reform or even in working together. For example, although the advantages of cooperatives were evident, these made little headway in the highlands, and where they existed members tended to suspect their leaders and each other of corruption and putting self-interest first. What had been demonstrations to press their claims they now saw simply as time-wasting "politics." When a 1964 military coup removed the MNR from power and brought a crackdown on miners and urban workers, the peasants stood aside.

In Peru, the epicenter of highland rural agitation was the valley of La Convención north of Cuzco. Malaria kept much of the valley uninhabitable until the 1940s, when new public health measures encouraged increased migration from the nearby sierra. But new arrivals found that the land already belonged to large haciendas, forcing them into a *colono*-like situation of labor rent (*condiciones*) on the hillsides above the valley bottom. With the arrival of a road and trucks in the mid-1950s many of these tenants began to shift to coffee production. The new crop proved so profitable that soon they were hiring workers to fulfill the *condiciones* they owed, allowing them to concentrate full time on coffee. The *hacendados*, for their part, now tried to break existing rent agreements to regain control of the slopes and profit from the new crop. A growing number of conflicts resulted—over contracts, over working hours, and over the disposition of improvements to the land made by the tenants.

In the late 1950s renters and small holders began to organize and to file claims and protests with the government. In the process they made contact with lawyers in Cuzco and through these with labor organizers and leftist activists. Some of these came to La Convención to help with the struggle, but with one notable exception, leadership of tenant and peasant groups remained in local hands. The exception was Hugo Blanco, a self-described Trotskyite from Cuzco who arrived in the valley in 1960, working first as a laborer and then becoming active in the local organizations, where he led a labor boycott of the haciendas. His election to the head of the main confederation in 1962 split the movement between his more radical wing and that of the older, traditional leaders who sought improved conditions, not revolution.

In April of 1962 the government attempted a compromise between the landowners and the tenants, abolishing *condiciones* but requiring instead cash rent. The tenants refused. A military coup in July of that year reiterated the demand, but residents of La Convención continued to ignore it, and the army did not press the rent question. Effectively, then, by the early 1960s the ex-tenants had broken the power of the local landed elite, ended the labor requirement, and gained de facto possession of their plots. With these successes, however, a familiar pattern emerged: conflicts over land boundaries, subcontracting arrangements, and labor relations increasingly dominated the attention of the population, and cooperation and interest in further change collapsed. When in 1965 Cuban-style guerrillas appeared in the area, they received little support.

Conclusions

While export agriculture and raw material production continued to expand and diversify in the half-century after 1930, what was new for Latin America was rapid urbanization and industrialization. By the 1980s Latin American metropoli were among the largest in the world, more than half the population of some countries lived in cities, and countries such as Mexico and Brazil exported manufactured products not just to Africa and the Middle East but to the United States and the European Common Market as well. The populations of the cities no longer grew chiefly from international immigration, as they had in the first years of the century, but as a result of migration from the countryside, augmented by a spiraling birthrate. Migrants were attracted to the towns by economic opportunities and by the educational and health services available there. More importantly, though, they were increasingly being expelled from the countryside by the concentration of land ownership and the transformation of what had been areas of peasant food production into export plantations and cattle ranches. At the same time, the mechanization and rationalization of agriculture greatly reduced labor requirements, even as output went up. Both for those who remained in the rural labor force and for those who went to city, work more and more took on the characteristics of capitalist free labor.

As employers and, more reluctantly, workers abandoned traditional paternalistic forms, the state was unable or unwilling to compensate by providing the "safety net" of social services that underpinned market-driven work relations in North Atlantic industrial societies. When economic downturns hit the cities or were reflected there from the primary product sectors, workers were cast from poverty into misery with little recourse. Some sought survival in the "informal" economy, while others supported unions and political parties that promised change. For a generation the populists, aided on occasion by military or foreign interventions, managed to keep this discontent within limits that were acceptable to local elites and international capital. By the 1960s and 1970s, however, unrest was increasingly hard to control. The urban poor and working classes, educated by populist rhetoric, had become more sophisticated, and the economic cycles seemed both more violent and their effects more widespread. Labor organizations were expanding even into the countryside. With the evident economic and political bankruptcy of populism, the military, supported by the United States, intervened in country after country to preserved elite control and guarantee investments. Without the impediments of popular protest or elections, these governments could carry out the austerity programs promoted by the IMF and international capital and for which the workers and the poor inevitably paid.

After half a century of industrialization, the 1980s and 1990s witnessed a conscious and dramatic reversal. Under the thrall of neoliberalism and trapped by huge debts run up in the 1970s, Latin American governments stripped away the incentives and protections that had been used to promote import substitution industrialization, and business after business failed: in the first two years of NAFTA, for example, Mexico lost upward of 2 million jobs, as small and medium-sized industries oriented toward the domestic market buckled under a flood of imports. The economy created too few new jobs, and most of those were in the *maquiladora* sector, with low wages and few local backward or forward linkages; real manufacturing wages in Mexico in 1996 were below those of 1981, and the value of the minimum wage had declined fairly steadily since the late 1970s. Estimates for 1996 were that it took 4.8 minimum wages to support a family of four in Mexico City, but the average family wage was only 2 to 3 minimum wages.

Local businesses that did survive, often in cooperation with or under the control of foreign investment, rationalized production, recapitalized with more modern and more efficient equipment, and cut employment. Similarly, huge "factories in the fields," also often linked to foreign investment, more and more dominated export agriculture, raising productivity and lowering employment. Put another way, cheap labor no longer guaranteed competitiveness or profitability for Latin American producers, particularly as they now had to compete with even cheaper workers in Africa and Asia. In large areas of Latin America, as in parts of the United States, the labor force was bifurcating into a small, relatively well paid elite associated with the modern parts of the economy, and a growing, effectively useless mass population. In the North Atlantic economies, a large middle class allowed some displaced workers to find employment in service industries, albeit at low wages and under the constant threat of unemployment. Because of welfare transfers, even the unemployed in the United States and Europe could at least play the role of consumers, helping to sustain the economy. In Latin America, on the other hand, with only a tiny middle class and a limited welfare system, the mass of the population had less and less purpose, unable either to work or to consume.

Conclusions

There was nothing inevitable and very little that was accidental about the way work and work relations developed in Latin America. Forms of work in the New World resulted from the interplay of internal and external circumstances and conditions. By "external" we mean chiefly the shifting forms of the world capitalist economy and the demands and opportunities these presented to Latin America. By "internal" we refer to factors such as possible crops or commodities, the availability of a labor force, and the political and social conditions that frame relations of production. Having analytically separated internal from external, it is necessary to immediately reverse field and admit that they only exist in combination. In fact, it is possible to imagine many different ways in which these elements could combine, or be combined, to produce various production and labor forms, and most such variants have existed. Timing matters; some forms of work, for example, slavery, are viable in certain moments of history and not in others. The question then becomes who or what determines the specific combination in a given instance, and how and why do these combinations change, or not change, over time? Work, both specific processes and the social and political relations in which these are embedded, results from decisions made by individuals and groups. Rarely were they the only choice available, and the final outcome almost always was the product of struggle.

A dominant characteristic of New World work relations has been a relative scarcity of labor. Short-lived situations, for example, the early post-conquest years or government policies of subsidized immigration, created temporary conditions of labor surplus, but these surpluses soon dissipated or came only at high and unsustainable costs. With persistently low ratios of population to available land, there are several paths labor relations could take, and, interestingly, we find the two limit cases in North America: northern yeoman farmers and southern slave agriculture. That is, one solution is to allow the development of a small farmer economy based on family labor and progressive integration into national and international markets. Of all Latin America's commercial crops, only coffee and tobacco proved adaptable to family farming, and only in the latter case did this form predominate. In most areas even coffee moved toward large-scale production and coerced and/or wage labor forms.

A surplus of land to labor tends to drive up the cost of labor. This may make the price of export commodities uncompetitive in world markets and will certainly cut into the profits of elites—which reminds us, mathematical models notwithstanding, that all economics is political economy. Economic decisions respond to the interests, real or imagined, of those groups or classes with the power to make and impose decisions, and the strong tendency is for these to arrive at decisions that benefit, or are imagined to benefit, their group or class. In the large-scale production that dominated the history of most Latin American exports, economic and political elites generally chose to mobilize labor not by offering attractive wages, preferring instead to impose political and economic controls on the population to force them to work. For most of Latin America's history, most labor outside the peasant sector has been coerced work, paid or not. This is not because poor Latin Americans shun work, and anyone who has seen a small farmer laboring in his own plot would never call him "lazy," but because the mass of the population has been reluctant to work for others under conditions so obviously structured to its disadvantage.

The chief internal determinant of labor relations in Latin America has been the availability of a work force. "Availability" is determined by several factors. One, as suggested above, is simply the size of the population that can be set to work. This has varied dramatically between places and over time. For example, early post-conquest Indian slavery and *encomiendas* depended on a large—indeed an almost infinitely large—indigenous population, practically a "free good." As that population declined and the number of would-be European employers expanded, new forms of labor organization directed by the state came to dominate. These, in turn, gradually gave way, at least in the central areas, to the rationing of labor by market mechanisms, although until the present day labor relations in Latin America continue to be heavily conditioned by political power.

"Availability" is also influenced by cultural understandings of who or what group can or should do what sort of work. The most commonly used cultural codes for structuring labor relations are gender and race. Most societies define "men's work" and "women's work," but what is more interesting is how these definitions change as circumstances change. Labor shortages in late Bourbon Mexico or on the sugar plantation during the harvest, for example, led to temporary redefinitions of what women could do, though almost never did these redefinitions extend to positions of authority. By contrast, periods of labor surplus prompted similar shifts, but ones that now allowed men to push into what had been women's work. In the 1990s unemployment along the U.S.–Mexican border converted almost half the *maquiladora* jobs to work for men. Similarly, ideas about race and racist stereotypes affect labor relations and forms of work: for example, established prejudices may say that white men cannot do field work in the tropics, or Indians are too lazy to be left uncoerced, or blacks are capable of three or four times the work of Indians. What is most notable about such stereotyping, of course, and this is not unique to Latin America, is the way in which it tends to reinforce the power and position of existing elites and to condition attitudes toward other groups in ways that most benefit the interests of these elites. As with gender, race definitions that affect work change with time to meet new conditions. With an influx of European immigrants, black and mixed blood populations may no longer be simply inferior but useless.

Changing economic or political conditions also affect the availability of labor. This was most famously the case with African slavery, where changing moral values and a commitment to free trade prompted Great Britain to intervene in the international slave trade, condemning most New World slave economies to slow extinction. But there are other instances of such shifts. A peasant population that controls enough land or other resources to provide for its needs is generally reluctant to offer itself for wage labor, or it may demand wages that commercial producers think too high. Only extra economic coercion will induce them to enter the labor market, coercion paid for in part by the taxes of these same peasants and workers. Alternatively, population growth or government policies that limit access to land can help create a "surplus" of labor that must seek wage work in order to survive. There have always been regional differences, sometimes prompting internal migrations and an evening out of labor supply. Other circumstances may change. For example, a population suffering land shortages and forced into wage work may be able to recover some or all of its independence by shifting from subsistence agriculture to specialty crops or handicrafts that absorb more labor and provide higher returns. A resource shift such as the discovery of oil or the growth of tourism can create work alternatives, or political change may redistribute resources in ways that restructure work relations: Chilean land reform in the early 1970s increased employment in the rural areas and cut down the flow of women willing to migrate to the cities to work as servants.

As these suggest, an important determinant of labor relations is the existence of possible alternatives that create competition for workers. To be effective these have to be available and be understood to be available. For example, it does not matter if better paying or safer jobs are to be had in a neighboring town if the workers have no access to them. They may not have access because there is no road or bus service, and such service may not exist because it would not be profitable or because local employers fear competition for workers. For this reason, agricultural employers often oppose local construction of factories. In recent years a common outlet for "unabsorbed labor" has been migration to the cities, but for rural inhabitants who are deeply involved in the life of their communities or whose religion practices link them to the graves of ancestors and telluric deities, such migration may not be culturally available. The building of a hydroelectric dam or political violence such as that which racked highland Guatemala in the 1980s, may give them no option, forcibly removing whole populations and creating new, if not necessarily better, work relations.

Intertwined with the internal conditions of Latin America have been changes in the external situation. Nothing has had more influence than the spread of capitalism. Of course, capitalism itself has changed dramatically, shifting from merchant capitalism in the sixteenth and seventeenth centuries to industrial capitalism in the late eighteenth and nineteenth centuries to a post-industrial world in the years after World War II. The object of merchant capitalism was the accumulation of metallic wealth—gold and silver—and the normal means of acquiring this were mining, theft, and exchange. Where possible Europeans at first traded for what they wanted, leaving local labor forms intact, as in the early Brazilian log wood trade, or they sought to adapt these forms to the new uses, as the Spanish did with the *mita*. Initially postconquest slavery involved European exploitation of the indigenous population, but this quickly gave way to an entirely new form. Europeans introduced a third population, Africans, into the Americas specifically for use as enslaved labor, and this slavery soon operated on a scale unprecedented in Europe, the Americas, or Africa. African slavery in the Americas was a form of work created specifically to meet New World conditions and one of the most pervasive and long lasting.

During the eighteenth century North Atlantic capitalism moved beyond the buy low/sell high exchanges of mercantilism to embrace innovative schemes of organization and new energy sources and labor relations, creating industrial capitalism. This fundamentally altered Latin America's relationship to the capitalist world and with it local processes and relations of work. From a source of metallic wealth and luxury commodities such as sugar and dye products, Latin America became a supplier of bulk food, food substitutes, and raw materials vital to Europe's agricultural and industrial development. It also constituted an important market for European, and increasingly U.S., manufactures, to the enormous detriment of local Latin American artisans and handicraft industries. African slavery, in the decline in both Latin America and North America in the late eighteenth century, underwent a sudden resurgence, but only in specific areas and linked to certain activities. In other areas the demand for unprecedented numbers of workers to service new export commodities overwhelmed incipient free labor. The effect was to amplify and intensify the use of labor coercion and forced wage labor across Latin America, from vagrancy laws in Argentina to *mandamientos* in Guatemala and debt peonage in Yucatan. Latin American states and local and foreign elites were not disposed to wait for the working of the capitalist leviathan to create adequate numbers of free workers and instead used economic and political policies to force erstwhile independent peasants and farmers into wage labor.

But the leviathan did work. Over time, rising populations and declining access to resources created genuinely free labor, men and women with nothing to sell and no means to survive but their labor. In other cases the rural population still had access to land but not enough to live off and had to migrate seasonally to earn wages to supplement what they made from their own cultivations. Such "semi-proletariats," for example, as the migrants that came each year from the Peruvian sierra to cut cane and pick cotton on the coast, were particularly valuable because they could be paid below subsistence and supported themselves on their own plots most of the year when their labor was not needed. By the turn of the twentieth century, free and semi-free labor predominated in Latin America, but coercion did not disappear. Employers, and the states that they controlled, maintained legal and extra-legal coercion to cheapen labor and to make certain that unions or worker-based political parties did not gain strength. In the more developed countries everyday repression gave way during the 1930s and 1940s to populism. Populism served much the same purpose of keeping the working class from posing a threat to the existing economic-political system, though at the price of occasionally enacting reforms favorable to the poor and at the long-term cost of politically educating, and even radicalizing, a generation of workers.

In looking at external circumstances that have conditioned work in Latin America, it is necessary to consider also political relations and geopolitics. It mattered, for example, whether a given area was or had been a colony of Great Britain or of Spain or Portugal. Beginning with the Enlightenment, the ideological and economic revolutions that convulsed Europe for two centuries were largely external to the Iberian countries. Industrial capitalism and popular democracy arose not within Iberian culture but came from without; they were literally "things out of place." The more so in the Iberian New World. These imported ideas were consciously and unconsciously modified to fit the circumstances of the Spain's and Portugal's colonies and the new republics. Industrial capitalism arrived in Latin America as imported technology, and in the process lost many of the social and political components that formed the basis of European and North American democracy. Like it or not, however, the new technologies revolutionized work and the workplace and, in turn, the family and community. This was profoundly threatening to existing elites. It was bound to be doubly so for those without experience in democracy, indeed, those whose very existence depended on denying social and political rights to the majority of the population. Elites in northern Europe and northern North America adapted to the subversive influences of industrial capitalism through a gradual democratization, an accommodation that undercut Karl Marx's anticipated revolutions. By contrast, elites in Latin America, as in the southern United States, astride mass populations they despised and feared, attempted a partial shift restricted to technology alone, without the attendant social and political changes. This resulted in a blocked, or partial, transition to capitalism that created societies shot through with contradictions, societies without the mechanisms necessary for the nonviolent resolution of these contradictions.

One thread that runs through the history of work and work relations in Latin America, and the title of more than one book, has been an evolution toward freedom. For many the very proof of the superiority of the West has been the triumph of free enterprise capitalism and free labor. But it is important to remember what has been lost, without falling into fantasies about happy peasants. The price of freedom is a loss of security, as post-1990 Eastern Europe has discovered. It is hard to argue against the sense that for those at the upper ends of society and the economy, this has been a valuable stimulus to change and progress, but for the less well placed the costs have been high and the rewards largely remain distant. Are *maquiladora* workers better off than landless ex-peasants? Almost certainly. They think so, and they flood the cities hoping for a job. Is a street hustler, selling cigarettes one at a time, better of than a member of an eighteenth-century landed peasant community? Possibly, and even probably if you think in terms of the health care and education potentially available to him or her. But at some point the potential must be realized in order to validate the system. In a period of capitalist triumphalism, it is worth remembering that socialist revolutionaries never imagined that the working class was getting poorer or that a revolution would grow out of simple impoverishment. Rather, they argued that it was the relative enmiseration of the poor, and the growing concentration of wealth in fewer and fewer hands, that would provoke revolution. Nothing is more characteristic of the last quarter of the twentieth century.

Notes

Introduction

1. *The Compact Oxford English Dictionary*, 2d. ed. (New York: Oxford University Press, 1998), 2338.

Chapter 1

1. Charles Gibson, *The Spanish Tradition in America* (New York: Harper and Row, 1968), 41.

2. Ibid., 56.

3. John Hemming, *Red Gold: The Conquest of the Brazilian Indians* (Cambridge: Harvard University Press, 1978), 29

4. Lewis Hanke and Jane M. Rausch, eds., *Peoples and Issues in Latin American History: The Colonial Experience* (New York: Markus Wiener, 1993), 87.

5. Bernal Díaz de Castillo, *The True History of the Conquest of New Spain, 1517–1521*, trans. A.P. Maudsley (New York: Farrar, Straus and Giroux, 1966), 143–46.

6. Brian Loveman, *Chile: The Legacy of Hispanic Capitalism* (New York: Oxford University Press, 1979), 61.

Chapter 2

1. Peter Bakewell, *Miners of the Red Mountain: Indian Labor in Potosí* (Albuquerque: University of New Mexico Press, 1984), 143.

2. Archivo General de Centro América (AGCA) [Guatemala City], A1.14.25 158 3183.

3. AGCA, A1.22.20 153 3036.

4. Robert Smith, "Forced Labor in Guatemalan Indigo Works," *Hispanic American Historical Review* 36, no. 3 (August 1956): 321.

5. Leslie Bethell, ed., *Colonial Brazil* (Cambridge, UK: Cambridge University Press, 1987), 158.

6. Charles Boxer, *The Golden Age of Brazil, 1695–1750: Growing Pains of a Colonial Society* (Berkeley: University of California Press, 1962), 184.

7. C.L.R. James, *The Black Jacobins: Toussaint L'Ouverture and the San Domingo Revolution* (New York: Vintage Books, 1963), 12–13.

8. John K. Chance, *Race and Class in Colonial Oaxaca* (Stanford: Stanford University Press, 1978), 178.

9. Roberto Moreno, "Régimen de trabajo en la minería del siglo XVIII," in *Labor and Laborers Through Mexican History*, ed. Elsa Cecilia Frost, Michael C. Meyer, and Josefina Zoraida Vásquez, with Lilia Díaz (Tucson: University of Arizona Press, 1979), 262.

Chapter 3

1. B.R. Mitchell, ed., *International Historical Statistics: The Americas, 1750–1993*, 4th ed. (London: Macmillan, 1998), 47, 54–55.

2. Bernard E. Bobb, *The Viceroyalty of Antonio María Bucareli in New Spain, 1771–1779* (Austin: University of Texas Press, 1962), 28.

3. Consulado de Comercio, "Apuntamientos sobre la agricultura y comercio del Reyno de Guatemala," in José María García Laguardia, *La génesis de constitucionalismo en Guatemala* (Guatemala: n.p., 1968), 313.

4. Leon Campbell, *The Military and Society in Colonial Peru, 1750–1810* (Philadelphia: American Philosophical Society, 1978), 45.

5. Laura de Mello e Souza, *Desclassifcados do ouro: a pobreza mineira do século XVIII* (Rio de Janeiro: Graal, 1982), 175.

6. Maria O. Dias, *Power and Everyday Life: the Lives of Working Women in Nineteenth Century Brazil*, trans. Ann Frost (New Brunswick, NJ: Rutgers University Press, 1995), 61.

7. Susan Deans-Smith, *Bureaucrats, Planters, and Workers: The Making of the Tobacco Monopoly in Bourbon Mexico* (Austin: University of Texas Press, 1992), 214.

8. David McCreery, "'This Life of Misery and Shame': Female Prostitution in Guatemala City, 1880–1920," *Journal of Latin American Studies* 18 (July 1986): 335.

Chapter 4

1. James R. Scobie, *Argentina: A City and Nation*, 2d. ed (New York: Oxford University Press, 1971), 118.

2. *Recopilación de las leyes de Guatemala*, vol. 1 (Guatemala City: 1881), 457.

3. B.R. Mitchell, ed., *International Historical Statistics: The Americas, 1750–1993*, 4th ed. (London: Macmillan, 1998), 64–65.

4. Brian Inglis, *Roger Casement* (New York: Harcourt Janovich, 1974), 178.

5. Both quotes from Charles Bergquist, *Labor in Latin America: Comparative Essays on Chile, Argentina, Venezuela, and Colombia* (Stanford: Stanford University Press, 1986), 123–24.

6. Ana Lúcia Duarte Lanna, "Santos–Transformações urbanas e mercado de trabalho livre, 1879–1914," in *História econômica da Primeira República*, ed. Sergio Tomás Szmrecsányi (São Paulo: USP, 1996), 314–15.

7. David S. Parker, "White-Collar Lima, 1910–1929: Commercial Employees and the Rise of the Peruvian Middle Class," *Hispanic American Historical Review* 72, no. 1 (February 1992): 56.

Chapter 5

1. B.R. Mitchell, ed., *International Historical Statistics: The Americas, 1750–1993*, 4th ed. (London: Macmillan, 1998), 51 and 56–57. These figures would be much larger if the entire metropolitan area were included.

2. Kenneth P. Erickson, *The Brazilian Corporate State and Working Class Politics* (Berkeley: University of California Press, 1977), 35.

3. Hobart Spalding, *Organized Labor in Latin America* (New York: New York University Press, 1977), 165.

4. Judith Evans, Paul Heath Hoeffel, and Daniel James, "Reflections on the Argentine Auto Workers and Their Unions," in *The Political Economy of the Latin American Motor Vehicle Industry*, ed. Rich Kronish and Kenneth S. Mericle (Cambridge: MIT Press, 1984), 153.

5. June C. Nash, *We Eat the Mines and the Mines Eat Us: Dependency and Exploitation in Bolivian Tin Mines* (New York: Columbia University Press, 1993), 30.

6. Thomas M. Klubock, "Working-Class Masculinity, Middle-Class Morality, and Labor Politics in the Chilean Copper Mines," *Journal of Social History* 30, no. 2 (winter 1996): 443.

Sources and Additional Readings

Chapter 1

Aiton, A.S. *Antonio de Mendoza, First Viceroy of New Spain.* New York: Russell and Russel, 1967.

Bethell, Leslie, ed. *Colonial Spanish America.* Cambridge, UK: Cambridge University, 1987.

Bowser, Frederick P. *The African Slave in Colonial Peru, 1524–1650.* Stanford: Stanford University Press, 1974.

Chance, John K. *Race and Class in Colonial Oaxaca.* Stanford: Stanford University Press, 1978.

Charney, Paul. "Negotiating Roots: Indian Migrants in the Lima Valley During the Colonial Period." *Colonial Latin American History Review* 5, no. 1 (winter 1996): 1–20.

Clendinnen, Inga. *Ambivalent Conquests: Maya and Spaniards in Yucatán, 1517–1560.* Cambridge, UK: Cambridge University Press, 1987.

Cobo, Bernabé. *History of the Inca Empire.* Translated by R. Hamilton. Austin: University of Texas Press, 1979.

Coe, Michael D. *The Maya.* 6th ed. New York: Thames and Hudson, 1999.

Cook, Alexandra Parma, and Noble David Cook. *Good Faith and Truthful Ignorance.* Durham: Duke University Press, 1991.

Cook, Shelburne, and Woodrow Borah. *Essays in Population History.* 3 vols. Berkeley: University of California Press, 1971–79.

Díaz de Castillo, Bernal. *The True History of the Conquest of New Spain, 1517–1521.* Translated by A. P. Maudsley. New York: Farrar, Straus and Giroux, 1966.

Frost, Elsa C., Michael Meyer, Josefina Zoraida Vásquez, and Lilia Díaz, eds. *Labor and Laborers Through Mexican History.* Tucson: University of Arizona Press, 1979.

Gibson, Charles. *Aztecs Under Maya Rule: A History of the Indians of the Valley of Mexico*. Stanford: Stanford University Press, 1964.

———, ed. *The Spanish Tradition in America*. New York: Harper and Row, 1968.

Hassig, Ross. *Trade, Tribute and Transportation: The Sixteenth Century Political Economy of the Valley of Mexico*. Norman: University of Oklahoma Press, 1985.

Hemming, John. *Red Gold: The Conquest of the Brazilian Indians*. Cambridge: Harvard University Press, 1978.

Kamen, Henry. *Spain, 1469–1714: A Society in Conflict*. 2d ed. London: Longman Group, 1991.

Lockhart, James. *Spanish Peru, 1532–1560: A Social History*. 2d ed. Madison: University of Wisconsin, 1994.

———. *The Nahuas After the Conquest: A Social and Cultural History of the Indians of Central Mexico, Sixteenth Through Eighteenth Centuries*. Stanford: Stanford University Press, 1992.

Loveman, Brian. *Chile: The Legacy of Hispanic Capitalism*. New York: Oxford University Press, 1979.

MacLeod, Murdo. *Spanish Central America: A Socio-economic History, 1520–1720*. Berkeley: University of California Press, 1973.

Melville, Elinor G.K. *A Plague of Sheep: Environmental Consequences of the Conquest of Mexico*. Cambridge, UK: Cambridge University Press, 1994.

Palmer, Colin. *Slaves of the White God: Blacks in Mexico, 1570–1650*. Cambridge: Harvard University Press, 1976.

Rout, Leslie B. *The African Experience in Spanish America: 1502 to the Present Day*. Cambridge, UK: Cambridge University Press, 1976.

Sauer, Carl. *The Early Spanish Main*. Berkeley: University of California Press, 1966.

Service, Elman. "The Encomienda in Paraguay." *Hispanic American Historical Review* 31, no. 2 (May 1951): 230–252.

Sherman, William. *Forced Labor in Sixteenth Century Central America*. Lincoln: University of Nebraska Press, 1978.

Villamarín, Juan A., and Edith E. Villamarín. *Indian Labor in Mainland Colonial Spanish America*. Newark: University of Delaware Latin American Studies Program, 1975.

Wolf, Eric. *Sons of the Shaking Earth: The People of Mexico and Guatemala*. Chicago: University of Chicago Press, 1974.

Chapter 2

Andrien, Kenneth J. *The Kingdom of Quito, 1690–1830: The State and Regional Development*. Cambridge, UK: Cambridge University Press, 1995.

Bakewell, Peter. *Miners of the Red Mountain: Indian Labor in Potosí*. Albuquerque: University of New Mexico Press, 1984.

———. *Silver Mining and Society in Colonial Mexico: Zacatecas, 1546–1700*. Cambridge, UK; Cambridge University Press, 1971.

Barrett, Ward. *The Sugar Hacienda of the Marqueses del Valle*. Minneapolis: University of Minnesota Press, 1970.

Bauer, Arnold J. *Chilean Rural Society from the Spanish Conquest to 1930*. Cambridge, UK: Cambridge University Press, 1975.

Bethell, Leslie, ed. *Colonial Brazil*. Cambridge, UK: Cambridge University Press, 1987.

Boxer, Charles. *The Golden Age of Brazil, 1695–1750: Growing Pains of a Colonial Society.* Berkeley: University of California Press, 1962.

Brockington, Lolita G. *The Leverage of Labor: Managing the Cortés Haciendas in Tehuantepec, 1588–1688.* Durham: Duke University Press, 1989.

Cole, Jeffery A. *The Potosí Mita, 1573–1700: Compulsory Indian Labor in the Andes.* Stanford: Stanford University Press, 1985.

Conrad, Robert E. *World of Sorrow: The African Slave Trade to Brazil.* Baton Rouge: Louisiana State University Press, 1986.

Curtin, Philip D. *The Atlantic Slave Trade: A Census.* Madison: University of Wisconsin Press, 1969.

Cushner, Nicolas. *Farm and Factory: The Jesuits and the Development of Agrarian Capitalism in Colonial Quito, 1600–1767.* Albany: State University of New York Press, 1982.

———. *Jesuit Ranches and the Agrarian Development of Colonial Argentina, 1650–1767.* Albany: State University of New York Press, 1983.

———. *Lords of the Land: Sugar, Wine, and Jesuit Estates of Coastal Peru, 1600–1767.* Albany: State University of New York Press, 1980.

Danks, Noblet Barry. "The Labor Revolt of 1766 in the Mining Community of Real del Monte." *The Americas* 44, no. 2 (October 1987): 143–65.

Deeds, Susan M. "Rural Work in Nueva Vizcaya: Forms of Labor Coercion in the Periphery." *Hispanic American Historical Review* 69, no. 3 (August 1989): 425–49.

Farriss, Nancy M. *Maya Society Under Colonial Rule: The Collective Enterprise of Survival.* Princeton: Princeton University Press, 1984.

Ferry, Robert J. *The Colonial Elite of Early Caracas: Formation and Crisis, 1567–1767.* Berkeley: University of California Press, 1989.

Flory, Rae, and David Grant Smith. "Bahian Merchants and Planters in the Seventeenth and Early Eighteenth Centuries." *Hispanic American Historical Review* 58, no. 4 (November 1978): 571–94.

Hoberman, Louisa, S. *Mexico's Merchant Elite, 1590–1660: Silver, State, and Society.* Durham: Duke University Press, 1991.

Hoberman, Louisa S., and Susan Socolow. *The Countryside in Colonial Latin America.* Albuquerque: University of New Mexico Press, 1996.

James, C.L.R. *The Black Jacobins: Toussaint L'Ouverture and the San Domingo Revolution.* New York: Vintage Books, 1963.

Klein, Herbert. *African Slavery in Latin America and the Caribbean.* Oxford: Oxford University Press, 1986.

Ladd, Doris M. *The Making of a Strike: Mexican Silver Workers' Struggles in Real del Monte, 1766–1775.* Lincoln: University of Nebraska Press, 1988.

Larson, Brooke. *Colonialism and Agrarian Transformation in Bolivia: Cochabamba, 1550–1900.* 2d ed. Princeton: Princeton University Press, 1998.

Martin, Cheryl English. *Rural Society in Colonial Morelos.* Albuquerque: University of New Mexico Press, 1985.

Phelan, John Leddy. *The Kingdom of Quito in the Seventeenth Century: Bureaucratic Politics in the Spanish Empire.* Madison: University of Wisconsin Press, 1967.

Schwartz, Stuart. *Sugar Plantations in the Formation of Brazilian Society: Bahia, 1550–1835.* Cambridge, UK: Cambridge University Press, 1985.

———. *Slaves, Peasants and Rebels: Reconsidering Brazilian Slavery.* Urbana: University of Illinois Press, 1992.

Sharp, William F. *Slavery on the Spanish Frontier: The Colombian Chocó, 1680–1810*. Norman: University of Oklahoma Press, 1976.

Simpson, Lesley B. *Studies in the Administration of the Indians of New Spain, III: The Repartimiento System of Native Labor in New Spain and Guatemala*. Berkeley: University of California Press, 1938.

Smith, Richard. "Indigo Production and Trade in Colonial Guatemala." *Hispanic American Historical Review* 36, no. 3 (May 1959): 181–211.

Van Young, Eric. *Hacienda and Market in Eighteenth-Century Mexico: The Rural Economy of the Guadalajara Region, 1675–1820*. Berkeley: University of California Press, 1981.

Wortman, Miles. *Government and Society in Central America, 1680–1840*. New York: Columbia University Press, 1982.

Zulawski, Ann. *They Eat from Their Labor: Work and Social Change in Colonial Bolivia*. Pittsburgh: University of Pittsburgh Press, 1994.

Chapter 3

Alier, Verena M. *Marriage, Class and Colour in Nineteenth Century Cuba*. 2d. ed. Ann Arbor: University of Michigan Press, 1989.

Arnold, Linda. *Bureaucracy and Bureaucrats in Mexico City, 1742–1835*. Tucson: University of Arizona Press, 1988.

Arrom, Silvia M. *The Women of Mexico City, 1790–1857*. Stanford: Stanford University Press, 1985.

Barbier, Jaques A. "Elites and Cadres in Bourbon Chile." *Hispanic American Historical Review* 52, no. 3 (August 1972): 416–45.

Beezley, William H., Cheryl English Martin, and William E. French, eds. *Rituals of Rule; Rituals of Resistance: Public Celebrations and Popular Culture in Mexico*. Wilmington: Scholarly Resources, 1994.

Bobb, Bernard E. *The Viceroyalty of Antonio María Bucareli in New Spain, 1771–1779*. Austin: University of Texas Press, 1962.

Booker, Jackie R. *Veracruz Merchants, 1770–1829: A Mercantile Elite in Late Bourbon and Early Independent Mexico*. Boulder: Westview Press, 1993.

Boyer, Richard. *Lives of Bigamists: Marriage, Family, and Community in Colonial Mexico*. Albuquerque: University of New Mexico Press, 1995.

Brading, David A. "Government and Elite in Late Colonial Mexico." *Hispanic American Historical Review* 53, no. 3 (August 1973): 389–414.

Burkholder, Mark, and D.S. Chandler. *From Impotence to Power: The Spanish Crown and the American Audiencias, 1687–1808*. Columbia: University of Missouri Press, 1977.

Campbell, Leon G. *The Military and Society in Colonial Peru, 1750–1810*. Philadelphia: American Philosophical Society, 1978.

Cornblit, Oscar. *Power and Violence in the Colonial City: Oruro from the Mining Renaissance to the Rebellion of Tupac Amaru (1740–1782)*. Translated by E. Glick. Cambridge, UK: Cambridge University Press, 1995.

Deans-Smith, Susan. *Bureaucrats, Planters, and Workers: The Making of the Tobacco Monopoly in Bourbon Mexico*. Austin: University of Texas Press, 1992.

Dias, Maria O. *Power and Everyday Life: The Lives of Working Women in Nineteenth Century Brazil*. Translated by Ann Frost. New Brunswick, NJ: Rutgers University Press, 1995.

Gibbs, Donald L. "The Economic Activities of Nuns, Friars, and Their Convents in Mid-Colonial Cuzco." *The Americas* 45, no. 3 (January 1989): 343–62.

Graham, Sandra L. *House and Street: The Domestic World of Servants and Masters in Nineteenth-Century Rio de Janeiro.* Cambridge, UK: Cambridge University Press, 1988.

Hahner, June E. *Women Through Women's Eyes: Latin American Women in Nineteenth-Century Travel Accounts.* Wilmington: Scholarly Resources Books, 1998.

Johnson, Lyman, ed. *The Problem of Order in Changing Societies: Essays on Crime and Policing in Argentina and Uruguay, 1750–1940.* Albuquerque: University of New Mexico Press, 1990.

Karasch, Mary. *Slave Life in Rio de Janeiro, 1808–1850.* Princeton: Princeton University Press, 1987.

Kicza, John E. *Colonial Entrepreneurs: Families and Business in Bourbon Mexico.* Albuquerque: University of New Mexico Press, 1983.

Kinsbruner, Jay. *Petty Capitalism in Spanish America: The Pulperos of Puebla, Mexico City, Caracas and Buenos Aires.* Boulder, CO. Westview Press, 1987.

Kuznesof, Elizabeth. *Household Economy and Urban Development: São Paulo, 1765–1836.* Boulder, CO: Westview Press, 1986.

Lavrin, Asunción. *Sexuality and Marriage in Colonial Latin America.* Lincoln: University of Nebraska Press, 1989.

———, ed. *Latin American Women: Historical Perspectives.* Westport, CT: Greenwood Press, 1978.

Libby, Douglas C. "Reconsidering Textile Production in Late Colonial Brazil: New Evidence from Minas Gerais." *Latin American Research Review* 32, no. 1 (1997): 88–108.

McCreery, David. "'This Life of Misery and Shame': Female Prostitution in Guatemala City, 1880–1920." *Journal of Latin American Studies* 18 (July 1986): 333–53.

McFarlane, Anthony. *Colombia Before Independence: Economy, Society, and Politics Under Bourbon Rule.* Cambridge, UK: Cambridge University Press, 1993.

de Moreno, Christiana Borchart. "Beyond the Obraje: Handicraft Production in Quito Toward the End of the Colonial Period." *The Americas* 52, no. 1 (July 1995): 1–24.

Nazzari, Muriel. *Disappearance of the Dowery: Women, Families, and Social Change in São Paulo, Brazil (1600–1900).* Stanford: Stanford University Press, 1991.

Pike, Ruth. "Penal Servitude in the Spanish Empire: Presidio Labor in the Eighteenth Century." *Hispanic American Historical Review* 58, no. 1 (February 1978): 21–40.

Salvucci, Richard. *Textiles and Capitalism in Mexico: An Economic History of the Obrajes, 1539–1840.* Princeton: Princeton University Press, 1987.

Scardaville, Michael C. "Alcohol Abuse and Tavern Reform in Late Colonial Mexico City." *Hispanic American Historical Review* 60, no. 4 (November 1980): 643–71.

Socolow, Susan M. *The Merchants of Buenos Aires, 1778–1810.* Cambridge, UK: Cambridge University Press, 1978.

———. *The Bureaucrats of Buenos Aires, 1769–1810: Amor al real servicio.* Durham: Duke University Press, 1987.

Soeiro, Susan A. "The Social and Economic Role of the Convent: Women and Nuns in Colonial Bahia, 1677–1800." *Hispanic American Historical Review* 54, no. 2 (May 1974): 209–32.

Taylor, William B. *Magistrates of the Sacred: Priests and Parishioners in Eighteenth-Century Mexico.* Stanford: Stanford University Press, 1996.

Twinam, Ann. *Miners, Merchants, and Farmers in Colonial Colombia.* Austin: University of Texas Press, 1983.

Chapter 4

Adelman, Jeremy. "State and Labour in Argentina: The Portworkers of Buenos Aires, 1910–1921." *Journal of Latin American Studies* 25, no. 1 (February 1993): 73–102.

Amaral, Samuel. *The Rise of Capitalism on the Pampas: The Estancias of Buenos Aires, 1785–1870.* Cambridge, UK: Cambridge University Press, 1998.

Andrews, George Reid. *Afro-Argentines of Buenos Aires, 1800–1900.* Madison: University of Wisconsin Press, 1980.

Barickman, Bert. *A Bahian Counterpoint: Sugar, Tobacco, Cassava, and Slavery in the Recôncavo, 1780–1860.* Stanford: Stanford University Press, 1998.

Bauer, Arnold. "Rural Workers in Spanish America: Problems of Peonage and Oppression," *Hispanic American Historical Review* 59, no.1 (February 1979): 34–63.

Bergad, Laird. *Coffee and the Growth of Agrarian Capitalism in Nineteenth-Century Puerto Rico.* Princeton: Princeton University Press, 1983.

Bergquist, Charles W. *Labor in Latin America: Comparative Essays on Chile, Argentina, Venezuela, and Colombia.* Stanford: Stanford University Press, 1986.

Blackwelder, Julia Kirk, and Lyman Johnson. "Changing Criminal Patterns in Buenos Aires: 1890–1914." *Journal of Latin American Studies* 14, no. 2 (November 1982): 359–79.

Blanchard, Peter. *The Origins of the Peruvian Labor Movement, 1883–1919.* Pittsburgh: University of Pittsburgh Press, 1982.

Brown, Jonathan C.A. *A Socioeconomic History of Argentina, 1776–1860.* Cambridge, UK: Cambridge University Press, 1979.

Casanovas Codina, Joan. "Slavery, the Labour Movement and Spanish Colonialism in Cuba, 1850–1890." *International Review of Social History* 40, no. 3 (1995): 367–82.

Chomsky, Aviva. *West Indian Workers and the United Fruit Company in Costa Rica, 1879–1940.* Baton Rouge: Louisiana State University Press, 1996.

Chomsky, Aviva, and Aldo Lauria-Santiago, eds. *Identity and Struggle at the Margins of the Nation-State: The Laboring Peoples of Central America and the Hispanic Caribbean.* Durham: Duke University Press, 1998.

Conrad, Robert. "Neither Slave nor Free: The Emancipados of Brazil, 1818–1868." *Hispanic American Historical Review* 53, no.1 (February 1973): 50–70.

Duncan, Kenneth, Ian Rutledge, and Colin Harding, eds. *Land and Labour in Latin America: Essays on the Development of Agrarian Capitalism in the Nineteenth and Twentieth Centuries.* Cambridge, UK: Cambridge University Press, 1977.

Fowler-Salamini, Heather, and Mary Kay Vaughn, eds. *Women in the Mexican Countryside, 1850–1990: Creating Spaces, Shaping Transitions.* Tucson: University of Arizona Press, 1994.

French, John, and Daniel James, eds. *The Gendered Worlds of Latin American Workers: From Household and Factory to the Union Hall and Ballot Box.* Durham: Duke University Press, 1997.

French, William E. "Prostitutes and Guardian Angels: Women, Work, and Family in Porfirian Mexico." *Hispanic American Historical Review* 72, no. 4 (November 1992): 529–53.

Guy, Donna. *Sex and Danger in Buenos Aires: Prostitution, Family, and Nation in Argentina.* Lincoln: University of Nebraska Press, 1991.

Holloway, Thomas. *Immigrants on the Land: Coffee and Society in São Paulo, 1886–1934.* Chapel Hill: University of North Carolina Press, 1980.

Knight, Alan. "The Working Class and the Mexican Revolution, c. 1900–1920." *Journal of Latin American Studies* 16, no. 1 (May 1984): 51–79.

Knight, Franklin. *Slave Society in Cuba During the Nineteenth Century.* Madison: University of Wisconsin Press, 1970.

Korzeniewicz, Roberto P. "Labor Unrest in Argentina, 1887–1907." *Latin American Research Review* 24, no. 3 (1989): 71–98.

Lavrin, Asunción. "Women, Labor, and the Left: Argentina and Chile, 1890–1925." *Journal of Women's History* 1, no. 2 (fall 1989): 88–116.

McCreery, David. *Rural Guatemala, 1760–1940.* Stanford: Stanford University Press, 1994.

Mathew, W.M. "A Primitive Export Sector: Guano Production in Mid-Nineteenth Century Peru." *Journal of Latin American Studies* 9, no. 1 (May 1977): 35–57.

Munck, Ronaldo. "Cycles of Class Struggle and the Making of the Working Class in Argentina, 1890–1920." *Journal of Latin American Studies* 19, no. 1 (May 1987), 19–39.

Palacios, Marco. *Coffee in Colombia, 1850–1970: An Economic, Social, and Political History.* Cambridge, UK: Cambridge University Press, 1980.

Parker, David S. *The Idea of the Middle Class: White-Collar Workers and Peruvian Society, 1900–1950.* University Park: Pennsylvania State University Press, 1998.

Roseberry, William, Lowell Gudmundson, and Mario Samper K. *Coffee, Society, and Power in Latin America.* Baltimore: Johns Hopkins University Press, 1995.

Scobie, James R. *Argentina: A City and Nation.* 2d. ed. New York: Oxford University Press, 1971.

Scott, Rebecca J. *Slave Emancipation in Cuba: The Transition to Free Labor, 1860–1899.* Princeton: Princeton University Press, 1985.

Slatta, Richard W. "Rural Criminality and Social Conflict in Nineteenth-Century Buenos Aires Province." *Hispanic American Historical Review* 63, no. 3 (August 1980): 450–72.

Stein, Stanley J. *Vassouras: A Brazilian Coffee County, 1850–1900.* Cambridge: Harvard University Press, 1957.

Stewart, Watt. *Chinese Bondage in Peru: A History of the Chinese Coolie in Peru, 1848–1874.* Westport, CT: Greenwood Press, 1970 [1951].

Turner, Mary, ed. *From Chattel Slaves to Wage Slaves: The Dynamics of Labour Bargaining in the Americas.* Bloomington: University of Indiana Press, 1995.

Vanderwood, Paul J. *Disorder and Progress: Bandits, Police and Mexican Development.* Lincoln: University of Nebraska Press, 1981.

Weinstein, Barbara. *The Amazon Rubber Boom, 1850–1920.* Stanford: Stanford University Press, 1983.

Whigham, Thomas. *The Politics of River Trade: Tradition and Development in the Upper Plata, 1780–1870.* Albuquerque: University of New Mexico Press, 1991.

Chapter 5

Arizpe, Lourdes. "Women in the Informal-Labour Sector: The Case of Mexico City." In *The Women, Gender, and Development Reader*, ed. Nalini Visvanathan. London: Zed Books, 1997, 230–39.

Arizpe, Lourdes, and Josefina Aranda. "The 'Comparative Advantages' of Women's Disadvantages: Women Workers in the Strawberry Export Agribusiness in Mexico." *SIGNS* 7, no. 2 (winter 1982): 453–73.

Bethell, Leslie, and Ian Roxborough, eds. *Latin America Between the Second World War and the Cold War, 1944–1948.* New York: Cambridge University Press, 1992.

Boito, Armando. "The State and Trade Unionism in Brazil" *Latin American Perspectives* 21, no. 1 (winter 1994): 7–23.

Bunster, Ximena, and Elsa M. Chaney. *Sellers and Servants: Working Women in Lima, Peru.* New York: Prager, 1985.

Chaney, Elsa, and Mary García Castro. *Muchachas no más: Household Workers in Latin America and the Caribbean.* Philadelphia: Temple University Press, 1989.

Cohen, Youssef. *The Manipulation of Consent: The State and Working-Class Consciousness in Brazil.* Pittsburgh: University of Pittsburgh, 1989.

Erickson, Kenneth P. *The Brazilian Corporative State and Working Class Politics.* Berkeley: University of California Press, 1977.

French, John D. *The Brazilian Workers' ABC: Class Conflict and Alliances in Modern São Paulo.* Chapel Hill: University of North Carolina Press, 1992.

Frundt, Hank. "To Buy the World a Coke: Implications of Trade Union Redevelopment in Guatemala." *Latin American Perspectives* 14, no. 3 (summer 1987): 381–416.

Gil, Lesley. "Painted Faces: Conflict and Ambiguity in Domestic Servant–Employer Relations in La Paz, 1930–1988." *Latin American Research Review* 25, no. 1 (1990): 119–36.

Green, Duncan. *The Silent Revolution: The Rise of the Market Economies in Latin America.* New York: Monthly Review Press, 1995.

Hojman, David E. "Land Reform, Female Migration and the Market for Domestic Servants in Chile." *Journal of Latin American Studies* 21, no. 1 (February 1989): 105–32.

Horowitz, Joel. *Argentine Unions, the State, and the Rise of Perón, 1930–1945.* Berkeley: University of California Press, International Studies, Publication No. 76, 1990.

Iglesias, Norma. *Beautiful Flowers of the Maquiladora: Life Histories of Women Workers in Tijuana.* Translated by M. Stone and G. Winkler. Austin: University of Texas Press, 1997.

Keck, Margaret E. *The Workers' Party and Democratization in Brazil.* New Haven: Yale University Press, 1992.

Klubock, Thomas M. *Contested Communities: Class, Gender, and Politics in Chile's El Teniente Copper Mine, 1904–1951.* Durham: Duke University Press, 1998.

Kronish, Rich, and Kenneth S. Mericle, eds. *Political Economy of the Latin American Motor Vehicle Industry.* Cambridge: MIT Press, 1984.

Landsberger, Henry A., ed. *Latin American Peasant Movements.* Ithaca: Cornell University Press, 1969.

Maybury-Lewis, Biorn. *The Politics of the Possible: The Brazilian Rural Workers' Trade Union Movement, 1965–1985.* Philadelphia: Temple University Press, 1994.

Middleton, Alan. "Division and Cohesion in the Working Class: Artisans and Wage Laborers in Ecuador." *Journal of Latin American Studies* 14, no.1 (May 1982): 171–95.

NACLA Report on the Americas. (various issues.)

Nash, June C. *We Eat the Mines and the Mines Eat Us: Dependency and Exploitation in Bolivian Tin Mines.* New York: Columbia University Press, 1993.

Nash, June C., and Helen I. Safa, eds. *Sex and Class in Latin America.* New York: Praeger, 1976.

Nazzari, Muriel. " 'The Women Question' in Cuba: An Analysis of Material Constraints on Its Solution." *Signs* 9, no. 2 (winter 1983): 246–263.

Pereira, Anthony W. *The End of the Peasantry: The Rural Labor Movement in Northeastern Brazil, 1961–1988.* Pittsburgh: University of Pittsburgh Press, 1997.

Ranis, Peter. *Argentine Workers: Peronism and Contemporary Class Consciousness.* Pittsburgh: University of Pittsburgh Press, 1992.

Rock, David, ed. *Latin America in the 1940s: War and Postwar Transitions.* Berkeley: University of California Press, 1994.

Roseberry, William, Lowell Gudmundson, and Mario Samper K. *Coffee, Society, and Power in Latin America.* Baltimore: Johns Hopkins University Press, 1995.

Spalding, Hobart. *Organized Labor in Latin America.* New York: New York University Press, 1977.

Young, Grace Ester. "The Myth of Being 'Like a Daughter.'" *Latin American Perspectives* 14, no. 3 (summer 1987): 365–80.

Welsh, Cliff. *The Seed Was Planted: The São Paulo Roots of Brazil's Rural Labor Movement, 1924–1964.* University Park: Pennsylvania State University, 1999.

Wolfe, Joel. *Working Women, Working Men: São Paulo and the Rise of Brazil's Industrial Working Class, 1900–1955.* Durham: Duke University Press, 1993.

Winn, Peter. *Weavers of Revolution: The Yarur Workers and Chile's Road to Socialism.* Oxford: Oxford University Press, 1986.

Index

About the Author

David McCreery holds graduate degrees in Latin American Studies and History from Tulane University and in Social Anthropology from the University of London. He teaches at Georgia State University and has been a visiting professor at Tulane University, University of Wisconsin, and the Federal Universities of Minas Gerais and Goiás in Brazil. He is the author of *Rural Guatemala, 1760–1940* (1994). Since 1993, he has been working on the history of Brazil's western frontier during the Empire (1822–1889).